Routledge Revivals

British Politics and the Policy Process

In *British Politics and the Policy Process* (originally published in 1987), Grant Jordan and Jeremy Richardson provide an introduction to the workings of British political process and a guide to the ways in which it can be studied. They show how political decisions are taken and policies are adopted inside Parliament, in the political parties, and in cabinet, and how they are mediated and influenced by, for example, the civil service and pressure groups. In doing so, they draw widely on case study material, and systematically utilize the memoir material of ex-Ministers and civil servants to give a realistic feel for policy making at the centre of British politics.

This book is, however, interpretative as well as descriptive. The authors argue that Parliament is usually marginal to political decision making, and powerfully reject the thesis of adversary politics, which holds that British politics undergoes major change when there is a switch in party control of Government. This then is a textbook that will serve as an ideal introduction to students of British government and comparative politics, but which is also a stimulating and original contribution to current debates in political science.

British Politics and the Policy Process

An Arena Approach

A. G. Jordan and J. J. Richardson

Routledge
Taylor & Francis Group

First published in 1987
by Allen & Unwin

This edition first published in 2024 by Routledge
4 Park Square, Milton Park, Abingdon, Oxon, OX14 4RN

and by Routledge
605 Third Avenue, New York, NY 10017

Routledge is an imprint of the Taylor & Francis Group, an informa business

Publisher's Note
The publisher has gone to great lengths to ensure the quality of this reprint but points out that some imperfections in the original copies may be apparent.

Disclaimer
The publisher has made every effort to trace copyright holders and welcomes correspondence from those they have been unable to contact.

A Library of Congress record exists under LCCN: 86022227

ISBN: 978-1-032-94964-2 (hbk)
ISBN: 978-1-003-58259-5 (ebk)
ISBN: 978-1-032-94966-6 (pbk)

Book DOI 10.4324/9781003582595

British Politics and the Policy Process

An Arena Approach

A. G. JORDAN
University of Aberdeen

J. J. RICHARDSON
University of Strathclyde

London
ALLEN & UNWIN
Boston   Sydney   Wellington

Allen & Unwin, the academic imprint of
Unwin Hyman Ltd
PO Box 18, Park Lane, Hemel Hempstead, Herts HP2 4TE, UK
40 Museum Street, London WC1A 1LU, UK
37/39 Queen Elizabeth Street, London SE1 2QB

Allen & Unwin Inc.,
8 Winchester Place, Winchester, Mass. 01890, USA

Allen & Unwin (Australia) Ltd,
8 Napier Street, North Sydney, NSW 2060, Australia

Allen & Unwin (New Zealand) Ltd in association with the Port Nicholson
Press Ltd,
60 Cambridge Terrace, Wellington, New Zealand

First published in 1987

British Library Cataloguing in Publication Data

Jordan, A. G.
   British politics and the policy process:
   an arena approach.
1. Great Britain – Politics and government – 1964 –
I. Title   II. Richardson, J. J.
354.4107′25   JN318
ISBN 0–04–320185–7
ISBN 0–04–320186–5 Pbk

Library of Congress Cataloging-in-Publication Data

Jordan, A. G.
   British politics and the policy process.
Bibliography; p.
Includes index.
1. Great Britain – Politics and government – 1979 –
2. Policy sciences. I. Richardson, J. J. (Jeremy John)
II. Title
JN231.J67 1987   320.941   86–22227
ISBN 0–04–320185–7
ISBN 0–04–320186–5 (pbk.)

Typeset in 10 on 11 point Imprint by Computape (Pickering) Limited
and printed in Great Britain by Billing and Sons Ltd,
London and Worcester

Contents

Preface

While intended as a textbook, this none the less puts forward several arguments about the nature of British politics. For one thing, we are not impressed by the *adversary* politics notion put forward by some commentators and encouraged by the rhetoric of party politicians. Mrs Thatcher, for example, in *The Times* of 19 July 1985, was reported as claiming that 'we have changed the political landscape'. In Chapters 4 and 9 we question whether such dramatic claims can be justified.

Our aim is not to draw attention to the deficiencies of the Thatcher Government (indeed, we might be inclined to criticize their intentions more harshly than their performance). Our aim is to underline the constraints that bind, hamper and limit any government. These make the Utopian vision and expectations of party politics inappropriate.

One particular and important reason why we see continuity in politics, is that we see political activity as largely conducted in policy communities of interested groups and government departments and agencies. In these communities (or to use the American term, sub-governments) party politics has only limited impact. Of course, not all political activity fits this pattern: for example, if a Labour government came to office it could have American nuclear weapons removed from Britain. That might have unexpected political effects in areas of foreign policy; there might be unexpected practical problems of implementation, but a strongly held political conviction by the Prime Minister could no doubt be executed. But most desired goals cannot be secured simply by political will: they require the co-operation of other groups and institutions. Some goals can only be secured by the undermining of equally cherished ambitions. Thus, in fact, the operationalization of policy is often difficult.

We see it as a matter of fact that most political activity is bargained in private worlds by special interests and interested specialists. We are always prepared to concede that this is not the sole style of politics but, at the same time, as a prediction of how policies *are* handled we find it surprisingly robust. Thus, in the past few years, we have separately and jointly investigated several case studies that had the superficial look of radical change. For example, we looked at the proposed creation of a statutory Engineering Authority as suggested by the Finniston Committee; we looked at the creation of Enterprise Zones, and at the field of unemployment policy. In each area, our hopes of finding 'the atypical' example were frustrated, as radical objectives became compromised in the process of bargaining and implementation.

While we see this practice of group incorporation in decisions as a fact, we (more tentatively) also approve of it as an expression of a *value*. One of the most important developments in political study in the past twenty years is renewed attention to the 'twin channels' of democracy – that democratic practice is not simply to do with elections, but with consent, consultation and co-operation.

However, we return to the point that politics is not always like this. The 1984 miners' strike, for one prominent example, cannot be presented in our terms of group negotiation. Nor is mob activity in the inner cities the kind of politics which we shall discuss. Completing this book at the time of the Tottenham riots underlines for us that the term 'politics' encompasses very different processes. We are all familiar with Clauswitz's 'War is nothing more than the continuation of politics by other means'. Perhaps, instead of his continuum, we need to contrast the *negotiative* politics with the politics of *direct action*. In no sense is the latter type of politics the only type and we would see direct action as the overspill, the failure of negotiative politics. Of course, our type of analysis has little to say about the problem of Northern Ireland, but perhaps it gives a pointer to the kind of solution that needs to be found. We do not, however, attempt to cover such a topic. Nor do we attempt to cover, say, the House of Lords, or practices in local government, the EEC, the judiciary, or the role of the police. Some of these topics need a specialist knowledge which we lack, and we feel none of them are necessary for a book with this orientation.

In recognizing that our version of British politics is not uncontroversial, we have attempted to sustain and support our argument by drawing not only on our own case study material, but also that of many researchers. (One of the good features of the subject has been the accumulation of a number of solid, empirically based studies of British politics.) Thus, to academics such as Michael Moran, Gavin Drewry, Richard Rose, Ivor Crewe, and others, we owe a debt. We also draw liberally upon the contributions of politicians and civil servants such as the late Richard Crossman, Edmund Dell, Sir Leo Pliatzky, Joel Barnett, Sir Douglas Wass, and others. Although the publication of such 'insider' knowledge is sometimes criticized, we feel that without that corpus of work our level of political knowledge would be seriously weakened; however we define democracy, to lower that level would be undesirable. We hope that none of those quoted will mind too much the interpretation which we put on their words.

The above have mainly assisted with their published work; others (both academics and practitioners) have assisted more directly and personally. Between us we have learnt much from departmental colleagues, such as Tom Mackie, Brian Hogwood, Bill Miller, Mark Franklin, Frank Bealey, Clive Archer, and others. We have also benefited from the advice of Peter Hennessy, Fred Twine, and others; to begin the list is to appreciate that it is impossible to complete it. We are also grateful to the Nuffield Foundation for its financial support for much of our work on policy communities. To those who typed this – Lorna Cardno, Helen Stuart, Jenny Albiston, Grace Hunter, Helen Innes, Fiona Docherty and Alison Robinson – we are duly grateful. Those who imagine university life as unstressed, gentle and contemplative could start their necessary re-education by looking at secretarial facilities: no group in Britain can have become more productive, more rapidly, with increased work and fewer staff than university secretaries. We are grateful to Susan Jordan for preparing the index and to Elise Sochart for reading the proofs.

We thank, too, Allen & Unwin for some patience over the writing of this book – and to our families for their patience because of the writing of this book. This book is dedicated, then, to Rachel, Steven, Grace, Alex and Innes, in the hope that they find a political system that is not too noticeably different. The old ship may be leaky, the supplies running low, but we would rather not keep the company of the visionaries who build their new Titanics.

PART ONE

Introduction

CHAPTER ONE

The Contemporary Language of Policy-Making

A starting-point for our analyses of the policy process is David Ricci's comment, in *The Tragedy of Political Science* (1984, p. 10), that in the 1970s in the USA the output of newly published books on politics clamouring for attention approached 400 per month. The mountain of literature that intimidates the new observer will, in Ricci's words, 'only marginally include items that were universally considered important to political learning and practice in the past'. In other words, the modern subject of politics – and, in particular, the policy-making variant – is not based on a close textual reading of Hume, Mill, Locke, Aristotle, or even Marx. Terms, once fundamental – such as absolutism, justice, nation, patriotic, rights, society, or tyranny – are largely used only by political theorists interested in Great Thinkers of the Past. The new lexicon contains words such as attitude, cross-pressure, conflict, game, interaction, socialization and system (Ricci, 1984, p. 299). These words are now used without explanation – the new vocabulary.

Discussions of politics, and in particular policy-making, thus frequently use a specialized language, indeed jargon. Ideally, one would wish to distinguish between unnecessary circumlocutions which obscure and a specialist terminology necessary to allow precision. In practice such a distinction would be arbitrary, for opinions vary. Certainly not all of the old language was an aid to understanding. For example, when one has absorbed the concept of the 'Queen in Parliament' (which some hold to be vital) what has one mastered? Does the term aid comprehension of political power in this country? W. J. M. MacKenzie's reaction (1982, p. 40) to the work of Dicey, one of the late Victorians, perhaps gives support to this undeferential view. Writing of Dicey he says, 'such is his self confidence that it is hard to grasp that except when he writes technically as a lawyer he writes largely nonsense'. Worse, some of the work of the modern German philosophers, such as Habermas, bring to mind Hobbes's attack on Suarez: 'What is the meaning of the words, "The first cause does not necessarily inflow anything into the second, by force of the essential subordination of the second causes, by which it may help it to work" . . . When men write whole volumes of such stuff, are they not mad, or intend to make others so' (quoted in Ricci, 1984, p. 227). Some of the received language is simply unhelpful. What is *primus inter pares*, but a logical absurdity? Some terms are significantly wrong. For example, individual ministerial responsibility may well be obsolete in any strict sense. Some terms are misleading. Thus, while a debate takes place in the academic literature between Cabinet government and prime ministerial government notions, both may be correct in their own restricted senses.

In the case of the newer language that has developed (or at least accumulated), predictably, the more successfully that terms have entered common currency, the more imprecise their content has become. This is a language, however, that has sufficient technical content to be remote from ordinary use. Arguably, these terms are important as hints at theory. Since most work lacks an explicit theoretical orientation, it is often necessary to 'decode' from the language to find the theoretical position. Certainly, sets of terms are associated with distinctive ways of looking at political life.

This chapter is not designed as a summary of theory; it is much less ambitious. It is, at most, a summary of some of the issues raised in the theories. It is also skewed to draw attention to the kinds of theory that underpin our own approach. Some twenty or more authors are mentioned in this review. They are selected not on the criterion that to understand one, or more, or all of these is to understand politics and policy-making, but that to know their terminology will help us understand the arguments in the literature in the past twenty-five years. The authors introduced here have had a residual impact on our way of looking at the policy process.

Golembiewski (1960, p. 971) has observed that, 'political science and the social sciences in general are characterized by a fantastic discontinuity – one of the unfortunate consequences (and causes) of the research trends which periodically sweep across them. A chapter of this kind in the 1960s, reflecting the then current literature, would have had to devote considerable attention to ideas such as 'power' and 'class'. The discussion of power perhaps culminated in Steven Lukes's brief book, *Power* (1974). Although the debate flared up in an exchange in *Political Studies* in 1979 between Nelson Polsby and Ken Newton, it otherwise seems to have been simply laid aside in the literature. Thus the problem for the student of politics is that controversies are not resolved. (Lukes starts his discussion by quoting Parsons's (1957, p. 139) earlier lament that, 'Unfortunately, the concept of power is not a settled one in the social sciences, either in political science or in sociology.') The tendency is simply to ignore the problems which tried earlier generations. Thus the language of political science is an aggregation of disparate approaches and not the consequence of some evolutionary survival of the most useful. Put more bluntly: when they find the questions impossible to resolve, political scientists have found other questions.

Organizing Ideas

CYCLE

The first clutch of theorists mentioned here have in common the concept of *cycle*: one ordering image of political activity is to see it as phased behaviour leading from stimulus to new or adapted policy. In this form, this is a banal idea, but arguably this is the clarity of hindsight. The works of Karl Deutsch and David Easton were pitched at different targets, but both authors have a core similarity. Within their models are assumptions about political society – the cybernetic approach emphasizes the responsiveness of the policy-makers to the demands.

Deutsch, in his *The Nerves of Government* (1966), applies ideas of Norbert Wiener and others on the control of organizations. His discussions are exceedingly abstract and not a natural starting point for anyone interested in questions such as prime ministerial power or the outcome of by-elections.

The central perception is perhaps *feedback*, and Deutsch (1966, p. 88) defines that in a quotation as: 'In a broad sense (feedback) may denote that some of the output energy of an apparatus or machine is returned as input . . . (If) the behaviour of an object is controlled by the margin of error at which the object stands at a given time with reference to a relatively specific goal . . . (the) feedback is . . . negative . . ., that is, the signals from the goal are used to restrict outputs . . .' The work is difficult but the metaphor of the book's title has been potent.

Easton's approach is suggested by the base model (see Figure 1.1) that he offers in *A Systems Analysis of Political Life*.

The style is illustrated in his chapter on 'The regulation of the flow of demands: reduction process'. He said:

> In this chapter I shall assume that numerous and capacious enough channels are available to carry demands to the various parts of the system for further consideration. The problem becomes one, not of too many demands and too few channels, but of enough channels operating so effectively that they let too many demands through . . . Under conditions where a system is able to process its demands so

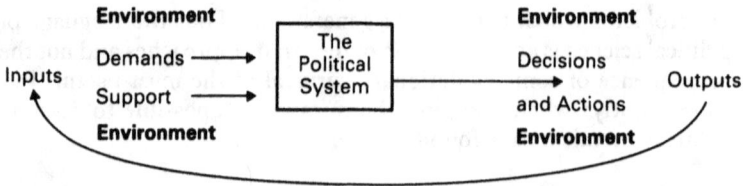

Figure 1.1   *A simplified model of a political system.*
Source: Easton, 1965, p. 32.

that an excessive volume may reach the output points, measures of various kinds must be taken to prevent input overload.

He suggests that there must be demand reduction through the aggregation of individual demands or by *intra system gatekeeping* to regulate access (p. 133). The image of the overloaded channel and the strategic importance of the gatekeeper is clear, but Easton's hope that his 'modest and small step' (p. 440) will be built on appears frustrated. It is difficult enough to absorb the 500 pages of his early effort, without wishing for more complex approaches. It is unlikely that political life is to be captured by a two-by-two table – but improbable that we can easily handle models much more complicated.

BEHAVIOURALISM

Still in the general field of 'cycles' and endorsements of the notion of 'a political system', one of the most ambitious efforts at providing a vocabulary for political science is the early work of Gabriel Almond. He considered the intellectual inheritance – separation of powers' and the like – and found it wanting. It was a case, he said, of endeavouring to handle the complexity of political phenomena of the modern world with a legal and institutional vocabulary.

Almond was self-consciously a behaviouralist. In the 1950s and 1960s behaviouralism (or behaviourism) was the theoretical revolution in (especially) American social science. Definition is, as usual, problematic. The approach did (does) certainly entail empirical observation, a distinction between explanation and ethical evaluation, a generally 'scientific' orientation and ambition. Dahl predicted (1961, p. 769) that the success of the behavioural revolution would be its absorption into the routines of the subject:

Where will the behavioural mood, considered as a movement of protest go from here? I think it will gradually disappear. By this I mean only that it will slowly decay as a distinctive mood and outlook. For it will become, and in fact already is becoming incorporated in the main body of the discipline ... As a separate outlook it will be the first victim of its own triumph.

It might reassure those who find these matters unclear that Dahl, himself, observed (1961, p. 763) that the most striking characteristic of the 'behavioural approach' was ambiguity and that, like the Loch Ness monster, while one could say with considerable confidence what it was *not*, it was difficult to say what it *was*. David Ricci (1984, pp. 138–43) successfully shows that behaviouralism was the belief of the most prominent political scientists (as indicated by the presidency of the American Political Science Association) – and that this belief which they shared was tantalizingly imprecise – though the testability ideas of Popper (for example, 1972) seemed to be somewhere at the heart of it all. As with most revolutions, the prospectus was attractive. A process of falsification would eradicate mistakes from the accepted stock of political knowledge and small-scale empirical knowledge would contribute to an overall synthesized knowledge. Even Ricci's broad vision, however, failed to find any coherence to the next intellectual wave – post behaviouralism. He saw it only as a shared determination to leave something – that is, behaviouralism – behind.

Almond (in Almond and Coleman, 1960, p. 4) claimed that the terms he was using were not simply additions to the old vocabulary, but part of a process of developing or adapting a new one. He continued: 'And, to put all of our cards on the table, this is not only a matter of a conceptual vocabulary; it is an intimation of a major step forward in the nature of political science as a science.' The assumption was that each political system necessarily performed particular functions. The functions identified were (p. 17):

(A) Input functions
(1) Political socialization and recruitment.
(2) Interest articulation.
(3) Interest aggregation.
(4) Political communication.
(B) Output functions.
(5) Rule making.
(6) Rule application.
(7) Rule adjudication.

The terminology blurred the simple distinction of 'structure' and 'role'. Almond claimed that different institutions could be multifunctional. For example, courts could adjudicate *and* legislate; the bureaucracy could be a *source* of legislation, and so on. While this approach was once the stuff of political science journals, it cannot be said to be the current diet; but the terminology survives – without much cognizance of its original context.

POLICY CYCLE

It is a leap from the general and abstract literature of systems to the attempt at social science policy relevance of modern public policy and policy analysis, but there is the shared concept of the political cycle. One early version of policy cycle approach is found in Mack (1971, p. 136) – what she calls a deliberative staged, recursive, administrative process (DOSRAP). Mack makes the point that the life history of the decision cycle is seldom clearly segmented, but five sub-divisions can be identified.

(1) Deciding to decide: problem recognition.
(2) Formulating alternatives and criteria.
(3) Decision proper.
(4) Effectuation.
(5) Correction and supplementation.

While this kind of cycle is developed for very different intellectual purposes from that of, say, Deutsch, it shares the sense of politics as a dynamic process and it confirms the importance of politics as a *learning* system. More elaborate versions of the policy cycle can be found in W. Jenkins (1978, p. 12), or Hogwood and Peters (1983, p. 8), for example.

Models are used in two important different senses: a *descriptive* model of how policy *is* made, and a normative model of how policy would be *better* made. All models have either a descriptive or normative nature, but the difference is especially vital in the public policy field where the whole subject has a broadly normative, reformist thrust – with a current interest in evaluating policy proposals and impacts. Even where the model is no more than descriptive, it might well be that all features would not be appropriate in all cases. Hogwood and Gunn (1984) set out their sophisticated version of the policy cycle as:

(1) Deciding to decide (issue search or agenda-setting).
(2) Deciding how to decide (or issue filtration).
(3) Issue definition.
(4) Forecasting.

(5) Setting objectives and priorities.
(6) Options analysis.
(7) Policy implementation, monitoring and control.
(8) Evaluation and review.
(9) Policy maintenance, succession, or termination.

They immediately note that the list is not definitive and can be adjusted, and that it is not a description of what happens to every issue, but is a framework for organizing what does happen – or does not (p. 4). Thus, like the systems models above, this is an *organizing idea* and an *ideal type* by which to evaluate specific examples. Much confusion surrounds the ideal type notion. First, it is worth observing that 'ideal' does not mean 'best', 'sought after', 'preferred' but, rather, 'idealized', that is to say, simplified but exhibiting essential characteristics. Thus one can have an ideal type of something, such as fascism, which in terms of value judgement would not be desirable. Secondly, however, the usefulness of the ideal type is that it bears some kind of approximation to the possibilities discussed. 'It's only meant as an ideal type' is not a satisfactory defence of a model, if that ideal type is so distant from perceived reality to make it irrelevant.

RATIONALITY

Rationality is a major concern within public policy – how decisions should be taken. The Hogwood and Gunn example of a policy cycle exhibits that interest in identifying and judging between alternatives which characterizes rational approaches. The term 'rational' can cover a range of decision-making techniques – particularly, if it is argued that rationality is about *intentions*. Behaviour almost inevitably is intended to be rational. One particular application of rational choice/means-ends analysis is in voting and political partici-pation. Here the basic work is probably Downs' *An Economic Theory of Democracy* (1957), – but the subject has also been pursued by Buchanan and Tullock (1962), and others. A similar 'economic' theory of rational action has been applied to participation in pressure groups by Olson (1965).

If laymen were asked to outline rational decision-making behaviour, they would probably set out some kind of means-ends analysis a sort of commonsense rationality. This process of rational choice would include features (derived from Lindblom, 1959), such as:

(a) isolate objectives (ends)
(b) determine alternative policies (means) to achieve objectives

(c) select the most appropriate means to secure desired ends

(d) analysis is comprehensive

(e) theory is often heavily relied upon

This kind of rationality characterizes approaches such as Planning, Programming, Budgeting Systems (PPBS) or corporate management – techniques which broadly assess the impact of selected (costed) options in the light of specified goals and allow choice of the most effective.

This kind of approach is pervasive and persuasive. Indeed, Jordan (1984b) has argued that the planners involved in an oil-related housing project felt it necessary to translate and distort their descriptions of perfectly legitimate reiterative procedures to fit this kind of goal-directed rationality. None the less it is *a* rational rather than *the* rational approach. A major competing framework was offered by Lindblom, and his co-authors. It is summarized in his paper, 'The science of muddling through' (1959). The title given to the piece dramatically underlines that while 'muddling through' is usually seen as a criticism of policy-making, as a process it may have its own intrinsic merits. (Braybrooke and Lindblom [1963] use the phrase 'systematic and defensible strategy'.)

In support of incremental, learning-from-experience approaches, Mack (1971, p. 172) has noted that 'Learning models are the prose of ordinary behaviour; people use them whether they know it or not. They "play it by ear"; "don't cross bridges until they come to them"; "try and try again". Only planners speak a special language.'

The ideas of Lindblom are perhaps most accessible through his discussion in 1959. Lindblom considered what a hypothetical administrator could do were he asked to formulate a policy in regard to inflation. Lindblom argues that he could:

- try to place all related values in order of importance e.g. full employment, reasonable business profits, protection of savings, etc.

- then all policy outcomes could be rated as best maximising these values (this would require prodigious research to discover intensity of values held in society)

- he could then consider all possible policy alternatives

- he could then compare his possibilities to determine which best delivered the best combination of values.

- he would take advantage of any theory available – he might consider strict central control and the abolition of all prices and markets on the one hand and elimination of all controls on the other.

As opposed to such a comprehensive and synoptic type of response, Lindblom outlines an alternative, simpler approach whereby the administrator sets (perhaps subconsciously) a simple aim of keeping prices level. While this would be a 'goal', the administrator would recognize that he was perforce 'ignoring many related values and many important consequences of his policies'. His next step would be to outline the relatively few policy alternatives that suggested themselves. In comparing these alternatives he would not usually find theory of much practical assistance, but would instead rely on experience of past attempts and, by choice, would proceed with small steps to allow the prediction of consequences of further such steps.

He would find that the various policy options combined objectives in different ways. For example, one policy might offer price-level stability with more unemployment; another less price stability, but less unemployment. The choice would, therefore, combine the process of choice of instrument and choice of value. A further key feature of this approach would be an expectation of repeated adjustment of policy. There is a kinship to the behavioural stress on testing and learning.

This second approach is clearly that preferred by Lindblom and (because of the small-step aspect) is generally referred to as 'incrementalism'. Lindblom also referred to it as 'successive limited comparison' – a form which emphasizes the reiterative nature of the technique.

The other major critic of 'commonsense rationality' has been Herbert Simon. Three different models can be abstracted from his *Administrative Behavior* (1958) (See also the more difficult *Models of Bounded Rationality*, 1982.)

(1) Behaviour Alternative Model (1958, p. 67) The task of decision involves three steps:

(1) the listing of all the alternative strategies;
(2) the determination of all the consequences that follow upon each of these strategies;
(3) the comparative evaluation of these sets of consequences.

Like Lindblom's incrementalism this approach eschews early identification of 'ends'. Some notion of preference is needed, but this delayed choice prevents agonizing over choices which are, in practice, not feasible.

(2) Bounded Rationality Model The core of this second idea is implicitly expressed in Simon's discussion (1958, p. 241) of the 'The Area of Rationality':

When the limits to rationality are viewed from the individual's standpoint, they fall into three categories: he is limited by his unconscious skills, habits and reflexes: he is limited by his values and conceptions of purpose, which may diverge from the organization's goals: he is limited by the extent of his knowledge and information. The individual can be rational in terms of the organization's goals only to the extent that he is *able* to pursue a particular course of action, he has a correct conception of the goal of the action, he is correctly *informed* about the conditions surrounding his action. *Within the boundaries laid down by these factors* (our emphasis) his choices are rational – goal oriented.

Earlier he expressed the limitations as follows:

Actual behaviour falls short, in at least three ways, of objective rationality . . . :

(1) Rationality requires a complete knowledge and anticipation of the consequence that will follow on each choice. In fact, knowledge of consequences is always fragmentary.

(2) Since these consequences lie in the future, imagination must supply the lack of experienced feeling in attaching value to them. But values can be only imperfectly anticipated.

(3) Rationality requires a choice among all possible alternative behaviours. In actual behaviour, only a few of all of these possible alternatives ever come to mind. (p. 87)

Lindblom's version of this kind of perspective is contained in *The Intelligence of Democracy* (1965, p. 171). There he observed that partisan mutual adjustment decision-making, 'imposes on no one the heroic demands for information, intellectual competence, time, energy and money . . .' that a more ambitious, centralised synoptic approach would demand.

(3) Satisficing model Simon is often linked with the useful and important idea of *satisficing* – though the textual references are slim: '*The central concern of administrative theory is with the boundary between the rational and the non-rational aspects of human social behaviour.* Administrative theory is peculiarly the theory of intended and bounded rationality – of the behaviour of human beings who *satisfice* because they have not the wits to maximize' (1958, p. xxx). Perhaps one should add that the burden of the argument is not only that policy-makers have not the wit (intelligence) to maximize, but they also lack information and often, in particular circumstances, it is more sensible to *satisfice* rather than maximize.

The important difference between Simon and Lindblom is probably in their level of optimism about the limits of rationality. Simon is obviously uncomfortable with the 'learn to love it' advice of Lindblom and favours management education and improvement. (See *The New Science of Management Decision*, 1977.)

The major exchange on incrementalism is possibly between Yehezkel Dror and Lindblom in *Public Administration Review* (Dror, 1964; Lindblom, 1964) in which Dror objected that the benefits of the system advocated by Lindblom would emerge only when:

(a) existing policy is broadly satisfactory,
(b) there is continuity of problem,
(c) there is continuity of resources.

He saw these conditions pertaining only under circumstances of unusual social stability:

Under conditions of stability, routine is often the best policy, and, change being at a slow rate, incremental change is often optimal. But even in the most stable societies, many of today's qualitatively most important problems are tied up with high speed changes in levels of aspiration, the nature of issues and the available means of action, and require therefore a policy making method different from 'muddling through'. (p. 154)

Lindblom's main point in his rejoinder is that he had admitted that incrementalism was best restricted to certain contexts – but that in both the Western democracies and stable non-democracies, such as the Soviet Union, the three conditions propitious to incrementalism were largely met.

In his 1979 essay, 'Still muddling, not yet through', Lindblom said that it was now textbook orthodoxy that in policy-making only small or incremental steps are ordinarily possible. However he went on:

But most people, including many policy analysts and policy makers, want to separate the 'ought' from the 'is'. They think we should try to do better. So do I. What remains as an issue then? . . . Many critics of incrementalism believe that doing better usually means turning away from incrementalism. Incrementalists believe that for complex problem solving it usually means practicing incrementalism more skillfully and turning away from it only rarely'. (1979, p. 517)

Broadly the 1979 vintage is a defence for the designed, deliberate and conscious incompleteness of analysis that is incrementalism over the accidental incompleteness that (necessarily) is failed synoptic analysis. (The other important incrementalist defence is Dempster and

Wildavsky's article in 1979 which, like Lindblom's, spelt out different types of incrementalism.)

One important difference between most versions of rationality and the incrementalist position is the allowance built into incrementalism for multiple actors with competing values (this, after all, is surely the normal situation in the real world). In Lindblom's 'The science of muddling through' (1959) one of the features of 'successive limited comparisons' is that the test of a good policy is that analysts can agree on it – without having to agree on ultimate goals. In 'Still muddling, not yet through' (1979) Lindblom was still arguing that social problems can be attacked by 'resultants' of interactions rather than 'decisions' arising out of someone's particular understanding: 'Understanding a social problem is not always necessary for its amelioration . . .' (Brewer and de Leon [1983, p. 87] cite Bellman and Kalaba's point that the irony is that to understand we must often 'throw-away information . . . We cannot, . . . grapple with a high order of complexity. Consequently, we must simplify.')

The discussion of the interaction of interests is discussed as *partisan mutual adjustment*. Although this is seen as different from political incrementalism, Lindblom concedes that the two are usually linked. He argues (1979):

> . . . policies are the resultants of the mutual adjustment; they are better described as happening than as decided upon . . . policies are influenced by a broad range of participants . . . the connection between a policy and good reasons for it is obscure, since the many participants will act for diverse reasons . . . In many circumstances their mutual adjustments will achieve a coordination superior to an attempt at central coordination, which is often so complex as to lie beyond any coordinator's competence.

PLURALISM

The conception of optimum outcomes as the unconscious, and perhaps unintended, consequence of competition by participants is a point of overlap with another major concept – *pluralism*. A link between the two literatures is Lindblom's joint work with Robert Dahl, *Politics, Economics and Welfare* (1953). The ideas of pluralism can be traced back to the nineteenth century (and much earlier), but contemporary pluralism has little to do with the archaeology of philosophy to which critics of pluralism attempt to bind it.

Two main concepts associated with Dahl – polyarchy and pluralism – are sometimes used interchangeably, but the emphasis is different.

Polyarchy has been held to include features such as:
Freedom to form and join organizations
Freedom of expression
Right to vote
A wide eligibility for public office
Right of political leaders to compete for votes
Alternative sources of information
Free and fair elections
Government policies dependent on public demands

In Dahl's use (see *Modern Political Analysis*, 1976, p. 81), *democracy* is reserved as an unattained and perhaps unattainable ideal type and the countries (such as the USA and UK) which *approximate* to democratic status are termed 'polyarchies'. That book does not list 'pluralism' in its index; and his *Pluralist Democracy in the United States* (1967) does not list 'polyarchy' in its index. Pluralism is linked less firmly to the electoral system as a means to democratic control. The basic elements of pluralism are multiple centres of powers, optimum policy development through competing interests. Polyarchy is a type of regime, which can have more or less pluralism: pluralism (in the senses of *conflictive pluralism* of enduring cleavages; or *organizational pluralism*, meaning the number and autonomy of organizations that must be taken into account) can also be found, more or less, in so-called hegemonic regimes (see Dahl, 1978, p. 19).

The most influential texts in the new pluralist literature of the postwar years were probably David Truman's *The Governmental Process* (1951), and various works by Dahl. Pluralism perhaps derived from intellectual dismay at the unsatisfactory portrait of voter-based democracy that was accumulating in empirical studies of the electorate: electoral democracy was simply not unfolding along the lines anticipated in classical theory. Schumpeter had found fault with the classical expectations and, indeed, even Schumpeter's (1976, p. 269) reformulation that democracy was 'that institutional arrangement for arriving at political decisions in which the individuals acquire the power to decide by means of a competitive struggle for the peoples' votes', was itself seen as optimistic.

Ricci (1984, p. 110) has made the disturbing observation that political scientists have managed repeatedly to find facts that disappoint democratic assumptions – and instantly put upon them a democratic interpretation more optimistic than that permitted by traditional liberal expectations. Thus he notes that E. P. Herring managed to turn the discovery of features, such as parties in disarray and confusion, as a matter for celebration; Francis Wilson managed to conclude that low electoral turnout did not violate democratic

needs. We can add the 'discovery' that strong pressure groups provide
– rather than destroy – the public interest, and so on. A. F. Davies, in
his *Essays in Political Sociology* (1972, p. 97), observes that when
Robert Lane in *Political Ideology* (1962) found an unsuspected lack of
group membership and group identification among the fifteen inter-
viewees in his study, he promptly hailed his subjects' disarming
vagueness about their political friends and enemies, the complete lack
of edge to their views and their failure to find political clues in class,
religion or ethnicity, as a major resource in flexibility and open-
mindedness for democracy.

One reaction to this difficulty in identifying significant voter-
control in the political process was élite theory – which, in various
formulations, broadly envisaged political power as restricted.
Although a range of middle-range issues might be the subject of wider
disputation, the 'commanding heights' were determined by, and in
favour of, the existing social/political élite. If concessions were seen to
be made to a broader base of society, they were, by definition, minor
or – in a less convincing argument – part of some consumerist,
materialist trap for the working classes to bind them to the system
(Mills, 1956; Domhoff, 1967).

In contrast to the élite model, the pluralist position assumed
widespread, effective, political resources. Dahl (1956, p. 145) had
defined the 'normal' process, as one in which there is a high
probability that all active and legitimate groups in the population can
make themselves heard effectively at some crucial stage in the process
of decision. A group originally excluded may none the less often gain
entry. This assumption of widespread effective influence is a basic
pluralist tenet. But Dahl continues:

> Clearly [the capacity to be 'heard'] does not mean that every group
> has equal control over the outcome. In American politics, as in all
> other societies, control over decisions is unevenly distributed;
> neither individuals or groups are political equals. When I say a
> group is heard 'effectively' I mean more than the simple fact that it
> makes a noise; I mean that one or more officials are not only ready
> to listen to the noise, but expect to suffer in some significant way if
> they do not placate the group . . . (p. 145)

Empirical work – particularly in local communities – did appear to
confirm that no consistent élite determined policy (for example,
Dahl, 1961; Polsby, 1963; Banfield, 1963). Among what we term
mainstream élitists were C. Wright Mills (1956) and Floyd Hunter
(1953), but the most significant counter-argument to pluralism was
put forward by Bachrach and Baratz (1970) (largely published in
article form in the *American Political Science Review* in 1962 and

1963). Bachrach and Baratz sided with the pluralist view that the élitist's basic premise of a stable, ordered system of power is unconvincing. However, they also criticized the basic pluralist tenet that the powerful will be revealed in key decisions. Essentially, they argued that power could be exerted not by success in a series of political struggles, but by preventing the issue emerging as politically contentious. This is the basis of their famous 'second face of power' concept: that power can be exerted as non-decisions. Non-decision in this sense is not indecision, but the capacity of the powerful to prevent issues that concern them from appearing on the political agenda.

Logic suggests that it is indeed feasible that the powerful can prevent the emergence of topics uncongenial to them, but given that so many topics are discussed that would displease what are presumably the favoured sections of society, it is difficult to imagine the nature of the suppressed agenda. And admitting this hidden veto can exist, is not conceding that there is, in practice, a machinery for consolidating élite preferences and for implementing a veto as Bachrach and Baratz suggest.

No tour of ideas would be complete without a Marxist reference, but Marxist analysis had limited impact in the British tradition of political science: even its distant cousins, élitism and corporatism, have been no more than passing waves. Certainly, ritual obeisance is regularly made to Miliband (1969) and to the issue of whether the state is an instrument of the bourgeoisie or relatively autonomous from it. But, arguably, the Marxist approach is essentially introspective: it becomes a debate on the 'true approach' and not on its use. While outside critics of the British academic political science community might haver about the dominance of Marxism, the interesting question is why Marxism is so marginal. (See Leys, 1983, or Coates, 1984 for sympathetic treatments.)

The most profound of the later attacks on pluralism (and given the importance of its author in the original pluralist pantheon the most unsettling), is Charles Lindblom's *Politics and Markets*. Lindblom (1977, p. 172) argues that, in several senses, business is a privileged participant in the political process of Western society. For example, many decisions are taken by businessmen which in other political systems would have to be governmental – 'Businessmen thus become a kind of public official and exercise . . . public functions'. Moreover, Lindblom argues that governments in market systems recognize the need for employment and growth, and for this reason governments accept a responsibility to assure high profits.

Notwithstanding critics such as Lindblom, some kind of pluralist theory underpins much political science. There is, however, no single authoritative pluralist source – much to the frustration of critics – and most broad pluralists enter their own reservations which often anticipate the points of critics. For example, E. E. Schattschneider, *The Semi-Sovereign People* (1960), effectively makes Lindblom's central point of class *bias* in the political contest.

CORPORATISM

A significant challenge in recent years to pluralism as an approach has come from the corporatism of Philippe Schmitter and his adherents. Corporatism was put forward by Schmitter (in Schmitter and Lehmbruch, eds, 1979, p. 14) as 'an explicit alternative to the paradigm of interest politics which has until now completely dominated the discipline of North American political science: *pluralism*. The concept assumes that interest groups do not merely attempt to influence governmental actions, but themselves become part of the decision-making and implementation system. In return for this participation in policy-making the groups – through the control of their members – make society more manageable for the state or government.

The main objections to this approach must be, first, that it is not as novel as it claims: only by suppressing or ignoring much of the discussion of pluralism can one present this as a new concern. Almond (1983, p. 202) made the point succinctly: 'The casualness of the search of the earlier literature and the distortion of its contents are serious weaknesses in an otherwise important contribution to the interest group literature.'

Secondly, the corporatists' imagery just does not fit the empirical picture. Policy-making in the Western democracies seems to better fit Schmitter's definition of pluralism (in Schmitter and Lehmbruch, eds, 1979, p. 16) than anything – namely, interest representation with spontaneous formation of groups, group proliferation, horizontal extension and competitive interaction. While it is now contended by corporatist theorists that corporatism can be a valuable ideal type without much empirical application, this was not the contention in the original Schmitter paper which expected to find by empirical inspection corporatist rather than pluralist practices, (pp. 9, 14).

Finally, corporatist theory allows for less rigorous (and hence more relevant) variants, for example, societal corporatism/liberal corporatism. These variants are difficult to distinguish from the well-observed practices of regularized relationships between interest groups and the bureaucracy which had independently been labelled 'corporate pluralism' in Scandinavia (Rokkan, 1966), and the USA (Kelso, 1978).

One term that separates writers in the pluralist tradition from those in the corporatist is the term 'state'. The pluralists appear to consider 'state' to be no more than a synonym for government. Other writers present the state as a vital and distinct concept. Ham and Hill (1984, p. 22) argue that 'it is necessary to give the state a central position in policy analysis'. Definitions of the state usually refer to aspects such as legal right to apply force, but beyond that the waters are muddy. While use of the term state is a clear signal that some kind of anti-pluralist position is being adopted, pluralists see little need to use the term, as 'stateness' is, in practice, fissured and fragmented. In other words, it is difficult to identify interests of 'the state' as opposed to contentious issues of constituent parts.

BUREAUCRACY

The pluralist and corporatist theories are linked by the stress on organized interests as the channel of citizen preference. Another major academic activity has been examination of the politics within the governmental machine.

In fact, as Jenkins and Gray make clear in their survey of 'Bureaucratic politics and power' (1983), there has been a widespread revolt against the rational-legal model of organizations which had its roots in Weber, but which was kept alive in prescriptive managerial texts. Instead of an image of bureaucracy as largely (and ideally) conflict free, empirically based perspectives have developed emphasizing different interests, sub-organizational rationality. Jenkins and Gray claim that 'organizations are viewed as aggregates of groups constituting bargaining systems. The making of decisions in the organization is the focal point for bargaining and conflict.' They cite Bacharach and Lawler's claim that organizational politics involves 'the mobilising of interest groups aimed at influencing authoritative decisions' (Jenkins and Gray, 1983, p. 181). One of the best reviews in this vein is Perrow's, *Complex Organizations* (1979), which interestingly sets out the features of different types of bureaucracy and types of theory about bureaucracy (classical management theory, human relations school, institutional school, and so on).

Thus one variant of the study of bureaucracy is pluralism in a new guise. Another approach, addressed by Jenkins and Gray, is public choice theory which we have skirted in consideration of the rational actor approach in relation to voting and pressure groups. The approach sees bureaucratic behaviour also following rational calculations of self-interest – see, for example, W. A. Niskanen, *Bureaucracy and Representative Government* (1971).

One of the most cited books in the contemporary subject – and deservedly so – is Graham Allison's *Essence of Decision* (1971) which, although on the specific topic of the Cuban Missile Crisis, has had an impact on a wide range of studies. His version of the crisis, described through several 'conceptual lens' – including one of *governmental* (or bureaucratic) *politics* – is based on an assumption that each participant's sense of priorities is coloured by their own concerns – 'Where You Stand Depends on Where You Sit' – and not some organization wide goal. The study of bureaucracy has been reclaimed as a branch of politics.

The policy-making movement has, we would claim, only a weak interest in the activities and pronouncements of political parties and parliamentary activities – for long the staple diet of British political study. Instead, what is of interest is the *cycle* of policy and the interactions among a widespread of participants – most notably special interest groups, policy professionals and civil servants. This certainly is the broad thrust of this book.

CHAPTER TWO

Problems in Studying the Political Process

Introduction

Sidney Low opens his book on *The Governance of England* (1914) by advising that the inquirer who follows Machiavelli's advice, 'to follow the real truth of things rather than an imaginary view of them', is confronted by the difficulty which forced from de Tocqueville the impatient aphorism that there is no constitution in England: 'elle n'existe point!' There are two lessons. First, Machiavelli's point that the superficial appearance is often false, or at least irrelevant. Second, de Tocqueville's observation – which is not that Britain lacks a *written* constitution, but that it lacks *any* constitution at all (though some might find de Tocqueville's conclusion too sweeping – arguably the conventions of the constitution are so malleable that they are unserviceable as tools of analysis). Using a different metaphor, Geoffrey Marshall (1984, p. 55) has described most British conventions as 'somewhat vague and slippery – resembling the procreation of eels'.

John Mackintosh began his book on *The Government and Politics of Britain* (1982, p. 31) by describing the 'Westminster Model' which he presented as 'an idealized version of British Government in the 1880–1914 period'. He, of course, also describes the substantial change *from* that model – principally a steady strengthening of the executive. He goes on: 'The capacity of the Commons to remove one government and install another, to amend legislation, to pick off ministers, to extract information and to push the government into changes of policy, has largely disappeared. While this may or may not be a desirable development, the mistake is to go on talking as if these powers existed . . .' As Mackintosh says, the outdated maxims are still quoted as if the political system has not fundamentally altered.

Another kind of difficulty is where the terminology of partisan political debate seems to miss the empirical scene. For example, in the discussion over privatization of the nationalized industries, it seems to be neglected that a government pursuing nationalization can still have weak political control over 'their' industry (for example, British Gas and the unsuccessful attempt to make them sell off their show rooms) and that any government will attempt to nudge, steer, encourage, control and support any large business, even if it is nominally private. The rhetoric of government and Opposition fails to match with feasible performance, constrained as it is by lack of resources and the need for co-operation of affected interests.

The issue of appearance and reality was, of course, also the theme of Bagehot's *The English Constitution*, first published in 1867. In a sly opening paragraph Bagehot quotes J. S. Mill: '"On all great-subjects", says Mr Mill, "much remains to be said" and of none is this more true than of the English Constitution . . . an observer who looks at the living reality will wonder at the contrast to the paper description.' As Crossman points out in his introduction to Bagehot ([1867] 1963, p. 6) this is an oblique criticism of Mill's *Representative Government* (1861) – which is so besotted by the power of the House of Commons that it allows only one mention of the Cabinet. Crossman also observes that, in turn, the Bagehot analysis became, in vital parts, *paper* description when power finally moved from the floor of the Commons to the great party machines and the bureaucracy. Crossman (ibid., p. 37) notes: 'Once he was safely dead and buried, the sceptic whose chief pleasure was the deflating of myths and the exposure of democratic pretensions, was himself admitted to the literary establishment; and the book in which he achieved such an exact separation of political myth from political reality became part of a dignified façade . . .'

A very different gap between the terms in use and the content of politics is noted by the journalist and former MP, W. F. Deedes, in discussing 'the lobby' and the language in the press of lobby reports. He gives examples of the formula: 'It was generally accepted in Westminster last night that the Government will . . .', 'Ministers have no intention of allowing themselves to be . . .'. As Deedes (in Mackintosh, 1978, p. 154) says, to a very narrow circle (which need not include a newspaper's readership) such a form of words indicates that the Prime Minister, her press secretary, or a senior Cabinet minister has been addressing off the record remarks to the press. But the remarks have to be decoded and translated, and the meaning is not accessible to the public. In a similar vein we can ask: why is there an attempt to suppress public knowledge of the Cabinet committee system which is the heart of government as practised? Or why is research on the subject of the 'usual channels' which organize and orchestrate parliamentary life not encouraged? There is, then, a failure of normal political discourse to engage with actual political behaviour.

One of the leading Western political scientists of the post-war years, Charles Lindblom, has proposed an extreme version of the mismatch between normal political discussion and political power. He claims that much of what we recognize as political behaviour and discuss as political science is spurious. He asks us to consider the view that popular control in both market and government is circular and that people are indoctrinated to demand – to buy and vote for – nothing other than what the decision-making élite is already disposed to offer them. The volitions that are supposed to guide leaders are, he says, formed by the same leaders (1977, p. 202).

Unfortunately, all those sources cited above are linked by the theme that we are not doing very well in understanding political society. Some things we can say with reassuring certainty: for example, Britain has first-past-the-post elections decided in 650 parliamentary constituencies. We can, again with certainty, set out matters such as turnout in elections, but even that quickly takes us into controversy. Is that turnout sufficiently high? If it falls, is it a sign of voter apathy or fundamental acceptance of the system? There is a drift from the certainty about the ingredients of good government. Twenty years ago a textbook could rehearse with assurance the advantages of an electoral system providing strong, disciplined parliamentary majorities. Such confidence has disappeared.

In the area of – to use Ricci's phrase – 'descriptive empiricism' (1984, p. 311), the problem is less severe and political science has accumulated findings with workmanlike efficiency. However, even this presents two problems. First, this exercise of apparently rather uncontroversial description has meant that we have had to address that gap mentioned above between the real world and the imaginary view. Ricci (1984, p.75) in discussing the major cross-national survey by Almond and Verba (1965), observed:

> In their analysis, the power of elites must be checked if democratic regimes are to be moderate and effective. [But] Voting studies had shown that citizens are neither sufficiently active nor competent enough to perform this service. It was a fact, however, that most citizens had not yet received word of their empirical irrelevance. And so they continued to participate in politics regardless of how little their efforts mattered.

The second problem raised by empirical work is that while the information is useful to arguments such as how the House of Commons works, or where power resides in the Labour party (though information has not by itself, finally settled any of these issues), the kind of information it is feasible to gather is remote from questions of a broad nature, such as why political regimes enjoy the support, or at least compliance, of their citizens.

On a matter such as why regimes are considered 'legitimate', some of the most convincing work is at the same time highly speculative. Christel Lane (1984) has argued that Soviet government is legitimated through a system of socialist ritual – from the October celebrations, through initiation rituals in the Young Pioneers, and individual *rites de passage* such as the Festive Registration of the Newborn. Lane links the rites of initiation with conscious efforts to invoke the past. The present regime is thus deliberately identified with the Revolution and the Great Patriotic War. Lane argues that the authority of the leadership is secured at least as much at an emotional as an intellectual level.

But Western societies also have their rituals and it might well be the case that, for example, voting is to be treated as an activity which is best seen as a means of legitimating the leadership rather than a means of determining policy outputs. Edelman's *The Symbolic Uses of Politics* (1964), is probably the most developed source of this view that the democratic political activity has a meaning, even if the democratic choice is weak. Legitimacy may have something to do with the formal electoral procedures adopted, but it may also have to do with outputs (legitimacy by results), or it may be founded on widespread beliefs in the rights of others – rights that cannot be negated merely because an electoral majority says otherwise.

These, then, are interesting areas – but poorly illuminated by political science. There is quantitatively an increase in terrorism in Western societies (Wilkinson, 1979) and this may simultaneously reflect a breakdown in legitimacy (from the terrorists) and yet, paradoxically, it could lead to an increased commitment to democratic procedures – as, arguably, has been the case in Italy. The terrorists may have underlined the consequences of a breakdown in democratic values and procedures. Yet at a point, undeniably, democracy is not compatible with violence. Violence could lead to a fragmentation of society as in Lebanon.

An industrial dispute is certainly *not* inconsistent with the strikers behaving democratically and accepting the state as legitimate. However, when a union is challenging and seeking to replace the government, or arguing that a law on industrial relations is not 'just' and need not be obeyed, then the position is less clear. While that sort of rhetoric might have been prevalent in the miners' strike of 1984/5 – with hindsight – the strike as an anti-system manifestation appears to have been shallow. The problem of interpretation is compounded when we build in to our considerations a norm that protest is legitimate in a democracy and must be tolerated. The most interesting questions appear to be those that we can resolve least well.

As an extension of this point – and in line with the rather pessimistic observations at the beginning of this chapter – the idea of governing 'overload' has been influential in political science. One of the best sources for this discussion is Anthony King's *Why Is Britain Becoming Harder to Govern?* (1976). King makes the point that government is now assumed to be responsible for everything. He gives the example of how, when the party conferences were cancelled in 1974 because of the general election in 1974, hoteliers and restaurateurs petitioned the Department of Trade for compensation. King (1976, p. 12–14) comments that government has come to be regarded as a sort of unlimited liability company, in the business of insuring all persons at all times against every conceivable risk. He went on:

> To be held responsible for everything is to feel compelled to intervene in everything. A Conservative Government [ie 1970–4] rescues Upper Clyde Shipbuilders and nationalises part of Rolls Royce; a Labour Government nationalised British Leyland and picks up the pieces after the collapse of Court Line, a privately owned airline and holiday company that was not particularly important to the national economy. Public is still public; private in 1976 is also public.

Matters such as sport are, by 1985, a matter of governmental concern – whether it is crowd safety, crowd behaviour, or sporting links with South Africa – or even the prestige of national success.

The electoral pressure is for any potential government to show an interest in all problems and to be confident that it can ameliorate the issue at hand. Put simply, the doctor who says he is not interested in the disease, or that it is incurable anyway, is going to lose patients. Electorally, hyperactivity is popular.

One of the difficulties is that problems are rarely solved once and for all. Because of the political storm in Scotland in 1985 after the rates revaluation, an arrangement was patched up for one year's relief. This only intensified the pressure for 1985–6. Success of one policy perhaps invents, creates, reveals a new issue. 'Policy as its own cause', in the words of Wildavsky (1980). The success in increasing the number of house buyers gives extra sensitivity to the mortgage issue. The economic benefit of North Sea Oil has a less welcome impact on foreign-exchange rates and hence on manufacturing industry and exports. The inter-connectedness of things makes for unintended and undesirable consequences.

In Sam Brittan's essay 'The economic contradictions of democracy', (reproduced in A. King, 1976), the main threats to liberal democracy are given as:

(a) the generation [in the minds of the voters] of excessive expectations,

(b) the disruptive effects of the pursuit of group self interest in the market place.

His main point is that the competitive party system has encouraged parties to issue political prospectuses which cannot be funded. He discusses the lack of budget restraint among voters. He points out how Opposition parties promise to do better and how the government must join in the electoral auction.

It might be that that kind of 'overload' discussion was time-bound. It perhaps reflected the political difficulties following the oil price 'hike'. Certainly, there was a concern with the inevitability of inflation – that now seems less inevitable. Also Anthony King's opening essay ties in the problem of governing with the observation that 'the tenure of governments is precarious and that for the foreseeable future it will be a lucky government that survives for more than a term'. No sooner did we get used to this new conventional wisdom of incumbency as a liability (the Americans began to discuss the no-win presidency), than Mrs Thatcher and Mr Reagan were re-elected.

The overload theorists present liberal-democracy in crisis. The crisis *in legitimation* is a related critique which stems largely from the political left. This view has been discussed by Professor Birch (1984, p. 143) in four principal propositions:

(1) That the liberal-democratic state is a means to legitimate, in the eyes of the political mass, the privilege of the capitalists and the capitalist system.

(2) That the political values of the capitalist class enjoy a position of what Gramsci called, 'an ideological hegemony'. Birch quotes Poulanzas as follows: 'The dominance of this ideology is shown by the fact that the dominated classes live their conditions of political existence through the forms of dominant political discourse: this means that often they live *even their revolt* against the domination of the system within the frame of reference of the dominant ideology.'

(3) That the liberal-democratic state adopts policies and tactics to protect its own legitimacy. One is the development of welfare so as to shelter disadvantaged groups from the inevitable hardship of capitalism. Another is to direct conflicts (for example, wage levels) which are sure to upset sizeable groups, outside the institutions of the state itself. This gives the state the illusion of neutrality.

(4) Fourthly, Birch notes the Marxist argument that the system of legitimation has broken down because of fiscal overload. So many groups in the population are dependent on public finance that the economic burden cannot be sustained – nor can social expenditure be cut because it would lead to electoral defeat *and* possible withdrawal of support for the regime itself. Thus both right-wing free market and neo-Marxist critics arrive at equally gloomy assessments of the liberal-democratic predicament.

We would agree with Birch that the talk of crisis is overheated. He points out that the Brittan type of discussion is undermined by the demonstrated ability of the Thatcher government to legislate on trade union policy and to control inflation. He notes that at the core of the work of Habermas is the claim that even if the liberal-democratic state overcame its economic problem, the legitimation crisis would remain. As Birch notes, this claim rests on Habermas's value position that, in the final analysis, *the class structure* is the source of the legitimation deficit. Birch (1984, p. 154) concludes, 'this seems to be a pure piece of Marxist faith which, if accepted, makes the rest of the analysis somewhat superfluous'.

As unemployment has greatly intensified since the development of the overload and crisis notions, the puzzle of the robustness of the democratic regimes is increased. Some commentators – such as Sir John Hoskyns, formerly head of the Prime Minister's Policy Unit and now director general of the Institute of Directors – are, as with the Marxists, unrepentantly pessimistic. In February 1985 he was still addressing the 'unsustainable post-war political economy' (*The Times*, 11 February 1985). However, such claims now seem extreme. Indeed, uniting the reformers of various parts of the political spectrum is their apparent belief that somewhere it is somehow possible to arrange political life so that harmony, economic well-being and administrative efficiency are possible.

Less optimistically, our level of aspiration for the political system is only that it staggers from crisis to crisis. There will be no calm after the storm: politics is the storm. Despair appears to be the tone whenever studies are written, for example, Lord Hewart's *The New Despotism* (1929), and Ramsay Muir's *How Britain Is Governed* (1930). Politics is about coping with the perennial problems of labour, wealth, investment, trade, and so on. The famous Harold Macmillan speech on 20 July 1957 in which he observed, 'most of our people have never had it so good', in fact ran on to talk about the mounting danger of inflation: 'For amidst all this prosperity, there is one problem that has troubled us ... ever since the war. It's the problem of rising prices.'

The democratic nature of society lies in part on reactive leadership – that the politically elected government in its actions bears some relationship to public wishes. (This principle is customarily suspended, however, when it is inconvenient. For example, the steady support for capital punishment as reported in successive opinion polls is ignored.) In our conventional way at looking at this, it is also common to allow that the political leaders influence demands: Bagehot ([1867], 1963) described how Parliament, 'ought to teach the nation what it does not know'.

Democracy is more than a set of electoral arrangements, and we would propose that the main democratic prop is the sense of restraint among the politically influential, that is, the elected politicians and the bureaucracy. However, on this sort of matter political science talks with much less confidence than about the empirical detail of practice. Far from being self-evident and clear, democracy entails different ideas and aspects (and even inconsistent elements). For example, it is commonly held that elected governments have a *right* to govern – but, at the same time, the government should secure the consent of those affected by a policy. These are age-old problems – better addressed in the discussion over the American Constitution than in Britain. In his *Dilemma of Democracy*, the Conservative minister, Lord Hailsham expressed concern about a position where 'a government elected by a small minority of voters and with a slight majority in the House regards itself as entitled and, according to its more extreme supporters, bound to carry out every proposal in its election manifesto . . . it seems to me that at any cost we must ensure that it cannot happen again' (quoted in Sedgemore, 1980, p. 47). Whatever the democratic principles, when it comes to hard cases – such as the abolition of the Metropolitan counties – government will tend to resort to the 'We have a majority, so there!' position. However, a notion of democracy which depends on an election every four years or so is clearly very crude. When a major interest (as in the case of the trade unions and the 1972 Industrial Relations Act) refuses to co-operate with legislation, the conflict between democracy as a matter of satisfying electoral requirements, and democracy as proceeding with consent is underlined.

Therefore, our position is that the role of political science in resolving the problems of a democratic society is weak. But that is not the role of political study: the role is illumination. To illuminate is not a trivial pursuit when the discrepancy between real truth and imaginary views remains so great.

The consequence of our view of the democratic process as being to an extensive degree non-partisan and non-parliamentary, with policy effectively made in specialist sectors (or in the American phrase sub-governments), is that far more attention needs, in our view, to be paid to the actual *process* of any policy decision. Bruce-Gardyne and Lawson (1976, p. 184) claimed: 'Interest groups cajole, the Bank of England warns, the civil servants guide, the back benchers plot, the departmental ministers propose and the Prime Minister disposes. But so often it is pure hazard which tips the scales in the end.' As one of their examples, they point out that Edward Heath would not have introduced a Bill on regional development initiatives in 1963 if the Opposition member, John Stonehouse, had not won first place in the ballot for Private Members' legislation. As Stonehouse wished to put forward a Bill to abolish Retail Price Maintenance (RPM), the Department was able to convince Heath, as Minister, to take up this cause.

They show how simple luck allowed the government to survive critical votes – where defeat would probably have forced Heath's resignation – which would probably have ruined his chances when the election for Leader unexpectedly cropped up.

As well as chance there is the matter of interaction, which means that policies are very often not the intended and calculated outcomes sought by any particular side in the argument, but the consequence of the bargaining process. In our case study (Jordan and Richardson, 1984) of the emergence of the Engineering Council after the recommendations of the Finniston Report (Cmnd 7794), Heisler's (1979, p. 286) underlining of 'the actual dynamics of the bargaining process' is sustained.

As well as being unpredictable and complex, policy-making in Britain is simply variable. The kind of process by which the government, say, decided upon and introduced the Industrial Relations Act 1971 (see Moran, 1977) was much more closed and partisan than, say, decisions on abortion politics (see Marsh and Chambers, 1981), or agriculture (see G. K. Wilson, 1977), or unemployment (see Moon and Richardson, 1985).

Later, in Chapter 4, we express some scepticism with the idea that *adversary politics* – and its image of sudden discontinuity in policies – is very useful in the study of British politics. Our contrasting emphasis is that the options of government are constrained, because irrespective of the electoral outcome, the problems that face government departments – and the pressures on departments – are likely to change little. While we readily acknowledge that policy style in policy sectors can vary, our work across a range of departments and issues suggests that a characteristic British style exists. It might be true that something like the past decade of local government finance does not fit our stereotype, but arguably the highly partisan nature of the clash has 'contaminated' possible bureaucratic resolution. (And,

at the same time, sub-communities on specific matters, such as fire
and safety, or building control, do continue their largely 'silent
politics'.)

The features of the British style are what we have termed elsewhere
(Jordan and Richardson, 1982) 'bureaucratic accommodation'. We
elaborate on this idea in Chapter 7. It is bureaucratic in its emphasis
on relationships between civil servants and civil service-like officers of
interest groups. It is accommodation-ist, in the sense that attempts
are made to resolve issues in sectors by the relevant 'professionals'.

Therefore in the study of the policy process our expectation is that
most political issues in Britain are resolved in the relatively private
and specialized worlds of policy sectors. That this is not a novel
interpretation is beyond dispute. The Webbs, for example, wrote
that:

> The real Government of Great Britain is nowadays carried on, not
> in the House of Commons at all, nor even in the Cabinet, but in
> private conferences between Ministers, with their principal
> officials, and the persons specifically affected by any proposed
> legislation or by any action on the part of the administration . . .
> The great mass of government today is the work of an able and
> honest but secretive bureaucracy, tempered by the ever-present
> apprehension of the revolt of sectional interests, and mitigated by
> the spasmodic interventions of imperfectly comprehending
> Ministers. (1920, p. 69, quoted in Fry, 1985)

To cite such authorities, writing in such a way, is to look at politics
from a different angle from the usual press and current affairs version
of politics, which would lay stress on ministers, parties and the
articulation of conflict. The departmental, civil service, consensus
'lens' is clearly *another* rather than a superior approach, but our
experience of case studies, and our reading of the experience of other
case studies, suggest that most policy outcomes have more to do with
the latter processes. For example, in Ovenden's (1978, p. 11) study
of the steel industry he found he had to move from his initial focus
upon Parliament and direct his attention 'to this enormous political
and industrial network'. In recent interviews with civil servants on
consultation practices, we have been impressed by the sheer weight of
consultation – quite at odds with the so-called 'Thatcher style' – and
the readiness of civil servants to use the language of political patrons
to the groups 'in their patch'. They were referred to as 'customer
groups', 'client groups' – even 'constituency groups'.

This sort of approach to British policy-making builds upon the
work of pressure groups in Britain in the 1960s, and upon a
succession of powerful case studies in more recent years. As an

approach, it also has points of contact with ideas which have developed in the USA about 'iron triangles', 'segmented pluralism', policy sub-governments, and the like (see Yates, 1982). The American ideas cover the broad identity of interest between the bureaucracy, its supporting interest groups, and its ostensibly controlling congressional committees which are frequently 'captured' by congressmen with constituency interests at stake.

Ripley and Franklin (1976, p. 7) have said of sub-governments:

Most of the policy making in which sub-governments engage consist of routine matters. By 'routine' we simply mean policy that is not currently involved in a high degree of controversy, policy that is not likely to change very much, and policy with which the participants most interested in it are thoroughly familiar . . . Since most policy making is routine most of the time, sub-governments can often function for long periods of time without much interference . . . If the members of a sub-government can reach compromises among themselves on any disagreements about a policy, they can reduce the chances of calling a broader audience together that might become involved in their activities and output . . . there is a strong incentive for them to reach compromises and avoid broadening the number of participants.

While, in Britain, Parliament is largely absent from the process, the key idea of *mutual support* between department and 'constituency groups' remains. This phenomenon verges on being universal throughout Western democracies. There is the well-known 'two-channel' characterization of Norwegian politics by Stein Rokkan (1966, p. 106):

Votes count in the choice of governing personnel but other resources decide the actual policies pursued by the authorities.

The extension of the franchise to all adults and the maintenance of a strict majoritarian rule of decision-making in the legislature made it possible for a movement of the hitherto underprivileged to rise to power. But the parallel growth of a vast network of interest organisations . . . made it impossible to rule by a simple '50 per cent plus' principle . . . The vote potential constitutes only one among many different power resources.

As well as intimacy of relations, a pattern of sectorization in group governmental relations has been widely documented. For Sweden, Ruin (in Richardson, ed., 1982, pp. 144–7) has argued that the sectorization and 'time consuming negotiations between government and interest groups' have been reinforced in the 1970s. Such comments are easily replicated for Denmark, Holland and even France.

Writing on the process of 'extended legislation' in West Germany, Wolfgang Zey (1985) has observed that 'The relatively free and legal access for organized interests is the cost for their backing, for their support in implementation.' He notes that the groups support governmental ends in publishing technical journals and gazettes and in informing the specialized world affected by proposals. Having been party to the policy-making, the groups have to prove the value of the participation by defending the outcome to the group members. In this way, details promulgated by the groups are possibly more acceptable than if stemming directly from government. In Canada, Pross has written (1975, p. 121): 'Pressure groups . . . are assumed to be integral to the functioning of the Canadian party system, now and in the past. Successful interaction between Canadian governments and pressure groups has been typified by consultations and the search for accommodation and consensus.'

As Pross says, while we know that these mutually supportive relationships exist, we are as yet unclear on how this process of reciprocity operates. Certainly, some kind of exchange over time exists between the bureaucracy and the group. An illustration of this frame of mind in Britain is the remark of the parliamentary director of the National Farmers' Union (NFU) who noted that: 'When a good deal has been obtained, of course we try to seek credit with our members – but not at the expense of damaging relationships with Government. . . . Tomorrow is another day and another issue' (Holbeche, 1986). Going back as far as Laski (1931, p. 84) there is a recognition of the exchange: 'Whenever a department touches a social interest, the associations which serve that interest ought to be related to the department for the purpose of consultative co-operation . . . No better means exists than the advisory committee for the reciprocal training of civil servants and the public . . .'

The 'British style' is therefore the consequence of 'deal-seeking' behaviour between realistic groups and consensus-seeking civil servants. This does not happen in all policy sectors at all times – as Holbeche (1986) observed: 'Some lobbies do seem to have difficulty in judging the art of the possible to what is on and what not – and they tend to be rather plaintive about a compromise solution that may have been worked out which does not meet all of their requirements. I think it is important to be realistic on this.'

We see the pattern of bureaucratic accommodation as a standard operating procedure of government – a procedural ambition – even though it may not be possible in all circumstances. There appears to be a 'logic' underpinning the development of the practice – which accounts for the emergence of similar procedures in very different political regimes.

Elsewhere we have listed some of the dimensions of this logic under five main headings (Jordan and Richardson, 1982, 1983). In brief, they are:

Sectorization – where policy is made in specialized communities.

Clientelism – where departments basically act as sponsor for 'their' groups.

Consultation – where policy proposals are routinely canvassed among interested groups.

Institutionalization – where commonly the access of groups is regularized in some kind of advisory machinery.

Exchange – where civil servants and group officers work together as policy professionals, to produce mutually satisfactory outcomes.

Distinctions need to be drawn between sub-governments and policy communities (see Jordan and Richardson, 1982, p. 89); there may well be worthwhile distinctions to be made in terms of issue areas: different issues can generate different styles (see Rhodes, 1985). It may well be that the tendency for accommodation is under threat in increasingly resource-stressed and densely populated policy environments (see Heclo, 1978; Gais, Peterson and Walker, 1984), but we would still feel that this broad approach of studying groups and departments with shared interests is the key to understanding the maintenance of a political system. If politics were simply conflict, political society could not exist.

We see striking relevance in Heisler and Kvavik's portrait (in Heisler, 1974, p. 48) of a 'European Polity'. They claimed that Western European countries could be characterized by 'a decision making structure characterized by continuous, regularized access for economically, politically, ethnically, and/or sub culturally based groups to be light levels of the political system ...'. Realistically, British democracy is to be found in the procedures for conflict resolution in specialized sub-governments and not simply, or even principally, in the largely illusory democracy of party politics.

The Arena Approach

In this book we attempt to cover the fact that decisions are determined in different ways by focusing upon five main arenas. They are the *public* arena where voters have a say in public policy by the fact of their electoral power. Even if one suspects that the actual difference between parties in government is commonly much exaggerated (arguably, it is only of limited importance, in terms of policy outputs, which party wins an election), it is very important to the politicians which party wins. Thus, as one of the considerations in the policy process, there is the sensitivity of the politicians to public moods.

A second arena which we discuss is *Parliament*. Although we might wish to play down its importance in comparison with some accounts, parliamentary processing is a necessary part of policy-making of the type which needs statutory backing. Similarly, the *party* is itself an arena for policy-making. Thus whether or not a future Labour government would reimburse the National Union of Mineworkers for the £1 million lost in the miners' strike of 1984–5 is a policy to be determined within the Labour Party and requires attention to the constitutional and political resources of the party leader, the conference and other elements.

Because of the centralization of power in the British political system, the *Cabinet* deserves to be considered as a separate arena of policy-making. All these arenas necessarily interrelate and the *bureaucratic* arena reflects much of the same pressures as the Cabinet, but in Chapter 7 we pay particular attention to the activities of civil servants and their relations with outside interests. As a final chapter in our discussion of arenas we look at the pressure groups (Chapter 8). In some circumstances, the actual group can be an arena – as in the political in-fighting within the RSPCA in recent years – but, in the main, we examine pressure groups because of their importance as actors in other arenas.

PART TWO

Policy-making arenas

CHAPTER THREE

The Public Arena

Introduction

One of the central themes of this book is that the classical ways of looking at the political system are often misleading. Thus a simple model suggesting that the electorate chooses a government, which then presents a coherent set of policies based on the party's election manifesto for parliamentary approval, misses much of the variety and complexity of how decisions are made and where power in society actually resides. Power is exercised elsewhere, often through a process of bargaining and negotiation between government departments (and within government departments), and between government departments and outside groups. It is, in fact, exceptional when political parties play a key role in bringing policies onto the political agenda and putting them into practice with parliamentary approval.

Nonetheless in Western societies the notion of *electoral democracy* is powerful. We, the voters, can turn a government out at the next election and replace it with another advocating a quite different set of policies. Thus the notion of the power of the voter is also linked to the notion of adversary politics in Britain – where parties are programmatic and oppose each other's policies with great force and determination. Hence, in theory, the voter can choose not only between competing teams of leaders, but also between competing programmes. A great deal of day-to-day political conflict, both within and outside the House of Commons, is part of a continuous extended election campaign, designed to win the support of voters.

Within political parties, policies are often judged by their potential electoral impact. Thus in 1984–5 Conservative backbenchers – many of whom would not be re-elected if government popularity fell – became restive about the possibility that the state pension system might be changed radically, as they feared that the proposed changes could lose them votes. In this sense, the voter is quite powerful, if only because politicians have a perception (perhaps inaccurate) of what the voter does or does not want. But, equally, politicians often disregard the wishes of voters (for example, on hanging, immigration, homosexual law reform, and so on) if their conscience, ideology, or relationship with powerful interest groups is pressing them to ignore popular opinion. Thus we must recognize that power is not always exercised in what we might call the *public arena*.

As introduced in Chapter 2, Stein Rokkan (1966) addressed the question of how societies achieve a successful balance between elections and the more private negotiations which take place between governments and interest groups (what we term in Chapter 7 the *bureaucratic arena*). He thought that there was a balance between 'numerical democracy' and 'corporate pluralism', or between elections and the symbiotic relationship between government departments and outside groups. Rokkan was puzzled by Norwegian society which was generally seen as rather democratic, yet (at the time he was writing) had had one party in office (almost continuously) for thirty years. (Sweden also had one party office for even longer – forty-four years – until 1976.) How could a country remain democratic under such a system – quite alien to the postwar British style, whereby parties are turfed out of office very regularly? His answer was that, although the Opposition might lose the election, the important interests which it represented could still be taken account of in other ways – they were not disenfranchised in practice. His 'model' was one of a two-tier system of decision-making. In a central passage he suggested that

> The crucial decisions on economic policy are rarely taken in the parties or in Parliament: the central area is the bargaining table where the government authorities meet directly with the trade union leaders, the representatives of the farmers, the smallholders and the fishermen, and the delegates of the Employers' Association. *These yearly round of negotiations have in fact come to mean more in the lives of rank-and-file citizens than the formal elections* (Rokkan, 1966, p. 107, italics added)

In this chapter we want to concentrate upon the first aspect of Rokkan's model – namely, the role that the ordinary citizen can play in making decisions and influencing the exercise of political power. Before turning to elections and voting – the most important means for the ordinary unorganized citizen to participate in the political process – we shall discuss the concept of participation and the various non-electoral means that the citizen has at his or her disposal.

Public Participation

As we shall see, the 1960s saw a tremendous increase in demands for 'participation' in political decision-making – a demand which has continued to accelerate. Indeed, the demand for 'participation' may itself be a reflection of the stage of development of most Western industrial democracies, as they enter the post-industrial era. Thus most post-industrial societies have achieved a very high level of wealth and education, with over half the population in service or communication industries. It has been suggested that these post-industrial societies develop new kinds of political values and demands: post- or non-material values (Inglehart, 1977). The demand for more participation in the governing process is a central feature of these new demands. No longer, so the theory states, do citizens merely demand from government that it should provide roads, schools, hospitals, universities, houses, and so on, but that it should create more opportunities for citizens to participate in deciding what governments should do. Participation is regarded as a good in itself.

But the idea that citizens should be offered the chance to participate has, of course, a very long history. For example, for Rousseau, participation in determining the general will is *the* political act. If citizens did not participate then the wrong *decisions* would be reached; that is, Rousseau believed that participation was functional. But it also served a broader purpose. Participation was a means of educating citizens. Through participation, men were 'forced to be free'. Similarly, J. S. Mill believed that one of the distinguishing features of a democratic society was that citizens could *share* in government. In practice, how are these lofty ideals fulfilled in Britain? Do we have a genuinely participatory democracy?

One difficulty in answering this question is that the term 'participation' is difficult to define! Parry defines political participation as taking part in the formulation, passage, or implementation of public policies (Parry, 1972). However, it is also difficult to define what 'taking part' means. One might exercise influence without formally taking part in the decision. (The reluctance of Conservative backbenchers to support radical change in the State Earnings Related Pension Scheme, SERPS, in 1985, is an example of citizen influence without formal participation.) In practice, 'the level of participation undertaken by any citizen will depend on the opportunities available to him, the political resources he commands, and the attitudes held by society in general, for example whether favourable to interest group activity or not' (Higgins and Richardson, 1976, p. 7). Whether citizens participate will also depend upon their own attitudes and perceptions of the political process, and the opportunities that the process presents to them. Cross-national studies suggest that levels of participation do vary quite considerably from one nation to another. Does this mean that levels of democracy vary in direct proportion?

In a classic study, Almond and Verba (1965) introduced the idea of a 'sense of civic competence', that is, a belief that citizens could influence governmental decisions. They sub-divided the notion of civic competence into 'subjective civic competence' (a belief that citizens could do something about a bad decision by government) and 'objective civic competence' (actual behaviour designed to influence government). Britain and the USA came out with rather high scores in the original Almond and Verba surveys (62 per cent and 75 per cent respectively), compared with West Germany, for example (38 per cent). Yet more recent evidence suggests that, as the West German democracy 'matures', the sense of civic competence is growing. Thus a 1974 survey produced a West German 'score' of 59 per cent (Conradt, 1980, p. 232). The percentage of German citizens who felt competent to influence unjust national legislation rose from 38 per cent in 1959 to 59 per cent in 1979, whereas it had increased by only 6 per cent over the same period in the UK.

Other data show that attitudes to *forms* of participation in the UK seem to be rather stable. Thus Kavanagh (1980, p. 170) notes that 'while there is no survey evidence to show widespread trust in the political authorities, outright cynicism or support for violence outside the law is confined to a small minority.' In terms of what citizens think that they would actually do to influence local and national government, the responses to the Almond and Verba questionnaire, administered in 1959, are very similar to the survey questionnaire by Marsh in 1974 (see Table 3.1).

Thus one needs to be cautious in believing that British politics – notwithstanding the troubles in Northern Ireland, the 1984–5 miners' strike, and the Handsworth and Tottenham disturbances in 1985 – should be characterized by mass, and often violent, participation. Though observers have claimed that waves of political protest have swept advanced industrial democracies (Barnes and Kaase, 1979, p. 13), Britain has experienced a gradual increase in political mobilization and participation, particularly via the formation of new pressure groups and the increased membership of existing ones. Groups formed in the 1960s – for example, Shelter formed in 1966 and the Child Poverty Action Group formed in 1965 – are now an accepted part of their respective policy fields.

Similarly, the environmental movement has grown to such a degree (particularly in the 1970s) that it has more members than all of the political parties put together. (This is also true of West Germany (see Richardson and Watts, 1985.) The view expressed by McKenzie in the mid-1950s, that pressure-group membership was a more effective channel of citizen involvement than political parties is even more valid today (McKenzie, 1958). As we shall see in later

Table 3.1   *What Citizens Would Do To Try To Influence Their Local and National Governments in 1959 and 1974[a] (in %)*

What citizens would do[b]	1959 (Almond and Verba)		1974 (Marsh)	
	Local	National	Local	National
Do nothing. Don't know	23	32	36	43
Contact politicians	45	44	40	45
Contact party	1	2	1	1
Vote	4	3	2	2
Form interest groups	3	3	3	3
Contact bureaucrats	3	1	2	—
Get up *ad hoc* protest group	34	18	32	18
Petition, use media	—	—	—	—
March, demonstrate	—	—	3	2
'Just protest'	—	—	3	1
Number		963		1,985

Source: Kavanagh, 1980, p. 150.
[a] The question was 'Suppose a regulation were being considered by ——— which you considered very unjust or harmful, what do you think you could do?'
[b] Total percentages exceed the sum of the individual cells, since some respondents gave more than one answer.

chapters, civil servants have been especially aware of the need to accommodate more and more groups into the policy-making and implementing process – so much so that the very large numbers of groups involved in some consultation exercises have become quite difficult to manage.

The pattern so far is that increased participation has been generally well ordered and has been successfully 'accommodated' into existing procedures. In that sense, the British system of government is rather 'open' in style – contrary to the popular view that government is closed and secretive.

Because participation has been perceived to be important and desirable, procedures have been developed to facilitate – at least in theory – public participation in policy-making. For example, the Skeffington Committee was set up in 1968 to investigate methods of securing participation and its recommendations, in turn, led to changes in the physical planning procedures. Also, the rules of public inquiries have been changed to make participation easier for citizens and *ad hoc* groups.

But what effect does the increased 'participation' have? Is the participation 'real' or is it 'sham' participation carefully (or cynically) designed to create the false impression that we can participate if we want to? Some environmentalists, for example, are frustrated by the outcome of public inquiries and feel that the proposed development goes ahead anyway, irrespective of their 'participation'. (For example, Stansted airport will be built, despite the opposition of local and national environmental groups, and the new docklands airport will be built in London, despite protests.)

But participation does affect political decisions. For example, the controversial plan to build a 290-foot office block at the Mansion House site in the City of London was rejected by the Secretary of State for the Environment in May 1985, despite the fact that the developer had spent twenty-six years and £10 million acquiring the site. The plan had been bitterly opposed by conservationists who regarded the minister's decision as a great victory for their efforts. Similarly, the animal rights' movement managed to persuade the government to introduce new legislation in 1985 restricting the use of animals in experiments. The new policy, outlined in a White Paper, *Scientific Procedures in Living Animals*, reflected proposals which some of the animal welfare groups had submitted to the Home Office in 1983.

It should, of course, be remembered that one man's successful participation may be another man's defeat. As one county councillor writing in *The Times* (29 May 1985) has observed, there may be an 'Iron law of Lobbyarchy: that when government attempts to involve the public in planning, the result is less power for the people and more power for the pressure groups. Your objections are only as strong as the pressure group you form'. Citing the example of plans to build 700 houses at Danley, in Sheppey, he notes that the existing local residents organized themselves to oppose the proposed development. They won, and he comments that 'the 700 houses will not be built at Danley because the people there got themselves organised; that will not stop them being built in a less suitable location a few miles away where people are less vocal'.

Thus it is important to note that procedures, which with every good intention have been introduced to facilitate participation in decision-making, are not entirely neutral in their effects as between different sections of the community. Because the most effective form of participation is through organizations, then participation tends to favour those who are best at organizing – not always those deserving of the most influence. Hence we need to be wary of arguments that 'more participation is a good thing', as this may further disadvantage certain interests in society, due to the fact that procedures designed to facilitate participation may have inbuilt biases.

There is, however, a much broader sense in which citizens affect public policies – simply by citizens 'doing things'. Thus the greatly increased female participation in the labour market has had a profound effect on the level of unemployment in the UK. By 1984/5 the government was able to demonstrate that there were more people *em*ployed in Britain than when the government took office in 1979 – yet *un*employment had virtually trebled in that period. Part of the reason for this increased unemployment was that more women (as well as more school-leavers) were demanding employment. At the time of writing (1985), it seems likely that the high rate of unemployment will force the government to change its policies before the next election. Thus the action of a group of citizens – in this case women – will have had a very direct political and policy impact.

Similarly, the action of state employees has a very direct effect on governmental policy. For example, it was calculated in 1984 that for every 1 per cent on public sector pay, public spending had to increase by £1,000 million, thus reducing the Chancellor of the Exchequer's room for manoeuvre in his budget. The rate of inflation (influenced by, among other things, wage claims and the behaviour of the City of London via exchange rates) has quite dramatic effects on the level of public expenditure. For example, the fact that the rate of inflation in May 1985 was nearly 7 per cent, compared with the original estimate of 4.75 per cent, cost the Treasury another £800 million on the social security budget. Yet another example of citizen action, or inertia, having profound policy implications was the very sharp decline in the number of students coming forward for training as mathematics teachers in Britain. Thus the number of students taking a postgraduate certificate of education course in mathematics fell by 12 per cent in 1984/5, despite the Secretary of State's desire to improve the level of mathematical attainment of British schoolchildren. Government policy was pointing in one direction, and citizen 'action', or 'inertia' was pointing in another.

Citizens do exercise power over governments – and greatly influence the nature of public policies – through our sheer inertia or unwillingness to behave in the way in which public policies prescribe. The fact that Britain lags behind West Germany and Japan in the mathematical attainment of its citizenry may be of concern to the government, and it may be very damaging to Britain's economic and industrial performance, but governments are probably powerless to do much about it in a democratic society. Of equal importance is the fact that public policies are often driven by citizen action. For example, the strong trend since the Second World War towards car ownership has forced governments (even socialist governments very sympathetic to public transport and to theories of transport co-ordination) to provide what the citizen (consumer) has demanded by way of bigger and better roads. We should, therefore, not neglect the power of the citizen as the consumer of public goods of various kinds, for example, roads, recreational facilities. Mrs Thatcher, for example, may wish to limit the growth of expenditure, but citizens will individually and collectively express more and more demands for more and more services to be provided. There is an analogy to be drawn between citizen power and consumer sovereignty. The consumer is not always king in the marketplace – he can be duped, cheated and manipulated – but he can also be very powerful. So it is with the citizen in the political process. Moreover, as in the marketplace, there are usually competing firms (political parties) willing to claim that they offer a better product. It is to the marketplace for votes that we now turn.

Elections, Voting and Policy-Making

The traditional notion of representative government is, in fact, in conflict with the stress on programmes in elections. For example, Lucas argues that:

> ... the tendencies are all towards playing down the role of the representative and playing up the importance of the electoral vote. The end result is the mandate. The people are asked to entrust themselves to a person or party for a term of years ... Democracy becomes an autocracy, in which decisions save one are taken by the autocrat, and the only decision left to the people is the occasional choice of an autocrat. (Lucas, 1976, p. 184)

He is very critical of our 'elective autocracy', because it fails to discriminate finely enough to take account of the individual, to remedy her grievances or to carry out her ideas.

Unlike many of our Western European neighbours we do not have a system of proportional representation (PR). Our first-past-the-post system, based upon single-member constituencies, gives no guarantee that the party which gains the most votes (aggregated over all constituencies) in a general election will actually form the government. A party can 'win' the election and become the government by winning individual constituencies by a very small margin, whereas its opponents may 'waste' votes by building up very large majorities in other constituencies. In an extreme example, a party can win a constituency with a third of the votes (even in a three-candidate contest). In 1945 in the Caithness and Sutherland constituency the result decided by only six votes:

E. L. Gander Dower (Conservative)	33·47 per cent
R. McInnes (Labour)	33·43 per cent
Sir A. Sinclair (Liberal)	33·10 per cent

Table 3.2   *Postwar Voting Record of Labour and Conservative*

Year	Conservative Elect-orate (%)	Votes cast (%)	Seats	Labour Elect-orate (%)	Votes cast (%)	Seats	Labour/ Conservative share of votes cast (%)	Total turnout (%)
1945	28·8	39·6	211	34·9	48·0	395	87·6	72·8
1950	36·5	43·5[b]	300	38·7	46·1	315	89·6	83·9
1951	39·6	48·0[b]	325	40·3	48·8	295	96·8	82·6
1955	38·2	49·7[b]	345	35·6	46·4	277	96·1	76·8
1959	38·8	49·3[b]	365	34·5	43·9	258	93·2	78·7
1964	33·5	43·4[b]	304	34·0	44·1	317	87·5	77·1
1966	31·8	41·9[b]	253	36·5	48·1	364	90·0	75·8
1970	33·4	46·4	330	31·0	43·1	288	89·5	72·0
1974 (Feb.)	29·9	37·9	297	29·3	37·2	301	25·1	78·8
1974 (Oct.)	26·1	35·8	277	28·5	39·2	319	75·0	72·8
1979	33·4	43·9	339	28·1	37·0	269	82·9	76·0
1983[a]	30·8	42·4	397	20·1	27·6	209	70·0	72·7

Source: Derived from F. W. S. Craig, *Britain Votes*, Vols 1, 2 and 3 (London: Parliamentary Research Service, 1977, 1980 and 1984); and F. W. S. Craig, *British Electoral Facts* (London: Macmillan, 1976).
   [a] In 1983 the SDP/Liberal Alliance polled 25·4 per cent of the votes and obtained 23 seats.
   [b] Conservatives and supporting parties.

With three major parties now in contention, the number of victories with less than an absolute majority of the votes in a constituency is likely to increase. In fact, 336 of the members of the House of Commons in 1983–7 were elected on a minority vote (Madgwick, 1984, p. 396). The 1983 election was particularly noteworthy (or notorious) for producing a large discrepancy between votes cast and seats gained. It was hailed as a massive landslide victory for Mrs Thatcher, but the Conservatives gained only 42·4 per cent of the votes cast, while gaining over 61 per cent of the seats in the House of Commons. The Alliance, supporters of PR, did particularly badly out of the electoral system. They gained 25·4 per cent of the vote (only 2·2 per cent behind Labour), but gained only 3·5 per cent of the seats in the House of Commons. Table 3.2 shows election results from 1945 to 1983 in terms of percentage votes and seats won.

   Figure 3.1 is a calculation of the number of votes required to elect MPs of different parties in the 1931, 1945 and 1983 elections. As can be seen from the figure, the Liberals (now opposed to the electoral system) were not always greatly disadvantaged by it. In 1931 they gained 6·5 per cent of the votes and got 5·2 per cent of the seats, whereas in 1945 they gained 9 per cent of the vote, but gained only 1·9

Votes per MP elected (thousands)

		% of votes	seats
1931	Conserv	55·4	77·1
	Liberal	6·5	5·2
	Labour	29·3	7·5
1945	Conserv	36·8	31·1
	Liberal	9·0	1·9
	Labour	48·0	61·4
1983	Conserv	42·4	61·1
	Alliance	25·4	3·5
	Labour	27·6	32·2

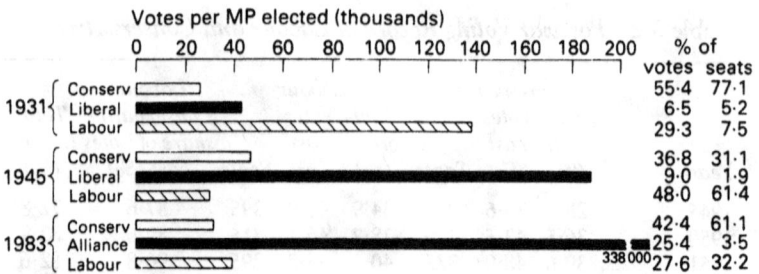

Figure 3.1   The landslide effect.
Source: 'Political Britain today', *The Economist*, 1984, p.8.

per cent of the seats. The geographic distribution of the votes is crucial.

The effects in local government elections can be even more dramatic. In the London Borough of Islington, Labour secured 65 per cent of the votes in 1978 but 100 per cent of the seats. By the 1982 local elections its share of the vote had fallen dramatically to 51 per cent, yet it still managed to get 98 per cent of the seats on the Council (*The Economist*, 1984, p. 8).

The most popular alternative to our first-past-the-post electoral system is the 'single transferable vote' system (STV). This is a system of multi-member constituencies – usually up to five members to be elected per constituency. Each party could run up to five candidates. The voter is required to list candidates in order of preference. (He or she can 'split the ticket', as the Americans say – that is, the voter may vote for representatives of more than one party on the ballot.) In order to decide which five candidates (out of however many have decided to enter the election), a system has to be devised for counting the preferences expressed by the voters. A 'quota' is determined which defines the number of votes a candidate needs in order to be elected. The quota is easily calculated as one vote more than the number of votes actually cast in the election, divided by the number of seats plus one. If, say, 150,000 votes were cast and the constituency has to elect five Members of Parliament then the quota is

$$\frac{150,000}{5 + 1} + 1 = 25,001$$

The voting slips are examined and first preferences are counted. Any candidate who gets at least the quota number of first preferences is elected. Any surplus votes, over and above the quota the successful candidate may have obtained, are distributed to the other candidates, according to the second preferences expressed on all the ballot slips for that candidate. If no one manages to reach the quota as a result of this redistribution of votes, then the bottom candidate (that is, the candidate with the lowest number of first preferences) is eliminated from the count, and the second preferences expressed on his or her ballot are redistributed to the other candidates. This continues until the five have reached the required quota.

As it happens, the UK has used such a system already – in the Northern Ireland Assembly elections of 1973 and 1982 (and for Northern Ireland district council elections, and in the European elections in Northern Ireland). However, both the Conservatives and Labour parties still resist a move away from the first-past-the-post system – seemingly, they prefer to have all of the power some of the time, rather than some of the power (in a coalition government) more of the time. There are, however, organized factions within both main parties who are compaigning for electoral reform, along with the Alliance and other parties. If the UK did have PR, then it is likely that we would have rather more coalition governments (although coalition government is possible under the first-past-the-post system as a consequence of a 'hung' Parliament).

Because of the nature of the electoral system, therefore, participation via elections is a very crude device for influencing policy, as so many votes are 'wasted' and have no direct influence on the election result. Despite this disadvantage, elections are about policies and election results do bring about policy changes. For example, there is no doubt that we would not have seen the massive privatization programme if a Labour government had been elected in1979 and 1983. Huge public corporations, such as British Telecom, British Aerospace, Britoil, British Airways, and British Gas, would have stayed in the public sector had it not been for the Conservative victory. A Labour Chancellor would have had the same temptation to sell assets but, under the pressure of public sector unions, it is difficult to imagine a Labour government developing a major privatization programme (although even Labour sold BP shares in book-balancing exercises).

Clearly, Mrs Thatcher's government has been quite different in style from that of her predecessor, Mr Callaghan, and has been radically different in some (but by no means all) policy areas (see Chapter 7). The centre of gravity (in policy terms) of the political parties is in a different place. This is clear from an examination of party manifestos. British parties are indeed programmatic, that is, they formulate quite specific policy proposals to place before the electorate. The manifestos contain much that is mundane and platitudinous, of course. For example, in the 1979 Conservative Manifesto Mrs Thatcher's foreword expressed her belief that 'for me, the heart of politics is not political theory, it is people and how they want to live their lives'. It is difficult to imagine any of her opponents disagreeing with that! Five main tasks were identified as priorities for a new Conservative government:

(1) To restore the health of our economic and social life, by controlling inflation and striking a fair balance between the rights and duties of the trade union movement.

(2) To restore incentives so that hard work pays, success is rewarded and genuine new jobs are created in an expanding economy.

(3) To uphold Parliament and the rule of law.

(4) To support family life, by helping people to become home-owners, raising the standards of their children's education, and concentrating welfare services on the effective support of the old, the sick, the disabled, and those who are in real need.

(5) To strengthen Britain's defences and work with our allies to protect our interests in an increasingly threatening world.

These statements of intent are unremarkable and relatively uncontroversial. But the manifesto contained other, very specific policy commitments. For example, on trade union reform the manifesto stated that 'all agreements for a closed shop must be drawn up in line with the best practice followed at present and only if an overwhelming majority of the workers vote for it in a secret ballot', and 'we shall ensure that unions bear their fair share of the cost of supporting those of their members who are on strike'. On industry, the manifesto pledged to 'amend the 1975 Industry Act and restrict the powers of the National Enterprise Board solely to the administration of the Government's temporary shareholdings, to be sold off as circumstances permit'.

The 1983 Labour Manifesto promised that 'within days of taking office, Labour will begin to implement an emergency programme of action, to bring about a complete change of direction for Britain'. As with the Conservatives, Labour had its fair share of platitudes listed in the manifesto. For example, on law and order, it stated: 'Labour's aim is to ensure that all sections of the community are safe on the street and at home, free from the fear that crime generates. We believe that the police should have the support of the community, have their rights safeguarded, and be fairly paid.' But the manifesto was also quite specific in its policy pledges. For example, it proposed to set up a National Investment Bank, to transfer the National Nuclear Corporation to the public sector and to stop Sizewell, and scrap the (Tory) Pressurized Water Reactor programme. Its emergency programme of action promised that a Labour government would provide a major increase in public investment, would begin a huge programme of construction, and would repeal Tory legislation on industrial relations. The party also promised to raise pensions by £1.45 per week for a single person and £2.25 for a married couple. Similarly, the Alliance had specific policy commitments in its manifesto – such as a pledge to introduce an effective pay and prices policy, and the introduction of compulsory secret ballots for trade union officials.

How important are these specific policy statements (irrespective of whether the parties would actually implement them if elected) to ordinary voters as they enter the polling booth? What *does* influence voters in their choice of parties? Had this question been asked twenty years ago, a fairly simple and accurate answer could have been given. The answer would have been that social class was the main determinant of voting behaviour, rather than party policies as stated in the election campaign. Indeed, Pulzer (1975, p. 102), writing only ten years ago, was repeating his view (first expressed in 1967) that 'class is the basis of British party policies; all else is embellishment'. There is now much evidence to suggest that the view that we voted according to our class is much less true than it was. It appears that the socialization process – whereby citizens acquire a particular set of political beliefs from parents, fellow schoolchildren, neighbours and fellow workers – no longer produces a highly stable and predictable electorate.

One electoral analyst, Franklin, has gone so far as to suggest that traditional voting allegiances have been so eroded over the last two decades that there is now a potential for quite radical change in British politics. Commenting on the 1983 election, he suggests that the outcome could have been very different. He believes that:

> the social structure that used to underpin traditional two-party voting has changed its nature in recent years, so that at least since 1974 the potential has existed for the right combination of political forces to reduce one or both traditional major parties either to the status of minor contender, or else to that of a more equal partner in what is no longer a two-party system. (Franklin, 1984, p. 367)

Franklin's study is one of several (for example, Heath, Jowell and Curtice, 1985) which have shown that the traditional strong links between voters and 'their' parties have become much weaker. Voters in the 1980s are much more volatile in their behaviour than voters were in the 1960s – a phenomenon also observed in many other Western democracies over the same period. (See Crewe and Denver, 1985). Franklin (1985, p. 112) notes that class voting was at its height in 1964, with two variables – parents' class and respondent's occupation – central to the traditional conception of class-based voting choice. The decline in class voting which he detects since 1964 is related to the decline in the importance of these two variables. Thus, 'the variables most central to the concept of class voting in 1964 are those whose importance in structuring voting choice declined the most' (ibid., p. 106). In a crucial passage he argues that:

> . . . the social forces which sustained the British two party system in 1974 no longer constituted a class system as this had previously been understood. In particular, the social mechanisms which remained in 1974 for transmitting party choice from generation to generation, and for reinforcing and sustaining this choice through adult life, were no longer such as to support any particular party system. (Franklin, ibid., p. 106)

The technical term for the decline in class voting is 'dealignment'. In a major study of voting trends in the 1970s, Särlvik and Crewe (1983, pp. 337–8) suggest that the boundaries of the traditional bases of the two major parties are being blurred and, as they have come to be seen as less significant, they have become easier to transgress – 'an increasing proportion of the voters cast their votes without any strong sense of allegiance to the party they choose to vote for in any particular election'. In Table 3.3, the Särlvik – Crewe analysis charts the steady decline in voter identification with the major parties up to 1979. (Though, in the 1983 election, Conservative and Labour party identification increased.)

The 1983 election was seen by some as a watershed in British politics. Certainly, the result appeared to be very dramatic. As Crewe notes, only the word 'disaster' does justice to the enormity of Labour's defeat, as it lost a quarter of its 1979 vote, itself the lowest for almost half a century. Its record in the south of England, outside London, was miserable, winning only 3 of the 176 seats and being relegated by the Alliance to third place in 150 seats (Crewe, 1984, p. 2). A MORI poll showed that the working class, Labour's traditionally solid base until de-alignment set in during the 1970s and 1980s, deserted the party in huge numbers, with Labour failing to gain a majority of semi-skilled or unskilled workers, or even of trade unionists. The June 1983 figures recorded by MORI suggest that the Conservatives took 40 per cent of the skilled manual vote, Labour took 32 per cent and the Alliance took 26 per cent. The figures for semi-skilled and unskilled workers were Conservative 33 per cent, Labour 41 per cent and Alliance 24 per cent; and for trade unionists were Conservative 31 per cent, Labour 39 per cent and Alliance 29 per cent. The 1983 BBC/Gallup survey showed that non-manual (middle-class) voters split as follows: 58 per cent Conservative, 26

Table 3.3 *Strength of Party Identification*

The table shows, for each election, the percentage of each party's identifiers who said they were 'very strong' supporters of their party.

Generally speaking thought of themselves as:	Percentage 'very strong' of each party's identifiers at the election in					
	1979 (%)	October 1974 (%)	February 1974 (%)	1970 (%)	1966 (%)	1964 (%)
Conservative	24	27	32	51	49	48
Liberal	14	14	12	26	35	32
Labour	29	36	41	47	50	51

Source: Sarlvik and Crewe, 1983, p. 337. Data from British Election Survey, May 1979, October 1974 and February 1974; Butler and Stokes, Election Surveys, 1970, 1966 and 1964.

per cent Alliance and 17 per cent Labour. Opinion poll evidence over the period 1963–83 suggests that class differences in voting declined from 76 per cent to 46 per cent over two decades (Miller, 1984, p. 368).

Heath, Jowell and Curtice (1985) also underline that there have been significant changes in the social/occupational composition which mean that, even if Labour retained the loyalty of the manual working class, it was the loyalty of a group shrinking in size. [Crewe (1986) disputes their contention that it is the shrinking of the *size* of the working class that explains Labour's decline – not a de-alignment of support from within the working class.] There remains an important puzzle – namely, the de-alignment at the level of the individual voter and the 'apparently contradictory tendency for constituencies to become more and more politically polarised' (Berrington, 1984, p. 119). Miller has drawn attention to the fact that if we look at *constituency* election results over the last two decades, two features of class polarization become apparent:

First, class polarization between constituencies is vastly greater than that implied by a simplistic interpretation of nationwide opinion poll results; second, class polarization between constituencies has not declined over the past two decades. *In short, the votes of individuals may no longer be very easily predictable from their social class, but the votes of parliamentary constituencies do remain easily predictable from their social class characteristics.* (Miller, 1984, p. 369, italics added)

Table 3.4 *Constituency Class Polarization 1979–83*

Party percent shares of the vote in different areas

		Solid w-c	Marginal w-c	Marginal m-c	Solid m-c
1979	Conservative	33	43	52	56
	Labour	56	43	30	25
	Liberal	10	13	17	18
1983	Conservative	31	41	51	55
	Labour	47	34	20	15
	Alliance	21	24	28	29
1979–83	Changes in				
	Conservative	− 2	− 2	− 1	− 1
	Labour	− 9	− 9	−10	−10
	Alliance	+11	+11	+11	+11

Sources: Miller, 1984, p. 371. *Analysis of data from BBC/ITN Guide to the New Parliamentary Constituencies* (London: Parliamentary Services, 1983) for estimates of 1979 votes according to 1983 boundaries; The Times, 11 June 1983, for 1983 votes; *Parliamentary Constituency Monitors 1983 Boundaries* (London: OPCS, 1983) for 1981 census data according to 1983 parliamentary boundaries.

Notes: (1) Constituencies have been categorized by their percent professional plus managerial plus non-manual as reported in the 1981 OPCS Census. Constituencies average 36% on that statistic. The four categories used in this table are the constitutencies with 15–25% (solid working class), 25–35% (marginal working class), 35–45% (marginal middle class), and 45–55% (solid middle). These names for areas are purely a shorthand for the precise definition and have no deeper meaning.

(2) Table based only on English (not Scots or Welsh) constituencies, where there was a Liberal candidate in 1979, where none of the MPs elected in 1979 stood under a different party label in 1983, and where fourth party candidates took an insignificant share of the vote.

Indeed, class polarization between constituencies did not decline in the 1983 election. Miller's evidence is summarized in Table 3.4.

Miller's argument (1978, p. 283) is that class polarization has become an attribute of communities rather than of individuals. Essenially, the argument is that constituency characteristics help to determine the voting habits of the people who live there – leading Miller to argue that 'the whole system of class polarization may be in a state of dynamically stable equilibrium with self-cancelling trends more likely than anything else'. The 'area effect' is disputed by Franklin who argues that it is *not* the case that one form of class voting has been replaced by another. His argument is rather technical, but rests upon an analysis of a range of variables which may influence voting.

Franklin believes that what he terms 'supportive variables' (compared with the key variables of parents' class and respondent's occupation) have come to bear more weight in predicting the voter's choice as class influence on the individual has declined. Thus, for example, he cites the influence of housing tenure as a supportive variable – patterns of housing tenure, in particular, will have tended to cluster geographically, so that more middle-class constituencies will tend to be characterised by high levels of home ownership while more working class constituencies will tend rather to be characterised by council-house tenancies' (1984, p. 458). The supportive variables – such as housing policy – are now more influential *because* class itself has declined as an influence on the individual's voting choice.

In fact, there is an area of agreement between the two analyses of the role of class as an influence on voting. Franklin (1984, p. 460) suggests that Miller is right to stress that electoral politics is becoming less and less about 'people like me' and more and more about 'people around here' (Miller, 1978, p. 283). The possibility remains, therefore, that there could be a re-alignment of voting based on region or unemployment.

There remains the important question of the role of issues in influencing elections results. Crewe (1984, p. 18), in commenting upon the 1983 election, argues that the evidence 'strongly suggests that, as in previous elections, policies counted for much more than personalities, and perceptions of the country's interest more than self-interest'. 'Issue voting' is now seen as a well-established concept in voting analysis. The Särlvik/Crewe (1983, p. 280) analysis of voting change between 1974 and 1979 came to the conclusion that there was a substantial relationship between opinions on issues and party choice. Crewe (1984, p. 18) quotes the BBC/Gallup survey of the 1983 election which asked how people would vote if they preferred the policies of one party but the leader of another – there was an 83 to 17 per cent split in favour of the former.

Franklin (1985, p. 146), too, is committed to the 'rise of issue voting' thesis. He recognizes that the dispute over the importance of issues in influencing voting is a complex technical one and not easy to resolve. Of various technical models of issue voting he believes that the most plausible model 'shows issue voting to have increased in step with the decline of class voting . . . what evidence we have been able to bring to bear points to the causal primacy of the decline of class voting in opening the way to an increase in the importance of issues in determining the electoral choice of British voters'. If Franklin (ibid., p. 152) is correct, then the British voter is 'no longer constrained to the same extent by characteristics largely established during childhood'.

Again, Miller (1984, p. 375) is doubtful about these conclusions. He concedes that policies are more influential than leaders in determining votes, but he points out that there is an important link between leaders and policies. The fact that people appear to be more influenced by policies than leaders 'does not mean that the personality of the leadership is irrelevant, it means that the function of the party leadership is to sell their party not themselves'. Issues and personalities cannot be easily separated. Thus, in the 1983 election, the poor and divided leadership of the Labour Party was bound to produce negative evaluations of policy. Interestingly, Miller suggests that one of the big problems for Labour in 1983 was that it was too 'programmatic' (though he does not use that term). He argues (1984, p. 378) that 'Labour leaders did their best to make their defence policy clear rather than obscure. Unfortunately they presented several clear but contradictory policies.' His conclusion on the important question of whether issues are more important than, say, class, or party leaders, is that general images of parties are more important than specific issues.

The 1983 election is especially interesting in terms of the role of issues. In many ways, it was a truly remarkable election result for the Conservatives – particularly because it was achieved in the face of extremely high unemployment (over 3·5 million). Indeed, the level of unemployment had trebled under the Conservative government of 1979–83 (it had doubled under the previous Labour government). It has been a long-established wisdom that mass unemployment would spell electoral disaster for a British government, yet the Conservative share of the total vote fell by only 1·5 per cent compared with the 1979 election. Unemployment was easily the most salient issue in the campaign. Since mid-1980 public opinion polls had indicated that unemployment was far and away the most important issue facing the country (apart from during the Falklands war). Examination of poll data suggests that, although the public perceived it to be the most important issue facing the country there had been a breakdown in the conventional corollary to this, namely, that the government was to blame for the state of affairs. Without this decoupling, the Conservatives would have faced a difficult task during the election campaign (Richardson and Moon, 1984, p. 29)

The government was effective in pressing home its own view that there was no alternative to its policies of trying to control public expenditure and reduce taxation. The electorate seemed to become conditioned to expect the worst as inevitable. For example, a Gallup poll in December 1982 showed that 43 per cent of respondents thought that unemployment could sometimes be justified as necessary during a period of adjustment, and only 57 per cent thought that high unemployment could be solved if a government really tried to apply the right measures – 36 per cent thought that no government could solve it. When asked how long it would be before unemployment would be drastically reduced, only 12 per cent chose any of the specified periods of three years or under, 47 per cent chose periods of between three and four years, 22 per cent said never, and 19 per cent did not know. Thus the government, by the time of the 1983 election, had managed to produce very low expectations of what could be done by any government (Richardson and Moon, 1984, p. 30).

This is not to suggest that such a key issue was 'neutered' by the Conservatives. Labour had a 16 per cent edge on the issue, but this was only 1 per cent up on the 1979 figure. As Crewe (1984, p. 20) notes: '. . . the issue only half worked for Labour. It damaged the Conservative vote without doing much to repair Labour's; at best it prevented Labour's disaster from turning into a catastrophe.' If we look forward, rather than backwards, it is unlikely that the successful 'damage limitation' will continue for the Conservatives. As the Labour leadership, after the replacement of Mr Foot by Mr Kinnock in 1983, appeared more united and credible, then so it began to undermine the 'there is no alternative' syndrome and so threaten the government's standing on unemployment. It is perfectly possible that the Labour leadership will be more effectively able to exploit the issue in the next election. Equally, we would expect the Conservative government to make more policy responses in an attempt to influence the electorate's perception of the issue. Thus, by early 1985, Mrs Thatcher was saying that if unemployment did not fall within a year or so, then the government would consider taking other measures. This was open recognition of the importance of the amalgam of issues, perceptions and policies in influencing voters.

It is to be expected that issues such as inflation, unemployment, defence, housing, welfare, and so on should be the 'stuff of politics', and that at least some voters might be influenced by what parties promise to do on these issues. But the issue agenda is also quite unpredictable. There is, however, wide disagreement on the significance of something like the 1982 Falklands war in influencing the election result. Crewe (1984, p. 19), whilst recognizing the dramatic effect that the Falklands war had on Conservative support prior to the election, discounts its effect in the actual election. His data suggest that foreign affairs and international peace were volunteered as factors by only 24 out of 4,141 respondents (0.6 per cent); Northern Ireland by a miniscule 3 (that is, 0.072 per cent). Only 1.4 per cent claimed that the Falklands affected their vote.

However, both Crewe (1984) and Miller (1984) note that the Falklands boost to Mrs Thatcher's and the government's fortunes dropped away much more slowly than did the salience of foreign affairs in the voters' minds. A MORI poll suggested that approximately half of the 'Falklands boost' was retained after the crisis had passed. The crucial relevance of the 'Falklands factor', according to Miller (1984, p. 374) is the long-term boost it gave to Mrs Thatcher's own personal image because, even when the Falklands itself was no longer in the forefront of people's minds, it evoked all kinds of codes and symbols. Our own view is that Miller is probably correct – namely, that this chance event was an important factor in constructing an image favourable to the Conservatives. Again, we see the unpredictability and volatility of the electorate at work.

This volatility should always be borne in mind. Thus, as we have seen, there are now serious doubts about statements about the importance of class which appeared to be perfectly valid in the 1950s and 1960s. Similarly, earlier statements about the importance of gender are now dated. The 1983 election was possibly a landmark in that, for the first time, surveys recorded that the Conservative Party drew less support from women (43 per cent) than from men (46 per cent) – even with a woman Prime Minister (Crewe, 1984, p. 14). For the whole of the period since the Second World War, until 1979, the Conservatives maintained a lead amongst women voters.

The young were influential in 1983, producing a 6 per cent swing in favour of the Conservatives. It was still true, in 1983, to say that Conservative support steadily increased from young to old. But it was 'along a much gentler gradient than in the past' (Crewe, 1984, p. 14). Moreover, while there may be an established connection between age and Conservative support, there is no agreement on the cause of the connection. The 'cohort' or generational explanation (Butler and Stokes, 1974 edn) stresses that electoral generations tend to retain a trace of the political creed which was dominant when they entered political life. Support for the Conservatives among the elderly can reflect their political views when recruited to the political scene: it need not reflect individuals becoming more Conservative as they age.

The very fact that voters' habits can and do change – and change more rapidly than they used to – quite possibly increases the effectiveness of citizens participation via the electoral process. The more volatile the voter, arguably, the more elected politicians will pay attention to issues and specific policies in an attempt to sway the vote.

CHAPTER FOUR

The Parliamentary Arena and Adversary Politics

A Parliament: Adversary Confrontation and Consensual Organization

Many a water wheel set up to attract the tourist finds difficulty in turning itself to maintain the illusion, far less to do work: the actual grinding is powered by an electric motor. There is much interest in the working of the House of Commons: whether the House contributes more to the policy process or to the tourist trade is a difficult question. As James Margach (1981, p. 79) put it 'The reality is that the modern Parliament has become in practice a central registry for recording votes and giving effect to decisions taken elswhere in the Cabinet and in Government Departments.' Such a conclusion is not novel. Writing in 1867, Bagehot stated: 'The legislature chosen in name to make laws, in fact finds its principal business in making and keeping an executive [i.e. government]' (1963, p. 66).

Ramsay Muir, in 1930, quoted Burke's view that 'The generality of people are fifty years at least behind in their politics' (p. 2). But even sixty years later there is, in places, a reluctance to acknowledge his point that a General Election exists to select a government and to send to Parliament a body of supporters strong enough to maintain it in office. Parliament, in this view, is an electoral college to choose the government (Muir, 1930, p. 13). Indeed, even this view can be seen as too generous to the actual role of Parliament. Like the American Electoral College itself, Parliament does not 'choose' but mechanically reflects the views of the mass electorate (Crossman, 1963, p. 39). The gap between constitutional principles and political practice is thus profound and long established. Low (1914, p. 19) noted: 'If we come down to our own times we find the paramount and unqualified authority of the House of Commons continually asserted, while the powers of that House are being steadily transferred to the Cabinet.' As Professor Griffith (1951, p. 436) put it: 'The theory of the Constitution is full of ghosts striving to tangle us with their chains.' A major problem for the student of politics is knowing what to ignore as academic sentimentality.

The problem with the emphasis on Parliament as an institution of the democratic society is that, when practice is discovered to depart from the story-book, belief in democracy suffers. What democracy is, if it is *not* constituency representatives determining policy on its merits in the forum of the House of Commons, is difficult to formulate. But it involves things such as a government not assuming that a majority of seats gives it the right to introduce and pass measures without further consultation with affected interests. Democracy has to do with things such as a willingness of leaders to expose themselves to close questioning by the media. 'Weekend World' or 'Panorama' are more difficult to fit into a definition of democracy than parliamentary question time; but in terms of the size of audience and the rigour of the questioning, the former seem the more effective instruments. It is more comfortable to discuss the facts of democracy. Thus the House of Commons sat on average for 172 days in the years between 1974 and 1983 with an average Monday to Friday sitting of 8 hours 54 minutes per day (*House of Commons Fact Sheet*, No. 28, 1984). However, understanding of the democratic system is not the sum of such empirical observations.

The jargon of Parliament is often puzzling, but rarely does it conceal anything profoundly important. For example, 'front-bench status' is the label for paid office holders in the government (about 100) who are by custom allowed to sit on the front bench of the government rows (and their Opposition counterparts). The figure includes the government Whips who are paid but, by custom, do not themselves speak. The so-called pay roll vote is augmented by what might be called the pay roll vote-in waiting: the more junior and unpaid parliamentary private secretaries who could expect future promotion (see Forman, 1985, p. 154). A 'three-line Whip' on a piece of legislation means that the party Whips (business managers) have underlined that piece of business three times in 'the Whip' – the document that is circulated to party members advising them of the times of key votes. A 'three-line' vote is the most serious type; other options, of course, include a two-line, one-line, or free vote.

Members cannot resign their seats – death, elevation to the Peerage, dissolution (of the House) or expulsion are the only causes, apart from legal disqualification, by which a Member can leave Parliament. The best-known and usual means by which Members disqualify themselves is to secure an office of profit under the Crown. Occasionally, this is a genuine office – as when Sir Thomas Williams, MP, was appointed a circuit judge in 1981 – but usually the offices involved are Crown Steward and Bailiff of the three Chiltern

Hundreds of Stoke, Desborough and Burnham, and that of the Manor of Northstead. These are purely nominal offices maintained to allow Members to resign, and these meet the requirements of the House of Commons Disqualification Act, 1975 (*House of Commons Fact Sheet*, no 39, 1985).

The parliamentary process is similarly complex. The 'bible' of procedure, *Parliamentary Practice* – commonly referred to as *Erskine May* – has now reached some 1,200 pages (including index) in its 20th edition. But the importance of the complexities is undermined by the efficiency of party control of the House of Commons and subordination of the House of Lords to the Commons.

Public Bills (see below) are the important type of Bill – the category includes major Bills introduced by the government. However, the term also covers Bills introduced by others outside the government – Private Members' Bills. Only the government can introduce Money Resolutions which increase public (that is, state) spending – unlike the position in the USA. This means that Private Members' Bills are, to an extent, pushed into matters of social reform (with few financial implications). And since matters of social concern are often thought to be appropriate to non-partisan treatment, Private Members' Bills which have no chance of passage if the government is actively hostile, have some chance of success in such fields. They follow processes distinct from Private Bills introduced by a particular interest, such as a local authority, or a commercial body. (Hybrid Bills which are Public Bills which have different impacts for certain persons in a general category, also have their own procedure. Such Bills are often in connection with works of national importance which affect a local area, for example, the Channel Tunnel Bills in the 1970s and 1987. It is difficult to generalize about the nature of such Bills as their precise status is so difficult to determine that it is often a matter of controversy.)

DELEGATED LEGISLATION

Although many important policies are enacted by Bills, some policy objectives can be attained without direct recourse to Parliament – for example, the influencing of interest and exchange rates, or the 'ear stroking' of interest groups, and so on. Other objectives can be pursued by means of delegated/subordinate legislation, for example, the Requisitioning of Ships Order of 1982 in connection with the Falklands' Task Force, or the establishment of a compensation scheme for the victims of crimes (see Miers and Page, 1982, pp. 4–5). Most delegated legislation takes the form of statutory instruments, but some non-statutory instruments, for example, Immigration Rules, must also be laid before Parliament as if they were such. Some

2,000 statutory instruments are issued each year. Indeed, while much academic attention is given to Public Bills, Walkland (1968, p. 17) has claimed that, in the twentieth century, subordinate legislation made by government departments has become the characteristic regulating device of a society which has developed politically to the stage where it needs comparatively few major policy adjustments, but much by way of technical improvements.

Parliamentary involvement in the statutory instrument process is varied: in the main, *de facto* scrutiny of instruments takes place in the often informal (though sometimes obliged by statute) consultation with affected interests that usually accompanies the drafting process. Some minor statutory instruments – for example, on the commencing date for some legislation to take effect – fall outside parliamentary review. They are self-implementing, and the change automatically takes effect on the date stated. There is, though, *negative* procedure whereby the proposed statutory instrument takes effect unless either House (usually within forty days) passes a Motion (or 'prayer') against. (In the case of instruments dealing with financial matters, only the Commons can negative the introduction.) There also exists *affirmative* procedure whereby the enabling Act requires that a Motion approving the statutory instrument must be passed within a specified time period (again often forty days). Except in very rare cases provided for in the parent Act, Parliament can only approve or reject a statutory instrument; it cannot amend.

The complications of statutory instrument procedure include the Joint (Select) Committee of both Houses on Statutory Instruments which does not look at the merits of an instrument, but has to ensure that the instrument is within the technical limits of the parent Act. Because of pressure of time on the floor of the full House, debates on statutory instrument motions can now take place in one or more Standing Committees. Statutory instrument procedure is thus complex – and, arguably, requires more effort for the non-specialist to follow than its significance perhaps deserves.

PUBLIC BILL PROCEDURE

First Reading Notice of presentation of a Bill is given on the Order Paper (that is written notice). The Speaker calls the Member introducing the measure (usually the relevant departmental minister). He bows to technically move First Reading. The Clerk (an officer of the House) reads out the short title of the Bill (which may have a longer official title). The Speaker asks, 'Second Reading, what day?' The minister or the Chief Whip (that is, the government's business manager) would then usually answer 'Tomorrow, sir'. This formula 'Tomorrow, sir' actually allows the government to choose any future day it wishes. The Bill is then printed and published. Invariably, the written notice stage discusses only a blank dummy, so the First Reading encapsulates the essence of procedure – traditional and theatrical. At this stage there is no debate, although if a Bill is introduced orally 'on a motion', a brief debate will take place. A Bill from the House of Lords is 'deemed' to have been read for the first time in the Commons whenever a Member of the House of Commons informs the Clerks (officials) that he or she will take charge of it in the Commons.

Second Reading This is the first substantive discussion. The length of debate will normally be prearranged by the Whips of the major parties – as will the sequence of main speakers. Government Bills are almost invariably passed. Again, in this context, the parliamentary language is unhelpful. Agreement 'that the Bill be read a second time upon this day six months' is a circumlocution for rejection.

Non-controversial Bills can be dealt with in a Second Reading Committee (which are Standing Committees – see below), and Bills which relate exclusively to Scotland are dealt with in the Scottish Grand Committee which consists of all the Members representing Scottish constituencies (*Erskine May*, 20th edn, p. 661). Both these types of Committee Second Reading are technically followed by a Second Reading from the House, but this is without debate and no more than ceremonial confirmation.

Standing Committee Most Bills go to Standing Committee. There are eight to ten of these committees depending on the volume of business. These have sixteen to fifty Members (usually towards the lower end of the range) which reflect party strength in the House. Up to two committees deal with Bills relating exclusively to Scotland (1st and 2nd Scottish Standing Committees.) For a Bill relating exclusively to Wales, the relevant committee will include all the Members sitting for Welsh constituencies.

The (non-Scottish) Standing Committees are labelled 'A', 'B', and 'C', and so on through the alphabet as required. There is no limit to their number, but they rarely go beyond 'G'. The allocation of Bills to committee is not controversial and is done by the non-partisan Speaker. Since all committees have a pro-governmental majority, the allocation has no real significance. Government Bills have precedence – except in Committee C. In Committee C, Bills follow their order of allocation. As the perverseness of parliamentary terminology has been indicated, it should cause no surprise that Standing Committees are now effectively *ad hoc* in membership: Committee A discussing a particular Bill might be entirely different in composition from Committee A as it discusses the next Bill allocated. The turnover of Members thus allows committees the opportunity to reflect specialized interests of Members. The Standing Committee is intended to give clause by clause consideration to a Bill, but lack of time might well mean whole sections are not effectively discussed.

Erskine May (p. 258) lays down that in committee the *details* of a measure are the primary object of consideration, and amendments which are incompatible with the principle of the Bill as agreed at Second Reading are out of order. This distinction between Second Reading general debate and Committee Stage discussion of detail need not be absolute. For example, in the case of the Scotland and Wales Bill 1976, the first amendment proposed to leave out Scotland and the second proposed to leave out Wales.

In 1941 the American Supreme Court construed the famous Tenth Constitutional Amendment – which states that all powers not delegated to central government, 'are reserved to the States, respectively, or to the people' – to mean 'that all is retained which is not yet surrendered' (Reagan and Sanzone, 1981, p. 10). In the same Lewis Carroll way we must appreciate that Parliament is a political body which serves the interests and purposes of the government. Parliamentary precedents as enshrined in *Erskine May*, are the kind of precedents which are binding and inviolable – up to the moment they are changed.

A passage in the Crossman *Diaries* (1977, vol. 3, p. 903), gives a sense of the usual flavour of the Standing Committee. Crossman, as secretary of state, had made a point of not attending the Standing Committee dealing with his National Superannuation Bill – leaving the committee stage to his ministers of state, David Ennals and Brian O'Malley. Crossman claimed that the only problem with the committee stage was on the Tory side, 'because they have somehow to spin things out until Whitsun so that the outside world doesn't conclude that there has been no real fight over the Bill'. However, when Crossman did put in an appearance he observed:

> . . .my attendance held everything up, because the Tories all seized the chance to show their political power to challenge and debate with the Secretary of State. We took the whole morning over a discussion that would otherwise have taken twenty minutes. Afterwards, Harrison [Assistant Government Whip] told me, 'That very often happens. Senior Ministers make it too political and we don't like them to come. It's easier for us to have the number twos and to get them into a quiet routine, just plugging along and

reading the briefs' . . . the sooner I was got out of the way and the backbenchers could go on writing their letters the better for all concerned.

Some Bills are considered not by Standing Committee but by a Committee of the Whole House. Bills so treated tend to be matters of major constitutional significance where all Members might be thought to have an interest, or matters of little controversy where the Committee Stage is a formality. As the House can move from its normal sitting, to Committee of the Whole House status – and back again – very rapidly, minor Bills are conveniently dealt with in this manner. Bills of great urgency, with party agreement, are thus also dealt with by a Committee of the Whole House.

Report Stage Most Bills go from Committee Stage back to the floor of the House for Report Stage. The government can use its majority to restore any unwanted amendments made in Standing Committee. In theory, Report Stage *can* be taken in committee (there seem few permutations of stage and arena not possible), but there are few instances.

Third Reading Normal practice is to move 'forthwith' from Report Stage to Third Reading. This often takes place without debate. Under recently changed rules, only verbal amendments are permitted on Third Reading (Standing Order Number 75). The scope of debate is thus even more limited than it is for the Second Reading.

Lords Stages and Amendments A Bill which has cleared the hurdle of the Commons would now go to the House of Lords for similar treatment. As the Lords and Commons must agree the same version of the Bill, any successful Lords amendments are considered by the Commons and accepted or rejected. In the case of Lords' rejection of a Commons' Bill, the Commons is advised of the reasons and it considers the points again. If the Lords persist with a version which is unacceptable to the Commons (that is, the government's majority in the Commons), the Parliament Act of 1949 allows that if the Commons passes the Bill again in identical fashion in the next session, it can obtain Royal Assent. This is, of course, a procedure to reduce the Lords power of 'veto' to a power of delay.

Royal Assent As the final technicality of the legislative process, the Crown must give Assent to a Bill: this has not been withheld since 1707. The Queen herself does not sign Bills: this is done formally on her behalf – because it is strictly a formality.

The volume of work in Parliament is summarized in Table 4.1.

Table 4.1 Volume of Parliamentary Work (Numbers and hours and minutes)

					Parliamentary sessions					
	1974	1974/5	1975/6	1976/7	1977/8	1978/9	1979/80	1980/1	1981/2	1982/3
House of Commons										
Numbers of days sitting[a]	87	198	191	149	169	86	244	163	74	115
Numbers of hours sitting	737	1,849	1,759	1,371	1,485	739	2,177	1,485	1,534	985
Average daily hours of sitting	8h 28	9h 20	9h 13	9h 12	8h 47	8h 35	8h 55	9h 07	8h 49	8h 34
Number of divisions	109	405	432	234	324	110	500	317	332	143
Parliamentary questions										
Oral[b]	1,660	3,611	3,199	2,481	10,226	5,470	12,453	8,175	8,991	6,125
Written[b]	3,852	33,447	39,121	29,058	28,630	12,952	39,912	22,688	23,439	17,095
Select Committees										
Number of committees and sub-committees	35	48	48	44	45	41	40	41	40	41
Number of meetings	287	800	860	676	741	354	968	851	801	602
Number of MPs involved[c]	219	291	294	254	244	222	277	309	310	294
Standing Committees										
Number of committees	15	19	22	21	16	17	20	21	21	21
Number of Bills considered	30	62	78	49	45	27	42	36	40	33
Number of Statutory Instruments considered	40	101	114	129	141	70	130	62	80	73
Number of sittings	128	441	552	248	229	177	576	388	395	328
Number of MPs involved[c]	498	578	584	546	533	456	567	530	538	524
House of Lords										
Number of days sitting	67	165	155	105	126	59	206	143	147	94
Number of hours sitting	350	930	970	596	737	345	1,268	920	930	619
Average daily hours of sitting	5h 13	5h 38	6h 15	5h 41	5h 51	5h 51	6h 09	6h 26	6h 20	6h 35
Number of divisions	17	119	146	45	96	21	305	184	147	89
Parliamentary questions										
Oral – brief (starred)	192	560	553	385	439	217	765	537	531	357
–debatable (unstarred)	23	35	41	36	46	23	68	31	50	36
Written	171	350	517	380	544	432	1,277	857	1,098	619

Source: *Social Trends*, no. 15, 1985 (London: HMSO).

[a] Includes certain formal sittings at the beginning of each new Parliament but excludes sittings of the House of Lords in its judicial capacity.

[b] The figures for 1977/8 onwards show the number of oral and written questions tabled. The figures for the previous sessions show the number of questions which received oral or written answers.

[c] Some Members serve on 2 or more committees but are only counted once.

THE DECLINE OF PARLIAMENT

While the mechanics of Parliament are complex, arguably too much time is spent on the subject in most accounts of the British political process and its procedures. Writing on the USA, Schattschneider (1960, p. vii) has remarked: 'While we were thinking about something else a new government was created in the United States.' We can similarly observe that while Britain has busied itself with parliamentary reforms, the importance of Parliament (the context in which these reforms have relevance) has been diminishing.

While the academic literature on politics has probably given undue prominence to the House of Commons and its reforms, the marginal role of Parliament has none the less been well defined. On the important area of finance, the distinguished former senior Treasury civil servant, Sir Leo Pliatzky (1985, p. 61), has noted that 'the formal procedures of the House for approving expenditure and taxation play virtually no substantive part in the decision-making process'. More generally, Jennings, in his *Cabinet Government* (1961, p. 18) commented: 'If the Government has a majority, and so long as the majority holds together, the House does not control the Government but the Government controls the House.' It might be argued that his conditional qualification is important – but the instances of its importance are, in reality, few. Thus there should be no surprise when empirical study underscores the marginality of Parliament. Moran's (1977, p. 97) study of the Conservative Industrial Relations Act of 1971 concluded: 'The parliamentary process was largely irrelevant to shaping the initial Bill into the final Act. Each amendment conceded or initiated by the Government required a parliamentary majority but the Conservative supremacy in both Houses meant that this was always assured.'

A classic statement of the superiority of government was given in Professor Griffith's *Parliamentary Scrutiny of Government Bills* (1974). Looking at the Committee Stages of Bills, Griffith found that 93.7 per cent of all successful amendments were moved (that is, suggested) by the ministers themselves (that is, government changing its own proposals). Only one ministerial amendment failed. Of course, the minister's mind *may* have been changed by the debate, but Griffith (1974, p. 197) does not encourage that view and concludes: 'Usually [government amendments] reflect later developments in the thinking of civil servants in the department, often reflecting pressures from interest groups ... for Government amendments at this stage, committee proceedings remain primarily the means by which amendments can be made, not the reason why they are made.' He found that only approximately 2 per cent of Opposition amendments succeeded.

His conclusions on the Report Stage were even more severe. In his examination of the 3,102 amendments in his three years of study, he considered a list of nine effective (non-governmental) changes of more or less importance – but none of major significance. He continued (1974, p. 206): 'On no occasion was the Government either defeated or forced to make a tactical retreat. As in committee, the visible result of a great deal of Opposition and Government back-bench activity was very small indeed.' Admittedly, Griffith did see a broader indirect impact of House activity – where government amendments did follow from points suggested by the Opposition or government back-benchers, yet he argued that 'we are left with some sense of great effort making for little result'.

In an earlier work, Griffith (1951, p. 291) noted:

When Parliament is called a Legislature what is meant is that no body or person can issue an order, rule, regulation, scheme or enactment having the force of law without Parliamentary authority. But it does not follow that Parliament is responsible for the whole of the legislative process ... In other words, 'to legislate' may mean either to authorise the action which turns a legislative proposal into law or to carry through the whole legislative proposal. In this latter sense legislation today is more a Governmental than a Parliamentary function.

Gavin Drewry concluded that, overall, Parliament 'legitimates' but does not 'legislate' (in Walkland and Ryle, eds, 1977, p. 74). This line of criticism is, unusually, not about British inefficiency, but that Parliament is an overeffective transmission belt in converting a Bill into law.

All this, however, is not to say that 'Parliament does not matter'. But it is leading to the conclusion that it does not matter in terms of changing legislation: the legislature is not in the business of the application of the individual legislator's judgement on legislation and on the best form of that legislation. Parliament matters because reputation matters. Back-benchers identify themselves for promotion by their performance, and ministerial careers advance or slip by their general reputation. One prominent back-bencher recently advised us: 'As for the impact on the political process, Parliament is pretty near to zilch.'

Professor Crick (1968, p. 245) has, however, articulated a more indirect argument about the role of Parliament in relation to policy: 'Parliament primarily serves to inform the electorate, neither to legislate nor to overthrow Governments.' Again, Griffith summarized this point about party reputations elegantly: 'The purpose of many Opposition amendments is not to make the Bill more generally acceptable, but make the Government less generally acceptable' (in Walkland and Ryle, eds, 1977, p. 98). Because it is well reported by the media, Parliament is a channel of information to the electorate, aiding the process of revaluation that leads to the maintenance or change of government at a general election.

And, while the measurable impact of Parliament is limited, it is true that most ministers and civil servants are very conscious of the potential of Parliament to cause difficulty and even embarrassment – most ministers do take their appearances in the House seriously. The mood of the House – or, at least, the mood of the government's supporters – does count. 'Having a word with the Whip' on an informal basis can lead to a governmental retreat. There is also the unmeasurable power of anticipated reaction – where the government does not introduce a measure because it is suspected that it would be a cause of unpopularity.

Examples of back-bench rebellion are now easier to produce than in earlier eras. There are, however, at least three types of rebellion. There is the symbolic rebellion where the object is to make a point without defeating the government (the 'law' is that the rebellion can be the size of the majority – less one). Rebellion can also be signalled within the parliamentary party machine or informally, rather than on the floor of the House, and the proposal can be dropped without being made public. In the case of the Civil Aviation Bill in December 1984, the government withdrew the Bill after a revolt by three Tory MPs in Standing Committee. The problem was not the Standing Committee defeats, which could have been reversed, but the political embarrassment of further revolts on the floor of the House at a later stage. The retreat on increasing the parental contribution from wealthier parents for student grants, also in December 1984, was made after noises in the Conservative back-bench Education Committee and after the public gesture of the signing of a motion by 138 Conservatives.

Another kind of rebellion is where it leads to government defeat on a minor specialist matter – for example, the defeat on the Films Bill, in December 1984, where four Conservatives voted against their party Whip. Defeat on marginal issues, as with some symbolic rebellions, can even be politically useful in blurring the government's image – over, say, petrol price rises in rural areas. In such an example, sitting rural Conservative Members can oppose the pro posals and thus undercut anti-Conservative feeling in the con stituency.

The third kind of rebellion is where the government is defeated on a major matter of policy – where confidence in the government is at issue. At one time, it would have been thought that this would promote a governmental resignation – and, indeed, the defeat on a relatively minor matter would, in some eyes, constitute the necessity of resignation. Harold Wilson, for example, in his memoirs considering the Labour government's small majority in 1964–6 commented: 'For all I know there might be enough members of the Flat Earth Society capable of bringing the Government down.' Morrison (1954, p. 165) – writing on the Labour government of 1950–1 with its majority of six – commented that almost any revolt or abstentions could bring the government down. Recent governments, however, have battled on through defeats on the Finance Bill, and on their main legislative proposals (for example, Scotland and Wales Bill, 1977). The fact that defeats have not brought down governments, has perhaps led to an increase in rebellions. The 'government will fall' argument no longer convinces – although obviously the situation of a minority government is very different. The Whips 'wolf' cry no longer has the same effect – over the Top People's Pay episode in July 1985, the Whips amended the line from the 'government will resign' (not credible), to a more convincing, 'Mrs Thatcher will go if you embarrass her'.

There are fundamental problems in measuring dissent – for example, the difficulty of distinguishing the MP not voting but 'paired' with an opponent, from the deliberate abstention. (The Tory Whips have also reintroduced a 'bisque' system to allow controlled numbers from their majority an early night.) More seriously, there is the possibility of influence being effective and hence not requiring public demonstration. Probably the well-educated modern back-bencher, possibly encouraged by Select Committee experience, is more likely to wish to show independence. However, while there were at least 21 revolts on the floor of the House in 1984/5 involving up to 70 Tories on Stansted (February 1985), 37 for postal ballots on the Trade Union Bill (July 1984), and 48 on the Top People's Pay issue (July 1985), it is noticeable that the *frequent* rebels are political mavericks, such as John Gorst and Anthony Beaumont-Dark, rather than prominent 'leadership in exile', such as Edward Heath, Sir Ian Gilmour, and Francis Pym (see *Daily Telegraph*, 29 July 1985).

Philip Norton's various works on dissent in the House (1975, 1980), have given a sense of scale to the impression of increased back-bench rebellion in the 1970s and 1980s. Richard Rose has used Norton's data to make the point that in the 1970–4 period of Conservative government 61 per cent of Conservative back-bench MPs voted against the government 'Whip' (instruction) on the floor of the House, one or more times. In the 1974–9 Labour government period 81 per cent of Labour MPs voted at least once against the party, and 89 per cent of all Opposition MPs did so. However, Rose (1983, p. 289) puts the matter in proportion by continuing:

One bite in the leg of the party whip does not make a dog dangerous. The suggestion that the House of Commons is now filled with rebel MPs, who roam the jungle freely rather than being caged is grossly misleading . . . Given that there are more than one thousand divisions in the course of a Parliament, an MP can bark a number of times yet still be voting with the party on 99% of all divisions.

His data also shows that in 1945–78 every government succeeded in having more than 90 per cent of their Bills passed (average of 96.6 per cent).

THE RITUALIZATION OF CONFRONTATION

Despite the adversarial rhetoric of the institution of Parliament, co-operation is required for its normal functioning. In his *Cabinet Government* (1961, p. 16) Jennings argued that party warfare was essential to democracy – yet democracy could not function if it was carried to extremes. He continued: 'An Opposition which could not accept the majority rule could make the parliamentary system unworkable. In practice, government is by consent and opposition by agreement.'

The jargon to describe the practice of orchestrating business in Parliament is 'the usual channels' or 'behind the Speaker's Chair'. Although parliamentary pleasantries are prone to be over-fulsome (for example, the ritual congratulations to a maiden speech by a new MP or thanks to a committee chairman), Harold Wilson's tribute to Mrs Thatcher on her being elected Leader of the Opposition in 1975 qualifies the image of party hostility:

I have formed the impression that there may well be a deep gulf between her and me in our respective political philosophies, but, having worked closely with her three immediate predecessors . . . I know that political disagreement between us need not mar the work that we have to do together in Parliament, and I look forward . . . to the meetings behind your Chair, Mr. Speaker, and to the informality . . . [and] intimacy which such meetings afford. (*Hansard*, 12 February 1975, col. 376, quoted in Wade, 1978, p. xiii)

The Chief Whips of the main parties, and the Leader of the House and his opposite number organize the topics for debate and an allocation of time for them. One Opposition Chief Whip has gone on record, as follows: 'I recognise that Governments have to govern and I get on extremely well with my opposite number and we understand each other's problems and, if there is certain business coming up and I don't want that next week for various reasons, he will agree and remove it. Eventually we settle the business' (King and Sloman, 1973, pp. 105–6). The timing of debate is thus normally closely controlled. Procedural convention allows the main parties to make the opening and closing speeches and Wade (1978, p. 11) describes how time is further 'bargained':

> As the debate reaches the stage at which Front Bench spokesmen are to wind up, Whips from both sides may retire behind the Chair to discuss the time at which their respective speakers wish to be on their feet. Agreement is reached and the Speaker is quietly informed ... (The Speaker may calculate that, if the Opposition is to start wind up at say, five past nine, with a division at ten o'clock and a particular MP who is on his feet has the good sense to finish at nine, this will give some other aspirant just five minutes.) The Speaker will send a message through one of the Whips that the member in question will be called on the understanding that he sits down promptly at five past nine. The member knows well enough that if he is fortunate enough to be called he must for his own future benefit adhere to this informal understanding.
>
> When the Minister finally reaches the conclusion of his speech, he must be careful to sit down before ten o'clock if that is the time of division, but not much more than a minute before. If he goes on too long he will be in danger of talking out the Bill ... If he stops say two minutes before ten ... some back bencher on the other side may jump up and the Speaker will feel obliged to call him.

As Wade makes clear, however, agreement behind the Chair does not discourage the Opposition from exploiting any technical openings left to them.

Crossman (Vol. 2, 1976), describes an example of how the 'usual channels' can be frustrated by back-benchers not keeping to the script. In moving a motion in connection with his procedural innovations in 1966, he had his own procedure problems:

> I had one very awkward hurdle to get over. I had to sit down just in time for the Speaker to get up and read the motion aloud before 9.30 – otherwise all the motions could fail if the word 'object' were spoken by any Member of the House. Of course, this meant that the two front benches had to collaborate through the usual channels ... Willie Whitelaw had agreed to fix this with us on condition that we made reasonable concessions ... [However]

After a time it was clear that the mood had changed and a spontaneous Tory rebellion was taking place ... The trouble was the usual channels didn't work on this occasion.

The orchestration of an apparently adversary occasion also extends to the pattern of the debate itself. While the selection of participants appears to be a matter at the spontaneous discretion of the Speaker, in fact the sequence is normally derived from a list drawn up in advance. Members write in asking to participate, and this allows the Speaker (and his secretary) to keep a balance of region, party, viewpoint, and so on, but the Whips also attempt to ensure that the mainstream of party thinking is reflected in the selection. The junior Whips act as messengers for the Speaker on this matter – passing on requests as to speech lengths.

Sometimes a deal on time cannot be struck and the government is obliged to introduce a 'Guillotine' (or Allocation of Time Motion). Since they have a majority, the 'allocation of time' request will almost invariably be successful.

Guillotines are rare: 36 Bills between 1881 and 1912; 14 Bills between 1921 and 1945; 30 Bills between 1945 and 1975; and 22 Bills between 1975 and 1983 (from *Fact Sheet*, No. 23, 1983, Public Information Office).

Of course, it is the potential threat of the Guillotine that probably explains why it is needed so seldom. But, on occasions, either feeling is genuinely running so high that the 'usual channels' cannot operate, or the Opposition wish to make some particular show to satisfy their supporters, and then the government must introduce a timetable to limit discussion on a Bill. On non-Guillotined Bills there is a tendency for the early clauses to be debated at more length than the later ones – when time is a pressure. Accordingly, there is some argument in favour of a timetable for the stages of all Bills. In May 1985 the Select Committee on Procedure recommended a Guillotine on controversial Bills – the timetable to be set by a new Legislative Business Committee.

The existence of the Whips, so important in the 'usual channels', is something of an ill-kept secret. The role of the Whip in organizing the House is not universally popular. The fact is, however, that parliamentary democracy without the Whips and 'usual channels' would be simply impossible. The importance of the Whipping system lies in organization not – as is often thought   in discipline. When asked what he did when MPs 'broke ranks', the former Labour Chief Whip, Bob Mellish, realistically answered: 'Well, first of all I get upset and then after that I have to live with it'. (King and Sloman, 1973, p. 108).

Parliamentary Question Time is widely celebrated as a platform of the British democratic system. It takes place on Monday to Thursday, at the start of business (2.30 p.m.). Departments answer question in broad rotation – decided by the government. (Business now generally runs from 9.30 a.m. to 3 p.m. on Fridays.) The prime minister answers questions for about fifteen minutes on Tuesdays and Thursdays at 3.15 p.m.

The minister (or prime minister) has notice of the question and hence has an answer prepared by civil servants, but supplementary questions are allowed and this means that in their preparation the minister and officials must anticipate the line to be followed in the supplementary. Questions for oral answer are distinguished by an asterisk on the Order Paper (or agenda). All unstarred questions, and questions not reached in the oral session (and not withdrawn by the Member) receive a written answer – which is also printed in *Hansard*. It is true that much ministerial time is spent in briefing for the sessions. (Mrs Thatcher usually works through lunch on Tuesdays and Thursdays in thorough preparation for PM's questions.) Civil servants, too, are very conscious that they must provide good defensive briefs for their ministers. None the less, experienced ministers such as Richard Marsh have not felt overextended. He claimed: 'Even the idea that our much vaunted Question Time is a significant part of our political system is a transparent nonsense for anybody who has ever been involved in it . . . There is nothing easier than Ministers stonewalling or even misleading Parliament in answer to Parliamentary Questions' (Marsh, 1978, p. 53). Brian Sedgemore – a former civil servant and junior minister – concluded (1980, p. 191): 'Even the weakest minister, providing always that he can read the supplementary answers prepared for him by his civil servants, finds it almost impossible to come unstuck. For the most part it is ritual, a primitive expression of the clash of political ideas . . .' One back-bencher put it to us even more cynically: 'Most of the words they say haven't passed through their own brains.'

The former MP, Christopher Price (1984), has set out a set of devices which ministers can use to avoid answering the question in the terms sought:

- Refusing to answer the question. This is both done by citing some precedent that questions on the matter are *not* answered, or by claiming the data are not available. (Sedgemore (1980, pp. 184–7) sets out three pages of barred topics which the Table Office will not accept.)

- Providing an answer, but phrasing it in such a way as to mislead or give no useful information. Even when the information is later discovered to be inaccurate (for example, Belgrano affair) – what can be done?

- Controlled timing. Price gives us an example of his own task (as parliamentary secretary to the then Secretary of State for Education Anthony Crosland) to 'plant' a written question which would be answered on Christmas Day – and so opposition was disorganized until after the New Year.
- The reply, 'I shall write to the Hon. Member'. This means that information is delayed – and the individual MP has to try to make a special effort to secure media interest if he or she thinks the topic merits it.
- The device, 'I shall place the document in the Library'. Although this reply sounds co-operative and well meaning, pressure groups, academic researchers, and others who might well be interested in the reply, cannot directly get access.

It is possible to reconcile the seriousness with which some ministers prepare for Question Time and the low opinion which some critics have of it as a process for establishing information. The minister generally enhances his or her reputation, in the Whitehall circles that count, by *denying* information. The main role of Question Time is gladiatorial and reputational. The main inquisitorial device at PM's Question Time is the use of questions such as, 'Has the PM any intention of meeting . . .?, or, 'Will the PM pay an official visit to . . .? These vague questions allow a supplementary – which is the real object of the exercise. One bizarre example (which also shows that questions are often friendly, and indeed prearranged) was when a Conservative back-bencher asked Mrs Thatcher to pay a visit to Pratts Bottom (*Hansard*, 24 March 1983, col. 1013). This permitted Mrs Thatcher to reveal that she knew the place well, but its main purpose was to allow her back-bencher to go on to say that the good citizens thereof wanted to show the Prime Minister their appreciation of a recent budget; he drew particular attention to their pleasure at the increase in mortgage relief. This gave the Prime Minister the chance to recite some well-rehearsed figures on the tax position of first-time house buyers (see Johnson, 1983, p. 123).

But Christopher Price, then an Opposition back-bencher, managed to ingeniously turn the discussion to the stop-and-search powers in the Police Bill, by noting that a journey to Pratts Bottom went through his constituency, and that his constituents would want to express their views on the Police Bill . . .! Procedural changes of 31 October 1984 were intended to curtail these 'disguised' questions – but with little obvious effect.

Although the mood of the civil service may well be changing (with the participation of prominent ex-civil servants in the Freedom of Information Campaign), the instinct is still to see the game of

Parliamentary Question Time as an exercise in damage limitation. The civil service might be required to give answers: there is no requirement to give gratuitously informative answers. This is summarized in a well-worn tale about the assistant secretary who is seen as a specialist in answering parliamentary questions. During a recess, the permanent secretary decides that the man deserves a little change and invites him to join him in the back of the departmental Rover on an official visit to the West Country.

The permanent secretary was asking his colleague to define the ideal parliamentary reply when he noticed that the driver had stopped at a minor crossroads and was consulting his map. The permanent secretary decided on more direct action and, winding down his window, called out to a very rural-looking farmhand: 'Look here, man, can you tell us where we are?' The farmhand replied blandly, 'Aye sir, you be lost'.

The permanent secretary was about to remonstrate with the man, when his assistant secretary took him by the arm and pointed out that this reply usefully crystallized the perfect parliamentary answer. It was brief. It was accurate. It added not one iota to existing knowledge.

REFORM OR OCCUPATIONAL THERAPY?

Various procedural changes have taken place in recent years with a view to modernizing Parliament – for example, in the Supply procedure by which the House votes money to pay for government spending. The twenty-nine Supply Days had become, in effect, divorced from financial scrutiny and were used for debate on any topic selected by the Opposition. Instead of relating to 'Supply', the Opposition days were used to criticize whatever government policy was topical. In July 1982 it was agreed that Supply Days would be abolished and, instead, nineteen days would be reserved for topics selected by the Opposition. In addition, three days would be devoted to discussion of particular items of the Estimates – the items to be debated to be selected not by the government but by the House's own Liaison Committee. (Of course, Members cannot propose *increases* in expenditure, that being a Crown (that is, government) right. Further timetabled opportunities for back-benchers to ventilate matters – perhaps of local significance – are given in the Recess Adjournment Motion and in the Adjournment Debates which follow the strictly formal Consolidated Fund Bill procedure. In 1985 the number of Opposition days was increased to twenty. Seventeen were reserved for the official Opposition party (Labour), and three to the Leader of the second largest Opposition party (Liberals).

These changes recognized that the Supply procedure had become an opportunity for omnibus debates unrelated to the Supply function. The increased opportunity for discussing back-bench points is, of course, an opportunity for publicity rather than decision. The main development in the House of Commons in recent years, however, has been in the Select Committee system. Many committees are involved in the running of the House and are technically select committees, but the focus of interest has been on the system of fourteen committees set up in 1979 to engage in scrutiny of the Whitehall departments. The debate on the new committees has been about the relationship betwen Parliament and the government. Is Parliament a collective body with responsibilities to control the Executive (government), or is it a forum for government versus Opposition conflict? Changes have generally been put forward as a means of restoring collective parliamentary control. For example, the 1979 Procedure Committee put forward its version of reform, 'with the aim of enabling the House as a whole to exercise effective control and stewardship over Ministers and the expanding bureaucracy of the modern state for which they are answerable'.

The Public Accounts Committee was set up in 1861 to supervise the rectitude of government spending; this continues as a major parliamentary institution. The other main committee of the older-style House was the Estimates Committee (which existed from 1912 to 1914 and 1921 to 1971). It had the remit of inquiring whether policies could be more efficiently implemented, that is, to report what, if any, economies – consistent with the policy implied in those Estimates – could be effected. However, it proved frustrating to Members not to pursue matters of *policy* as opposed to economy; and it was a temptation not always resisted. The drift to the discussion of substantive policy rather than technique was continued when, with Dick Crossman as Leader of the House, Harold Wilson's Labour government introduced specialist Select Committees.

The proposals are closely associated with Professor Bernard Crick and his *The Reform of Parliament* (1968). Crick's proposed committees differed importantly, however, from those actually introduced. His were: to inquire into the activities of departments; to take the committee stage of legislation; to examine the departmental estimates; and to scrutinize delegated legislation issued by the departments. The committees which emerged were not normally given a role in the legislative process.

The Estimates Committee moved, in 1965, to specialization by the use of sub-committees for Defence and Overseas Affairs, Economic Affairs, Social Affairs, Technological and Scientific Affairs, and Building and Natural Resources. The 'Crossman experiment' of 1966 saw the creation of specialist Select Committees on Science and Technology and Agriculture: the main attraction to the government in setting up committees dealing with these two topics appears to have been their lack of controversy (see Mackintosh, 1980, No. 2). It has been suggested that Crossman devised the Select Committees as a way of finding something to do for the intake of younger, enthusiastic Labour back-benchers of 1966. However, the tone of his diary (1976, Vol. 2, pp. 117, 130) is much less cynical than that interpretation suggests. The fact that his Cabinet colleagues were so reluctant to have a specialist committee examining their departments suggests that the reforms were seen as more than occupational therapy for the back-benchers.

Partly because of the lack of interest in agriculture on the part of Labour back-benchers, and partly because the committee was unpopular in Whitehall, the Agriculture Committee gave way in 1967 to an Education and Science Committee (although it was reappointed in a later session).

The Estimates Committee was succeeded in 1971 by an Expenditure Committee, with sub-committees on Public Expenditure, Defence and External Affairs, Trade and Industry, Education and the Arts, Environment and the Home Office, Employment and Social Sciences. The committee remit by now allowed consideration of policy as well as efficiency.

In this incremental reform, important precedents were established – for example, the willingness of ministers to appear as witnesses, the appointment of specialist advisers to assist the committees, the hearing of evidence sessions in public. Nevertheless, the essentially patchy coverage by the committees meant that the reforms looked incomplete. In 1979 the new Conservative government accepted the advice of the 1978 Procedure Committee Report and created a 'set' of committees which largely matched the Whitehall departments on a one-to-one basis. There were twelve original committees: Agriculture; Defence; Education, Science and Arts; Employment; Energy; Environment; Foreign Affairs; Home Affairs; Industry and Trade; Social Services; Transport; Treasury and Civil Service. Welsh and Scottish Affairs were quickly added. Again the remit included the study of both administration and policy.

Undoubtedly, the committees have been active: the agenda for the (randomly selected) final week of November 1984 alone, had seventeen Select Committee meetings – with witnesses as varied as Food from Britain, OXFAM, the Minister of Health, the Minister of Agriculture, and officials from the Treasury, Welsh office, British Gas Corporation, Department of Transport, and so on.

In 1979–82 there were, on average per year, some 321 formal

evidence sessions, 575 meetings, over 11,500 pages of evidence and over 1,300 pages of committee reports (see Jordan, Richardson and Dudley, 1984, p. 198).

The question of the impact of activity is, however, more open than that of the scale of the activity. The most favourable assessment is probably that of the House's own Liaison Committee (First Report, 1982) which claimed:

> Members will be aware of the many cases in which recent committee reports have directly affected Government policy or parliamentary debate. From the amendment of the 'sus' law, to the sensitive debate on the Canada Bill, from efficiency in the civil service, to 'misinformation' in the Falklands campaign ... Members' attitudes have been affected by what committees have done.

Drewry (1985, p. 364) concludes, less benignly:

> Consensus is a necessary goal for select committees if they are not to degenerate into arenas in miniature of inter-party battles ... But such consensus can be bought at the high price of excessive blandness and marginality as committees cast around for subjects that will not be too divisive and, at the same time, are not unduly destructive of good relations with departments from which much of the committees' raw material ultimately derives.

This alternative view of committee reform was anticipated by Henry Fairlie writing in 1968: 'The attempt to create important committees ... is an attempt to fashion mock political institutions within a constitution which cannot tolerate real ones '(quoted in Drewry, 1984, p. 30). This sceptical view – which seems increasingly prevalent – is that the examples cited by the Procedure Committee, far from being examples of the norm, are the limited total of minor cases.

In 1977 Stuart Walkland identified the main weakness of the reform movement of the 1960s, namely, the political context stemming from a majority of governmental supporters (Walkland and Ryle, eds, 1977, p. 244). He noted that 'Parliamentary committees of "advice and scrutiny" were invented, with little discussion of what would happen if the advice went unheeded or the scrutiny proved ineffective'. The role of the Whips in the new committee system is a subject of dispute. Clearly, if they still orchestrate activity, the possibility of controlling the government is slight. Yet, as Drewry (1984, p. 45) has pointed out, if the Whips *have* distanced themselves from the committees it is itself uncomfortable testimony to the perceived marginality of the committees. The charge against the committees (and the House) is not of lack of activity (as shown above); the issue is whether policy is affected. It is indeed arguable that the main impact of back-benchers is in their dealings with departments rather than through strictly parliamentary procedures. In January 1982, for example, over 20,000 letters were exchanged between MPs and Whitehall (see Mitchell, 1982, p. 185). The back-bench MP now acts as a local ombudsman – an informal role which has developed outside his or her traditional activities.

B   Extended Legislative Process – Consensual versus Adversary Policies

If we turn to look at policies – the nature of the outputs of the political system – rather than procedures of Parliament, we find the contrasting consensual versus adversary interpretations are repeated. If one is interested in policy changes, the extended legislative process of consultation with interested groups is probably of more relevance than the theatre of Parliament. In 1941 Laski claimed that 'the making of policy . . . is the more successful the larger the number of affected interests consulted in its construction' (quoted in Self and Storing, 1971, p. 218). In practice, this kind of rule of thumb is usually followed. As described later, in almost all policy areas close, even institutionalized, links exist between departments and client or affected groups.

Arguably, policy-making is, on the whole, less conflictual than the impression given by the superficial exchanges of Parliament. And policy-making is more marked by continuity than political parties would readily admit. There is Downs's (1974) 'law of compulsive innovation' which states that, 'Newly-installed administrations have a strong desire to reject what their predecessors have started and to emphasize programs they create themselves . . .' but there is also a counter-effect which means that governments are under similar pressures to those of their predecessors, and which leads to conformity with the past. Parliament hears little of this.

In a debate on the 30 October 1980 Paul Dean, MP claimed:

> By the time a Bill gets into Standing Committee it is in a rigid mould. The Government are too committed to it . . . It is understandable that Governments of all political colours have found it appropriate, indeed necessary, to consult outside interests at an early stage before they draft the details of their legislation. We have reached the stage when draft Bills are actually circulated round the outside interests. This seems a sensible precaution . . . but the only

people who are empowered by our constitution to enact legislation (i.e. members) are the last to be consulted ... This seems to explain why Standing Committees have become increasingly a ritual.

He went on to explain that ministers can use this consultation with outside bodies to reject points made in the House.

If they have been out-argued on an amendment during discussion of a Bill ... they appeal to their hon Friends sitting behind them by saying that the balance of the Bill has been so carefully drawn up and the Government have compromised here and there with interests outside that the whole balance of the Bill would be destroyed if the Government were to concede ... (*Hansard*, col. 741).

Lord Whitelaw, when Chief Whip, argued to the Procedure Committee:

Everyone knows that a Minister preparing a Bill is consulting all sorts of outside organisations and indeed must do so inevitably. The one lot of people he never consults in any way ... are Members of the House ... All too often the Bill is provided in a form agreed outside and then given to the House on a ... 'take it or leave it' basis. (1966–7, HC 539, para. 279)

Burton and Drewry (1981, p. 42) claim:

Indeed no one who has watched the House of Commons in action toward the end of an evening session ... or has regarded the House of Lords wrestling with a complex measure of social policy, and who has compared such scenes with what is known about the less public performances of civil servants, industrial executives, trade union negotiators or members of a departmental committee, can doubt that the effective power ... does not lie with parliament.

There are two, not fully compatible, threads of interpretation in British politics – (a) consensual and (b) adversarial politics. The former is to see postwar politics as 'Butskellism' – that fanciful amalgam of the names of the centrist Labour leader, Hugh Gaitskell, and the Conservative centrist, R.A.B. Butler. According to this interpretation of politics, competition between the two major parties pushes them to pursue the centre vote and leads them to adopt rather similar positions.

The second thread is that the post-war record of British politics has throughout been of conflict: that parties have listened to their ideologically sensitive members rather than the strategically important centre voters, and that successive governments have reversed the efforts of their predecessors.

A third option is to see British politics as being 'Butskellist' up to a point in time, but changing to conflict at some other time. But there is no agreement as to which period is what style: usually, indeed, 'today' appears to have adversarial politics and yesterday consensual – whenever 'today' happens to be. For example, in her *Diaries*, Barbara Castle (1980, p. 4) wrote that Mr Heath deliberately set out to polarize politics. She claimed:

> There must, he declared, be a radical new medicine for Britain's ills: more incentives, lower taxes, higher profits, less public expenditure. No government interference in industry and no subsidies. People must be made to stand on their own feet. And the unions must be brought to heel.

It was Heath in 1970, not Thatcher in 1979, who claimed : 'We were returned to office to change the course and the history of this nation, nothing else.'

Snapshots of earlier periods – the reaction to the Attlee government or the Wilson government – will equally confirm that pre-Thatcher politics were not entirely tea-party affairs. As long ago as 1930, Ramsay Muir was complaining that the British two-party system meant that 'the reins of government had passed by violent oscillations from one side to the other ... each side fiercely denouncing its opponents whenever it passed into opposition'.

Therefore, the argument that British politics was cosy Butskellism until the Thatcher 'experiment' misrepresents the intensity of political feeling throughout the 1950s and 1960s. The concept of adversary politics has always had some basis, even in the Butskellite era: steel and road transport were some of the issues on a see-saw of party politics which saw nationalization, denationalization and (for steel) renationalization. Conventional wisdom appears to make periodic reassessments of governments. The mood today appears to build up the Attlee government as more radical than the Wilson or Callaghan administrations of more recent years. The idea that we had consensus until recently is difficult to sustain – we cannot even agree when 'recently' began.

Most empirical analysis, however, fails to really sustain the image of adversary politics – at least in extreme form. Among the reasons making the adversary notion only partially valid are:

(1) The Opposition argues against the government's policy, but does not promise to change it. Thus for all the bitterness of the debate on comprehensive schools, the Conservative Government did not resurrect the system.

(2) The Government, in some policy areas, enacts Bills devised after consultation with affected interests – which the Opposition would themselves have been obliged to introduce in approximate form.

(3) Governments themselves are sometimes forced to reverse their own policies – or at least policy instincts. Thus the Conservative Government of 1970–4 felt that it was necessary to engage in limited nationalization, and the Labour government of 1974–9 sold off part of its holding of British Petroleum to raise cash.

The main reason for the weakness of an adversary explanation of Parliament is that most legislation is departmental in origin and reflects the reiterative efforts of Whitehall. Professor Rose concluded (1984, pp. 70–1):

> More than three quarters of all the legislation that a government introduces is derived from the ongoing policy process in Whitehall. Whitehall departments continuously nag at problems, whatever the colour of the party in office or the status of the parliamentary calendar. Civil servants consult with affected interests to see what can be done about problems of concern to departments, and committees are appointed. Months or years later, the moving inertia of the Whitehall machine produces a recommendation for legislation.

Nevertheless, at all times, examples will be found where the parties are in bitter conflict, and the confrontational parliamentary system demands that synthetic issues are discovered to sustain the conflict. 'Me-too-ism' produces problems of internal party management. There are frequent examples where governments have delivered marginal, but symbolically important, pieces of ideological red meat to back-benchers getting restless about the mainstream of policy. Given that the parliamentary system assumes conflict, it is easy for the impression to be picked up that conflict is endemic – it is as likely to be created to fit the arena.

One of the clearest expositions of the theme of a post-consensus politics is Raymond Plant's chapter on, 'The resurgence of ideology' in *Developments in British Politics* (Drucker *et al*, 1983). There it is claimed that there has been an end to the consensus which had prevailed from the late 1940s to the early 1960s. The 'fundamental parameters' of the earlier consensus were set out as:

- acceptance of the welfare state,
- acceptance of the mixed economy managed by Keynesian techniques,

- a duty on the government to secure 'full' employment, low rates of inflation and economic growth.

Plant is, however, obliged to concede that within the 'Butskellite' consensus, the parties had different priorities and that 'it would be absurd to suggest that modern Conservative policy is concerned to implement ... [neo-liberalism] as a complete ideological system' (p. 18). In effect, despite the boldness of his title, he has to both concede that past consensus was never complete and that the present dis-consensus is far from absolute.

If we look at his fundamental parameters (1983, p. 8) more closely, the idea that there was an identifiable 'Thatcher factor' leading to a 'marked change in climate' seems to be difficult to sustain empirically. It would be perverse of the Thatcher government not to want 'full' employment, low inflation and economic growth. It has not rejected a 'duty' but, like its Labour predecessor, has found it impossible to achieve. There is simply no evidence which has been advanced to suggest that the Conservative government (as opposed to individual members) does not accept the welfare state or the mixed economy. Whatever the instincts of the Prime Minister, her Brighton conference speech of 1984 made a point of boasting that the government had 'kept faith with nine million pensioners', and increased resources for the National Health Service.

When a Prime Minister claimed that 'We used to think that you could just spend your way out of a recession and increase employment by cutting taxes and boosting government spending. I tell you in all conscience that option no longer exists, and that in so far as it ever did exist, it worked by injecting inflation into the economy', it was Jim Callaghan, as *Labour* Prime Minister, who made the claim. The *Labour* Chancellor, Denis Healey, in his Letter of Intent to the International Monetary Fund proposed: '... an essential element of the government's strategy would be a continuing and substantial reduction over the next few years in the share of resources required for the public sector. It is also essential to reduce the public sector borrowing requirement in order to create monetary conditions which will encourage investment and support sustained growth and the control of inflation' (both quoted in Foster, 1984, p. 42). Although they were reluctant monetarists, the 1976 Labour Cabinet were, none the less unambiguously monetarist. They have perhaps been followed by the reluctant Keynesians.

The central Keynesian concept of public sector borrowing has been a feature of Conservative practice – if not Conservative advertisement. The Public Sector Borrowing Requirement (PSBR) – broadly the gap between government spending and revenue which has to be financed by borrowing – has stubbornly not declined as intended (see Table 4.2)

Table 4.2   Public Sector Borrowing Requirement Performance

	PSBR forecast	PSBR actual outrun
	(£ billion at 1978–9 prices)	
1978–9	9·3	9·2
1979–80	8·0	9·9
1980–1	6·0	13·2
1981–2	5·0	8·7
1982–3	3·5	9·2
1983–4	2·5	10·2

Source: Economic Progress Report nos 120, 160 and 188.

While PSBR has latterly been declining as a percentage of GDP, for a non-Keynesian government it is odd that its average annual PSBR is higher (at £10·5 billion) than the average for that of its Labour predecessor (at £8·4 billion); that public spending is now higher in real terms in 1984–5 than in 1979–80. While a 'tight' PSBR has frequently been taken as a measure of the current government's vigorous economic policy, in fact the Labour government of 1968/9 achieved a negative PSBR of over 1 per cent of GDP.

As Bulpitt (1986, p. 25) has noted, the idea that there ever was a Keynesian consensus is dubious. He shows that postwar budgets were in constant surplus – hardly evidence of a full employment commitment and he quotes Brittan (1983, p. 93) as follows: 'The truth is that, for most of this [postwar] period, neither the UK nor most other countries pursued demand management directed to full employment. The language of such policies was often used, but . . . the overriding aim was to maintain the currency parity.'

As an added thrust to these paradoxes, it should be noted that the asset sales (criticized by Labour) have been a means to permit extra spending. The cash realized has been treated as negative public spending – making resources available for projects which could not otherwise have been funded within the same PSBR limits. And in strong contrast with what might have been predicted from an ideological government, they have cut capital spending far more heavily than current.

In cash terms, in real cost terms (allowing for inflation) and, initially, as a percentage of Gross Domestic Product, there has been growing public spending. This is despite the 1980 Budget forecast which unambiguously saw spending in real terms consistently fall well below the inherited figure – down from £74·5 billion in 1978 terms to £71·4 billion by 1983–4. The actual pattern is shown in Table 4.3:

Table 4.3   Public Spending Increase 1979–85

	Cash	Cost in 1983–4 prices	Public expenditure as % GDP
1979–80	76·9	111·7	39·5
1980–1	92·7	113·5	42·0
1981–2	104·7	116·5	43·5
1982–3	113·4	118·4	43·0
1983–4	120·3	120·3	42·5
1984–5	129·6	not available	not available
1985–6	134.2		
1986–7	140.4 est		

Source: Economic Progress Report, No. 173 (1984), No. 182 (1986), No. 187 (1986).

Allowing for asset sales, the Sunday Times has calculated that the real spending figures are considerably higher than those conventionally produced (see Table 4.4).

Table 4.4   Real Spending Including Asset Sales

	1979–80 = 100	
	As published	Discounting asset sales, etc.
1982–3	105·9	107·4
1983–4	107·6	111·3
1984–5	109·4	114·7
1985–6	108·9	115·5
1986–7	109·2	117·4[a]

Source: Sunday Times, 10 November 1985.
(a) assuming a 2 billion increase in asset sales in 1986–7.

This might instructively be compared with the pattern in 1972–8, which shows the increase in the later Heath years and the sharp real decrease (in constant 1977 prices) of the Labour government in 1976–8 (see Table 4.5).

When the share of programmes of the (growing) public expenditure 'cake' is examined one finds that the pattern of change can only be described as incremental. While defence expenditure has increased in1979–83, so also has spending on health and social services and social security – the latter reflecting unemployment increases (see Table 4.6).

Table 4.5   *Decline of Public Spending under Labour*

	Public expenditure (£ million – 1977 survey prices)
1972–3	51,340
1973–4	54,501
1974–5	58,768
1975–6	59,184
1976–7	57,635
1977–8	54,850

Source: Economic Progress Report, No. 94, 1978.

Table 4.6   *Programme Shares of Planning Total, 1978/9 to 1986/7*
(in %)

	Outturn			Plans					
	1978/9	1979/80	1980/1	1981/2	1982/3	1983/4	1984/5	1985/6	1986/7
Programmes									
Defence	11·4	12·0	12·1	12·0	12·7	13·1	13·5	13·7	13·7
Trade Industry Energy and Employment	6·1	5·2	5·6	6·5	5·1	5·1	4·4	3·6	2·7
Transport	4·1	4·3	4·3	4·1	3·9	3·8	3·5	3·6	3·4
Education Science	11·8	11·6	11·8	11·3	11·2	11·1	10·3	10·2	10·1
Health and Personal Social Services	11·3	11·6	12·3	12·2	12·2	12·2	12·2	12·3	12·5
Social Security	25·0	25·2	25·3	27·3	28·6	29·4	29·4	29·9	30·5
Regional (b)	11·1	11·4	11·2	10·8	10·7	10·9	10·6	10·5	10·4
Other (c)	19·2	20·0	17·9	15·8	15·9	15·6	15·3	15·1	14·7
Adjustments									
Asset sales	–	–1·3	–0·4	0·1	–0·4	–1·0	–1·5	–1·5	–1·5
Reserve	–	–	–	–	–	0·1	2·2	2·8	3·5
Shortfall	–	–	–	–	–	0·2	–	–	–
Planning Total	100·0	100·0	100·0	100·0	100·0	100·0	100·0	100·0	100·0

Sources: Cockle (ed.), 1984, p. 14. Derived from *The Government's Expenditure Plans 1984–5 to 1986–7*, Cmnd 9143–1, table 1.3

(ᵃ) Estimated outturn.

(ᵇ) Scotland, Wales and Northern Ireland.

(ᶜ) Overseas aid and other overseas services; agriculture, fisheries, food and forestry; housing; other environmental services; law and order and protective services; arts and libraries; other public services; common services; local authority current expenditure not allocated to programmes (England).

This chapter does not deny that the parties sound very different in rhetoric: it does not deny that at some future date a Conservative or future Labour government could break out of the pattern of continuity. But case studies have tended to confirm the weakness of a simple adversarial interpretation. For example, Moran's study (1984, p. 39) of banking competition and credit control observed how: 'The Conservatives were elected to office in June 1970 committed to disengage government from the economy; nine months later the Chancellor, in his first full Budget, announced that plans were to be drawn up to disengage government from the banking industry.' Moran suggests that this 'striking coincidence' gives superficial encouragement to the adversary politics notion, but argues that this conclusion 'prompted by coincidence is wrong'. He quotes one senior Treasury official as claiming that 'Competition and Credit Control was seventy five per cent the Bank, twenty five per cent the Treasury, five per cent the politicians'. Moran continues: 'Even this may over state the politicians' influence. CCC had little to do with adversary politics ... Adversary politics is a theory of the esoteric politics of partisan argument in Parliament and in the country; it cannot make sense of those important policy changes which result from private negotiations between small elites removed from partisan politics.'

This non-fit of the adversary thesis is found in other recent case studies. Cox's study entitled *Adversary Politics and Land* (1984, p. 85), indeed found some adversarial qualities, but he concluded that landmarks such as the 1947 Town and Country Planning Act owed little to the role of adversarial politics. Cox saw the bulk of the Act as the result of civil servants and Labour ministers trying to work out a viable scheme in an incredibly complex technical area, rather than of ideological preferences. And where Cox's work does see adversarial reversal of policies, his examples and interpretation run through from 1939 – through the so-called consensual years of other authors. Cox labels his discussion of recent action as 'the enigma of the Thatcher Government' and shows how, far from adopting the simple *laissez-faire* approach of 1970–4, the Thatcher government's actions were, at best, ideologically patchy. He concluded: 'The Conservative Government had learnt the lessons of ideologically based adversary politics in the past, but only to a degree' (p. 196).

Deacon and Bradshaw's (1983, p. 96) review of social policy again finds that the language of political exchanges is not to be trusted – for example: 'The commitment of the Heath government to selectivity proved to be far less radical and far reaching than its rhetoric sometimes suggested.'

The most systematic discussion of the performance of party in government is Rose's, *Do Parties Make a Difference?* (1984). Partly basing his conclusions on Burton and Drewry's studies of legislation – published annually in *Parliamentary Affairs* – Rose shows that, in the House of Commons, consensus (no discussion on principle) was four times more likely than adversary behaviour in the years 1970–9. Rose concluded (1984 edn, p. 86): 'In the course of a year, MPs spend much of their time talking like Adversaries. But when the crunch comes ... Instead of incessantly dividing the House, the opposition tacitly accepts the enactment of legislation'.

And when Rose moves on to discuss behaviour when government and opposition change roles after an election, he still finds very limited adversarial actions – for example, 'A newly installed government repeals little of the legislation enacted by its predecessor'.

He points out (1984, p. 88) that when the Conservatives took office in 1970, they reversed only three measures passed in the two previous sessions of Parliament. They did not alter many of the measures they had voted against while in opposition. Similarly, he claims that although the Labour government of 1974–9 reversed eleven laws enacted by the Conservatives, this was only a small percentage of the legislative output of 1970–4 and many important Acts – for example, entry to the EEC, creation of independent radio, NHS and local government reorganization, the 1971 Immigration Act – were not repealed.

In following Rose and other critics of the adversary notion, we do not wish to argue that nothing changes when party government changes. There are clearly 'cases where the partisanship of the government counts – for example, the Conservative government's changes with regard to the trade union political (that is, Labour) contributions to parties. We consider some other major examples of party-inspired change in Chapter 9, though as *exceptions* to the normal style. But, in case after case, the data simply confirm neither the adversary change seen by critics of the government nor the radical change claimed by enthusiastic government supporters. For example, when the Minister of Health, Kenneth Clarke, went to an Association of Metropolitan Authorities seminar on restraints on social services he was able to claim: 'Actual spending on personal social services has risen massively over the last five years. It is 18% above the general level of inflation and almost one fifth as much again as was spent by the Labour Government in its last year of office'. (*Municipal Review*, April 1985).

Some examples of intended change can be found – for example, the civil service has been reduced in size from 732,275 in 1979 to 623, 972 in 1984. There is, perhaps, some manipulation of the figures in that certain tasks are now conducted by private contractors and some staff have been hived off to other public sector bodies – nonetheless the

Table 4.7   *Education Indicators*

Primary	1977	England 1979	1984
Average class size	26·9	25·9	24·7
Percentage of class with 31 or more pupils	35·1	27·4	19·1
Staff contact ratio	90·3	90·7	90·9
Secondary			
Average class size	21·4	21·0	20·4
Percentage of class with 31 or more pupils	13·0	10·3	7·1
Staff contact ratio	78·0	78·0	77·6

Source: *Better Schools*, Cmnd 9469, 1985, table 2.

goal has been met. It is perhaps significant, however, that this is the kind of issue where the government has maximum control – its own organization and staff. It depends on no other body for implementation.

The thrust of our rejection of the adversary thesis is that whatever the political gut instincts of governments, the pressures of the external environment force upon them policies which they would prefer to avoid. When he was Secretary of State for Energy, Tony Benn recognized the need to close coal mines that 'were out of line in economic terms' (*Hansard*, 4 December 1978). Joel Barnett, former Chief Secretary to the Treasury in the last Labour government, argued on 25 September 1979: 'The fact is that we had to cut public expenditure in the last five years and . . . we will (if re-elected) need to cut expenditure again . . . the laws of arithmetic don't change with a change of Government . . .'

Schooling is another area where the rhetorical differences are pronounced, but the statistical evidence of dramatic deterioration is underwhelming (see Table 4.7).

The real losers in public expenditure support have not been the schools, or hospitals, or social security, but industrial support.

Local government, too, is an example of partisan difference and behavioural similarity. In a debate on 24 October 1979 (*Hansard*, col. 551), Patrick Jenkin, as Conservative Secretary of State for Social Services argued (col. 551): 'It is not for me or the Government to seek to dictate to local authorities how they should achieve their spending cuts. Authorities must take responsibility for their own decisions and be prepared to account for them locally.' Yet, as Secretary of State for the Environment, Jenkin was later responsible for the 'rate-capping legislation'! And equally embarrassing for the

Labour side, under a Labour government the Rate Support Grant contribution to local authority spending fell from 66·6 per cent in 1975/6 to 61·3 per cent in 1978/9. Public spending on local government services in 1974/5 was £20·6 billion. By the end of that Labour government it was reduced to £18·4 billion (see Hansard, 24 October 1979, col. 458).

As Rhodes (1984, pp. 30–3) observes in his study of local government, it was the Labour government's decision to reclassify local expenditure as part of the national expenditure survey that promoted conflict between local and national government – 'national' expenditure precluded local decision. Rhodes says:

> It is clear that intergovernmental relations have become inextricably entwined with economic management whether the government of the day is Labour or Conservative: indeed the Labour government effected reductions in public expenditure every bit as great as those of the present Government ... *The most disturbing features of recent trends in intergovernmental relations are not, therefore, recent legislative changes but the continuities* ... If the ship of local government is heading towards the rocks, the hand on the rudder is as likely to be Labour as Conservative ... (Italics added)

Gamble and Walkland (1984, p. 174) in their study of postwar economic policies, certainly do not subscribe to the adversary politics version of British politics. Gamble concludes

> in many of its formulations the adversary politics thesis has suffered from the exaggerated rhetoric which it condemns ... When the whole field of economic policy is surveyed and not merely selective aspects, then the evidence suggests more continuity than discontinuity in economic policy – overwhelmingly so in the period between 1945 and 1959, but also in the period 1959–83. The adversary politics thesis ... exaggerates the role of politics in policy formulation and implementation and underplays the role of other bodies and institutions ...

A recent work on the Treasury (Young and Sloman, 1984, p. 35), claims that, 'Even officials who have left the Treasury, partly at least because they aren't wholly sympathetic to present policies, characterise culture-shock of Thatcherism as not so much about substance as style'.

Cox (1984, p. 21) argues that because power is located not only in government, but also in the social and economic structure of society, the government's power is circumscribed and limited. Thus he says, 'governments have to persuade, cajole and pray; they can only dictate to those politically, socially and economically weak interests in society which are totally dependent on the government's largesse for their survival'.

This introduces an important dimension to the adversarial discussion. Governments are not similar because they want to be, but because the contexts in which they operate tend to limit freedom. The run-down in local government finance since 1976, for example, is not a reflection of some bi-partisan consensus, but reflects demands elsewhere in the Budget and the fact that electoral approval is thought to impose a limit on tax increases. A major example of party convergence propelled by the external pressures is the job creation field. Moon (1983) shows that the first Conservative Budget (of 1979) indeed kept faith with the rhetoric of Opposition. Considerable reductions were made in the projected expenditure on the special Temporary Employment Programme, the Small Firms Employment Subsidy was restricted to special areas, and the Adult Employment Subsidy (AES) – which gave assistance to some employers who took on long-term unemployed – was abolished. Cuts were made in the planned expenditure on the Training Opportunities Scheme and Community Industry. However, Moon continues: 'Such adherence to rhetoric has proved extremely short-lived and the expenditure cuts referred to above were, with the exception of the AES, all reversed, in some cases within a matter of months.' As AES was, in any case, likely to have been axed by Labour because of a low 'take-up', the reversal was pretty well complete.

Few ideologically vital principles remain intact: in September 1985 the Confederation of British Industry (CBI) was informed that the British government was going to provide 'soft loans' to allow foreign customers to deal with British companies.

Barbara Castle's earlier claim (1980, p. 4) that, as Prime Minister in 1970–4, Edward Heath 'deliberately set out to polarize politics', can be contrasted with the assessment made by Burton and Drewry on the basis of their thorough analysis of all Public Bills in 1970–4. They reckoned (1981, p. 266): 'It is impossible to discern a firm strand of ideological principle in the mélange of enactments – merely a steady stream of negotiated departmental bills and incremental adjustments, broken up by a few significant policy innovations with a Conservative flavour.' Their assessment (1985) of parliamentary developments between 1981 and 1983 is equally unadversarial. They saw only 'piecemeal operations: a bit of privatisation here, a dose of trade union reform there, and an item of law reform elsewhere'.

Bagehot in 1867 (1963, p. 160) described how an Opposition, on coming to power, is often like a speculative merchant whose bills become due. Ministers have to make good their promises and they find difficulty in doing so. He said: 'They have said that the state of things is so and so, and if you give us the power we will do thus and thus. But when they come to handle the official documents, to converse with the permanent under-secretary – familiar with disagreeable facts, and though in manner most respectful, yet most imperturbable in opinion – very soon doubts intervene.' He concluded: 'And the end always is that a middle course is devised which *looks* as much as possible like what was suggested in opposition, but which *is* as much as possible what patent facts – facts which seem to live in the office, so teasing and unceasing are they – prove ought to be done.' While our academic colleagues might see 'Mrs Thatcher, as Prime Minister, imposing her hard-line monetarist policies in unwavering fashion' (Hanson and Walles, 1984, p. 319), we see Mrs Thatcher having more trouble with the facts of office than such generalization allows. Adversary politics is an interpretation aided by short memories and long gaps between changes in government.

CHAPTER FIVE

The Party Arena

Introduction

Conventionally, the British political system is described as a 'representative democracy', but it is worth the risk of over-pedantic precision to note that the idea of the representative representing his or her own constituents is weak in Britain (although MPs' attention to local issues and their local visibility has certainly risen). More accurately, we have party government – a rather different idea, whereby public wishes are reflected by their collective choice as to which party secures the greatest number of parliamentary seats. Public opinion is primarily reflected by party and the choice between programmes – not by representatives.

A common starting-point for contemplating political parties, therefore, is to see them as presenting competing philosophies or ideologies: party politicians and activists are particularly prone to have this self-image. Such an approach sees the public as being invited to choose between programmes which are arrived at by insight into the *real* needs and hopes of the public. If, by any chance, the party is not elected, the failure is clearly that of the public. (There is the old joke of the defeated party: 'the policies have been unpopular – time to get a new electorate.) A contrary view of the nature of parties – which is perhaps more common in American analysis – is to see the party as an organization in pursuit of a governing majority. Such parties, far from having enduring beliefs and enduring support, are 'catch-all' – prepared to adapt to popular opinion on key issues. The terms 'office-seeking' and 'voter-directed' have also been used. The former view of parties sees them as articulating major pre-existing interests; the latter sees the parties as aggregating a majority by whatever means possible.

David Cobham (1984, p. 30) has pointed out that both the New Right in the Conservative Party and the followers of the Alternative Economic Strategy on the political left reject consensus politics, with its acceptance of interest groups as legitimate expressions of opinion to be included with the government in a continuing process of negotiation and compromise. Cobham continues:

> They replace it by the trinity of the *manifesto*, in which each political party makes public its commitments over the wide range of economic, social plus other issues, of the *mandate* to carry out such commitments, which is obtained by the party which wins the most seats in Parliament, and of *governmental sovereignty*, by which the government and the government alone has the right to make policy and take decisions, untrammelled until the next election by the need to consult or negotiate with anyone else.

Thus, as Cobham notes, both of the traditional major parties have followers who subscribe to the manifesto/mandate version of democracy: that a majority of seats sanctifies the complete manifesto programme. Clearly, this interpretation is associated with the belief in parties as programmatic and ideological.

Arguably, this kind of belief is stronger in the Labour Party than any other. This can be explained by two main reasons. First, the Labour Party's image of itself as a means to *transform* society. Going along with that aim is the idea that a majority is a sufficient condition for that. The Conservative Party has recently been captured by those with radical goals – who have hence been attracted to the mandate idea – but, as the Conservative back-bencher Nigel Forman (1985, p. 52) has argued (from a 'wet' position), 'Historically speaking, the general conclusion seems clear: conscious political ideology does not really belong in the Conservative tradition.' In the Labour Party, however, the mandate argument has a special status. Unlike the Conservative Party, the Labour Party is technically, in Duverger's terms (1959, p. 63), a mass party. This refers not to the number of supporters, but the party structure – and the expectation that policy will flow from the members.

The doctrine of the mandate has been critically discussed by Finer (1980b). He demonstrates that manifestos have tended to become longer and more specific – in the Conservative case, rising from 3 commitments made in 1900 to 74 in 1979. In the Labour case, rising from 12 in 1900 to 133 in 1979. He argues that the commitments are unrepresentative of many party identifiers and even more unrepresentative of the values of voters at large. In discussing the 1979 election he shows that Labour supporters favoured *Conservative* policy on issues such as:

- banning secondary picketing 83·4 per cent to 16·6 per cent
- free vote on death penalty 87·6 per cent to 12·4 per cent
- sale of council houses 69·1 per cent to 31 per cent

Finer argues that the longer and more detailed the manifestos become, the more nebulous the mandate becomes – because the spread of commitments makes any single issue less central to the electoral decision.

The Organization of the Labour Party

Certain features of the Labour Party are explicable only in terms of the development of the party. The two main features of relevance are that the origin was extra-parliamentary: the Labour Representation Committee (LRC) was set up following a conference in February 1900 which called for 'a distinct Labour Group in Parliament'. Thus from the start there was the notion that the parliamentary representatives existed to further aims articulated in the movement outside Parliament. Secondly, 65 trade unions representing around 550,000 members were present at the first meeting – along with representatives of the Independent Labour Party, the Social Democratic Federation and the Fabian Society. The last group, the 'political' bodies, had only 23,000 members. Trade unions thus had a majority on the LRC (see Bealey and Pelling, 1958). Thus when the LRC transformed itself into the Labour Party in 1906 after the election of twenty-nine Labour MPs, trade unionism was built in as an element in the organizational structure. This has given an ambiguity, not to say confusion, over the organization of the party. It is an attempted reconciliation between a party of trade unionists and a party of individual constituency-based activists. By 1983 only 39 per cent of trade unionists voted Labour (Pinto-Duschinsky, 1985, p. 341) and only about 30 per cent of constituency activists (annual conference delegates) were working class. The potential for tension is clear.

The internal relationships within the Labour Party have always been more controversial than in the Conservative Party – even more so in the 1980s. Labour's mass organization is based on parliamentary constituencies. Partly because of the key function of selecting parliamentary candidates, the Labour constituency level is vital. It is based on two main bodies:

(1) Constituency Labour Party General Committee
(2) Constituency Labour Party Executive Committee.

The allocation of roles between these two bodies very much varies from constituency to constituency – reflecting the numbers willing to play an active part, and dominant personalities. The General Committee predominantly consists of delegates elected from local branches (five delegates for the first fifty members or part thereof, and one extra delegate for each subsequent fifty or part); trade unions are given a maximum of five delegates per branch, but frequently nominate less than the maximum. The Executive Committee consists of the officers, one representative from each local branch and trade union delegates. While constituencies attempt to mobilize voters, recruit members and can submit resolutions and send delegates to national conference, arguably the most significant constituency activity is the selection of candidates. Candidates need to be nominated by a ward, by the Executive Committee or by an affiliated organization (or by the National Executive Committee – NEC). The short list is prepared by the Executive Committee. Selected candidates appear in front of the wider General Committee and then exhaustive balloting produces an overall winner. The candidate needs then to be officially endorsed by the NEC (Clause X, 3).

The Labour Party headquarters maintains two lists of political candidates – those who are sponsored and those who are not. Sponsors are trade unions or the Co-operative Party, and sponsoring organizations contribute up to 80 per cent of election expenses. While usually one-fifth of candidates are sponsored, they are more likely to be found in the winnable seats and, therefore, they occupy a higher percentage of Labour's seats in Parliament. In the 1979–83 Parliament there were 148 sponsored Labour MPs – about 55 per cent of the total (Hanson and Walles, 1984, p. 56). A constituency can consider a candidate who is not on either of the official lists of candidates, but he or she would need NEC approval.

In 1985 there was a rare case of the NEC not confirming a constituency selection – Mr Russell Profitt in Lewisham East. The NEC disapproved of his candidacy because of the selection procedure used – in particular, the unconstitutional creation of black sections in the Lewisham local party and the participation of representatives of those non-approved sections.

While there is a system of regional organization (with regional conferences), the main interest is the link between the constituency and the national level and the national annual conference.

The power of the annual conference is the centre of the controversy over power in the Labour Party. The party constitution states that 'the work of the party shall be under the direction and control of the party conference', but various other bodies seem more practically placed to dominate – the National Executive Committee, the Parliamentary Labour Party and, above all, the leader of the Parliamentary Labour Party who may be Prime

Minister. The most celebrated version of the strong conference interpretation is Clement Attlee's description in 1937 which describes the conference as 'a parliament of the movement', and the 'final authority of the Labour Party'. He claimed (1937, p. 93) that: 'In contradistinction to Conservative conferences which simply pass resolutions that may or may not be acted upon, the Labour Party Conference lays down the policy of the Party, and issues instructions which must be carried out by the Executive, the affiliated organisations, and its representatives in Parliament and on local authorities.'

In this constitutional version, party policy is based on the decisions of delegates. A set of principles published in 1918 (which Attlee still saw as applicable in 1937 and which still remain in the party constitution) set out that the 'conference shall decide from time to time what specific proposals of legislative, financial or administrative reform shall be included in the Party Programme. No proposal shall be included unless it has been adopted by the Party Conference by a majority of not less than two-thirds of the votes counted on card vote.' (now Clause 5).

Three points need to be made to balance the impression given by that quotation. First, an earlier part of the 'Party Objects' states that the party existed, 'To give effect as far as may be practicable to the principles from time to time approved by the Party Conference'. 'As may be practicable' is less than an absolute insistence on implementation of conference decisions. Secondly, the document says that the National Executive Committee and the Executive Committee of the Parliamentary Labour Party shall decide which items from the Party Programme shall be included in the Manifesto, which shall be issued by the NEC prior to every General Election. Again, not all the programme seems to be automatically in the manifesto. Thirdly, and above all, the concept of party programme has somehow evaporated. For all its constitutional prominence, who now maintains the document? Who publishes and publicizes it?

Whiteley (1981, p. 162) has shown that party conference delegates are (70 per cent) likely to be white collar – almost all the blue-collar delegates are in skilled jobs. Fifty-seven per cent of delegates were from Registrar-General occupation groups I or II, with a high percentage of teachers and 'caring' professions.

A difference emerges here between the activists and the voters. Whiteley's list of preferences for a new leader in the party election won by Foot in 1980 is shown in Table 5.1

Some of Whiteley's other data, set out in Table 5.2, confirms a lack of identity of activist and voter opinion.

Table 5.1 *Preferences for Labour Leader*

	(1) *Left-wing candidate* %	*Prefer* *(2)* *Centre* %	*(3)* *Right-wing candidate* %
Labour voters	29	7	60
Labour conference delegates	59	2	26
MPs in first ballot	46	12	42

(1) Foot/Benn/Silkin (2) Shore (3) Healey/Owen/Williams

Table 5.2 *Views of Labour Activists and Labour Voters*

Conference Delegates (n = 254)	*Labour voters (n = 793)*
% who agree with a legally backed prices and incomes policy 19	% who believe that the government should set firm guidelines for wages and salaries 55
% favours reintroducing the death penalty for certain types of murder 8	% thinks that a free vote in the House of Commons on the death penalty is a good idea 88
% in favour of nationalizing profitable industry 81	% in favour of nationalizing more industry 32
% who disagree that trade unions have too much power 72	% also do not believe that trade unions have too much power 36

Source: derived from Whiteley, 1981 pp. 166–7.

While Welch & Studler have concluded (1983, p. 618) that political activists (in Britain) do not differ greatly from the general population in their policy opinions, they do see Labour activists to be slightly to the left of other Labour voters – and their data date back to 1974. Moreover, their definition of 'activist' generally includes all those who identify themselves as members of a party or are active on behalf of a party.

The belief that policy control should rest with the party members – that is, the activists who invest time and effort on behalf of the party – has a superficial appeal, but it has to be squared with the fact that the composition of the conference is *not* dominated by delegates of those constituency enthusiasts. By far the majority of votes at the conference (about 90 per cent) are cast by trade unionists who are affiliated by their union. There are claimed to be 325,000 individual members (*The Times*, 30 September 1985). Accurate figures are difficult to find, as constituencies may overcount for reasons of morale.

However, almost 6 million trade unionists are also represented as affiliated members, and there are 60,000 members affiliated through co-operative and socialist societies. As voting is by bloc, certain trade union leaders can, on behalf of their unions, outvote all the constituencies put together. The idea of the conference as a parliament of the activists which determines policy for the parliamentary wing to carry forward is thus at odds with the fact that these activists are outvoted by the unions. This does not fit into the picture of policy influence as a reward for effort. Given the importance of the union connection in terms of Labour sentimentality – and in terms of their cash and vote strength – there has, in the past, been a reluctance to criticize the trade union dominance of the conference but, in fact, in terms of any notions of democratic accountability it is an odd arrangement.

This is compounded by the fact that the number of union members affiliated is an almost arbitrary decision by the union. Unions can affiliate for any number of members they like (at 60p a head) up to a ceiling of the number of members of the union who have *not* contracted out of the political subscription (see Crouch in Kavanagh, 1982, p. 177). However, even the constituency total may be artificial. As each constituency had to affiliate for a minimum of 1,000 members, they did so even though membership was commonly less. Even now the minimum affiliation has been dropped, constituencies are granted a minimum of 1,000 votes each at the conference. This explains why the constituency vote there is about twice any of the estimates of the actual membership (see Table 5.3).

The votes at conference are obviously important, but the chain from constituency activists to conference decision is flawed. Nor are conference decisions translated into party policy (far less implemented) automatically as the programmatic party model would suggest. Of course, in the general run of things, party policy is sympathetic to conference policy, but on a succession of important issues a divide has emerged between the party leadership and the conference.

The conflict between the conference and the party leader is one of the traditional features of the party. In 1907 Keir Hardie 'declined to take advice, let alone instruction, from conference on matters such as women's suffrage' (Kogan and Kogan, 1982, p. 17). Until the 1985 set-piece battles on reimbursement of the National Union of Miners' funds, the most spectacular example of conflict was in 1960 when the conference voted by a majority of less than half a million (out of a total of 6·5 million) in favour of unilateral nuclear disarmament. (The leader of the Transport and General Workers' Union, Frank Cousins, was able to control a bloc vote in favour of the motion of 800,000 votes.) In 1985 when the conference decided by 3,542,000 votes to 2,912,000 that a Labour government should reimburse the miners,

Table 5.3   *Composition of Labour Party Conference*

Organization	Delegates	Number of Organizations	Votes
Trade Unions	602	47	6,189,000
Socialist Societies	12	8	42,000
Co-operative Organizations	6	2	24,000
Constituency Labour Party	623	607	626,000
Total	1,243	664	6,881,000

Source: Annual Report, 1984.

over 1 million votes were cast in favour of the motion by the Transport and General Workers' Union.

In 1960 the Labour leader, Hugh Gaitskell, did not accept that the conference vote should alter the views on disarmament of those in the official opposition and the rest of the Parliamentary Labour Party. He made the famous commitment to 'fight and fight and fight again to save the party we love'. The 1961 conference swung in Gaitskell's favour – mainly by a reversal of policy by three key unions. At least Gaitskell felt it necessary to reverse the conference decision, but Harold Wilson, when Prime Minister, felt it neither necesary to follow conference decision that the American Polaris submarine bases be withdrawn, nor that the decision be changed.

Conference opposition in 1967 to the Labour government's position on Vietnam was very embarrassing for the government, as was a 1968 call for a repeal of prices and incomes legislation, while the 1975 special conference voted by a majority of 2:1 to leave the EEC. The Cabinet, though divided, mostly followed a pro-European line. And Labour voters were estimated as favouring entry by 52·5 to 47·5 per cent (Minkin, 1980, p. 422).

The conference–leader conflict is usually resolved in favour of the leader. The leader can, in the end, do (or fail to do) what he wishes, and if the conference wishes to pursue the matter at a later date it will cause an embarrassment which political opponents can exploit. When Harold Wilson attended the 1968 Labour conference which was bitterly at odds with the Labour government, he argued:

Every resolution carried against the platform this week – and you have not been unproductive in this regard – we accept as a warning to the government. A warning not an instruction. No-one has ever seriously claimed that a government which must be responsible to Parliament can be instructed. This was repeatedly said from this platform under the last Labour government and never seriously challenged. (*Report of 67th Annual Conference*, 1968, p. 299)

However, a Labour Prime Minister has even more political clout *vis-à-vis* the party than a Labour Opposition leader, because he enjoys prestige from delivering electoral success. He also (probably) has the benefit of media attention and deference in projecting and promoting him as someone of qualitatively different importance. But Wilson was hinting at a different argument – that a Prime Minister is part of a different chain of accountability. The inner party democracy that would hold a Labour Prime Minister as the instrument of the conference, is at odds with the idea that the Prime Minister has obligations to the electorate as a whole.

Other problems with the conference-as-policy-maker idea include the lack of a conference facility for determining priority between desired goals; the inability of an annual conference to respond to new situations; and the fact that conference votes can reflect a very superficial and artificial majority produced by skilful compositing of resolutions rather than a clear policy stance.

A variant on the leader/conference conflict is the leader/National Executive Committee tension. The NEC has organizational power within the Labour Party to recognize and admit constituency parties, to control the 120-strong party bureaucracy at Walworth Road, and the 54 full-time constituency agents. The NEC has 29 members. The parliamentary leader and deputy leader, and a member of the Labour Party Young Socialists are members ex officio. The remaining 26 are elected at the conference as follows:

- 12 by an electorate of the trade unions represented at the conference
- 7 by an electorate of the constituency delegates
- 1 by affiliated socialist and co-operative societies
- 5 women elected by the whole conference
- Treasurer elected by the whole conference.

The trade union 'share' is, of course, greater than it first appears since their votes dominate the 'at large' section of the five women and the Treasurer. Members of the TUC General Council do not stand and hence trade union representation is second tier: the trade union representation *may* be Members of Parliament with strong trade union links rather than career trade union officials. Members of Parliament are usually elected by the constituency Labour parties and in the women's section – but they need not be unqualified supporters of the parliamentary leader. Thus the replacement of Doug Hoyle,

MP, by Sidney Tierney of the Union of Shop, Distributive and Allied Workers as chairman of the Home Policy Committee was hailed as a pro Kinnock move (*The Times*, 5 November 1984).

Historically there have been attempts by the chairman of the NEC to challenge the primacy of the parliamentary leader – or at least to attempt to control the freedom of the parliamentary leader. The most famous case here was when Professor Harold Laski was chairman of the NEC in 1945. In the unusual interval between the poll and the election result (to allow the collection of overseas service votes) Churchill invited Attlee to attend the vital Allied Conference at Potsdam. Laski tried to argue that Attlee could only attend as an observer and that he could not commit the Labour Party or a possible Labour government on matters which had not been discussed in the NEC or at meetings of the Parliamentary Labour Party.

The Conservatives sought to take advantage of the Laski issue. According to Jenkins (1948, p. 252) 'they spoke of the threat to the sovereignty of Parliament which would arise if the Prime Minister were to be primarily responsible to some outside body such as the National Executive Committee or the Labour party conference'. Churchill in his last broadcast election address tried the red scare by pondering that under a Labour government state secrets might have to be communicated to 'the [NEC] committee of 27 members, very few of whom are Privy Councillors'.

Attlee's rebuttal was firm. In reply to a lengthy and complex letter from Churchill (2 July 1945) Attlee noted: 'The new position with which you state we are confronted exists only in your own imagination.' Harold Laski retreated and pointed out that after the election, 'he would be returned to the obscurity from which he had emerged. He knew his place and it was generally known' (quoted in Morrison, 1954, p. 144).

Morrison, who served as deputy leader to Attlee, wrote: 'With the approval, so far as I know, of all the Labour candidates and the party generally, Mr Attlee held firm to the principles of parliamentary democracy ...' He explicitly argued that to have an outside body determine government policy would be like a Communist country – 'we should be losing our system of parliamentary democracy and moving towards single-party dictatorship' (1954, p. 144).

In fact the position of Chairman of the Labour Party (an annual appointment on a seniority system among elected members of the NEC) is not a position of premier political importance. Despite the ambiguity in the party constitution about where power lies, in practice the chairmanship has not been a major position.

Attlee's remarks in 1937 were arguably inappropriate for a party of government. Indeed, Robert McKenzie indicated (in Kavanagh, ed.,

1982, pp. 192–4) that conference domination was a controversial notion even in 1937, with clear prior examples of conference *not* having the uncontested authority to bind the Parliamentary Labour Party. McKenzie shows how a succession of prominent Labour leaders managed to get themselves in a tangle attempting to ride two horses. The 1973 conference programme asserted: 'Policy in the Labour Party is made by the members. The long-term programme of the Party is determined by Annual Conference.' The 1976 programme referred to the conference as 'the supreme parliament', of the party (Minkin, 1980, p. 330). The argument thus rumbles on.

The constitution of the Labour Party has not historically been a very useful guide to where power lies. Electorally successful parliamentary leaders are generally dominant. In practice, Labour governments cannot deliver change at a rate to satisfy the conference – and economic constraints also impose stress on the links to the trade unions. While it could be argued that the 40 per cent share in the leadership election (see below) and the preponderance of votes in the conference give the trade unions too much weight in Labour Party affairs, in practice these are clumsy and irregular channels of influence, and other devices such as NEDC (in office) and the TUC–Labour Party Committee have had to be invented to give more substance to trade union access.

THE LEADER AND THE PLP

The Parliamentary Labour Party (PLP) *can* be treated as a homogeneous body in discussions of whether, for example, conference can mandate the parliamentary party. It is possible, for example, to see a division between parliamentary party (including its leader) and the NEC, and the PLP and the conference. But there are also divisions *within* the PLP and often *between* factions of the PLP and the leader. Thus in 1970 when the Tribune Group (or left-wing Labour MPs) reaffirmed their commitment to conference sovereignty (Minkin, 1980, p. 329) it was a deliberate snub to the leadership. When in 1975, on the NEC, the chairmanships of the two major sub-committees were taken by the two MPs Ian Mikardo (international policy) and Tony Benn (home policy), this was less than of assistance to the Prime Minister.

A Labour Prime Minister has free selection of his Cabinet members and their allocation of posts. However, as is well known, in Opposition the fifteen places on the Parliamentary Committee of the PLP are elected. The leader has patronage, however, in his allocation of 'shadow' portfolios to the elected committee (and indeed his award of shadow portfolios to those not elected) – in all, about seventy front-bench spokesmen are needed. The Shadow Cabinet is largely synonymous with the Parliamentary Committee – but the leader can make use of the little elasticity. As part of the new mood in the Labour Party, an in-going Labour PM is now expected to appoint to his first Cabinet the elected members of the Shadow Cabinet.

However, in recent years, both the conference and the NEC have been more important. This eclipse of the PLP culminated in three important controversies: over the introduction of an electoral college for the election of the party leader; over the introduction of mandatory reselection of sitting Members of Parliament; and over control of the manifesto.

Those changes should perhaps not be regarded as reflecting views on *where* power should lie, but about *who* should wield power. To put it another way, the changes reflect a wish by the left of the party (in particular, the Campaign for Labour Party Democracy – CLPD) that the left-wing views among constituency activists should secure changes in the composition of the PLP and, indeed, in the leadership. The success of the left on these issues in September 1980 helped promote the creation of the Social Democratic Party in 1981 (see Kogan and Kogan, 1982).

ELECTION OF THE LEADER

Michael Foot was the last Labour leader selected only by the Labour Party MPs in the PLP. After the Bishop's Stortford conference which produced a compromise in 1981, trade unions were allocated 40 per cent of the votes, the PLP 30 per cent and constituency parties 30 per cent. Only MPs may stand for selection as leader and they need to be nominated by at least 5 per cent of other Labour Members. Similar provisions exist for the deputy leadership. While these changes were canvassed in the name of democratization, the fact that the franchise was only widened to constituency *activists*, rather than to one *member – one vote* has suggested to some that the motive was to increase left-wing influence and not merely wider participation. The electoral college need not, of course, guarantee a choice in line with left-wing wishes – the future sympathies of the trade unions will be all-important and, ironically, the trade union vote could, conceivably, be cast to frustrate a PLP/constituency choice.

The electoral college reform raised several issues that put other changes firmly on the agenda. The fact that non-Labour Party members in the trade unions could be voting in the trade union decision-making processes over the Labour leadership causes concern. Similarly, in arguments reminiscent of those which have been voiced (and followed) in the US Democratic Party, it is argued that (particularly) each trade union's vote should be cast proportionately so that a large union does not swamp the process with a bloc vote in favour of one candidate. The so-called 'three hats' problem where an individual could participate as a branch activist, as a trade unionist and as a member of a socialist society had also been identified. Finally, conference delegates from the constituencies, noting that the trade union 'weight' in the election is 40 pr cent, see the trade union vote (90 per cent) at the conference as too high.

RESELECTION OF MPS

The reselection of sitting MPs was a device to make MPs accountable to the constituency organization – with 'de-selection' and a change of candidate for the next election if views were incompatible. There were fewer examples of this than might have been expected at the height of the battle, but (a) some MPs 'volunteered' to go to avoid embarrassment, and (b) future *selection* could be a better guide to constituency views than reselection. The left-wing profile of constituencies was especially controversial because of the role of Militant tendency, ostensibly a Trotskyist group connected with the newspaper *Militant*, but it is argued by some that it is, in reality, a front for a strict political organization, the Revolutionary Socialist League. It has been claimed that the Militant tendency used a deliberate policy of 'entryism' to enter and capture constituency Labour organizations – leading the way to the promotion of MPs leaning towards Militant (see Crick, 1984). However, it would be far too sweeping to see the ideological swing in the constituencies as simply the result of Militant organization – though Militant has been part of the tendency to left-wing awareness. (A *Times* report of 7 April 1985 showed that Militant support had been exaggerated, with 40 per cent of its claimed membership of 6,000 not paying subscriptions.)

The fact that the 1984 conference refused the appeal procedure (backed by Neil Kinnock) – whereby a de-selected sitting Member could appeal to the full constituency membership – was significant in terms of the lack of weight accorded to the view of the new leader. However, the 1985 conference was generally seen as a triumph for Kinnock, apart from losing a crucial vote on the miners' issue. The revival of the 'strong leader' was confirmed in 1986.

While the focus of much discussion is about the conference as a means of policy-making and programme setting within the Labour Party, constituency influence through the selection process will possibly have a more significant long-term, if indirect, effect on the party.

CONTROL OF THE MANIFESTO

As noted above, the manifesto is, in constitutional theory, the product of a joint meeting of the NEC and the Parliamentary Committee of the PLP. However, in the past, it appears that if the party leader has decided that re-election is best furthered by the promotion of the leadership's own themes and arguments he can ensure that his version prevails (see Benn, 1979). Although the left has attempted to capture the manifesto as the sole charge of the NEC, prime ministers have the tactical advantage of being able to spring an election – as much a surprise to the NEC as to the Opposition.

Minkin (1980, p. 363), describes how, after months of detailed discussion and a mountain of expensive paperwork (in NEC committees and the Labour Research Department), the first draft of the manifesto came not from the party office but suddenly from 10 Downing Street. Minkin continues: 'The drafting committee of the NEC representatives and senior Ministers worked under circumstances in which most of the tactical advantage lay with the Party Leader.' He says that on one issue – the abolition of the House of Lords – NEC members were faced with what appeared to be a threat by the leader not to fight the election on the party manifesto if the item was included. The Prime Minister, James Callaghan, has been reported as interpreting the Clause V provision of the joint PLP/NEC arrangement to draw up the manifesto, to mean that each side has a veto if they do not *both* agree (Kavanagh, 1981, p. 18). And, at the end of the day, the Prime Minister could offer the electorate a personal statement that might differ from that of the NEC. Again the weight of advantage is prime ministerial.

In 1985 – when it appeared that the Labour conference would vote that a future Labour government would reimburse the National Union of Mineworkers for the costs incurred in the 1984–5 strike, and reinstate miners who had been sacked – Neil Kinnock, as Labour leader, announced that he would not fight the next election with retrospective indemnity for breaking common and civil law as a manifesto commitment. He would, if necessary, veto the item in the NEC/Shadow Cabinet committee framing the manifesto (*Sunday Times*, 22 September 1985).

The Organization of the Conservative Party

Like the Labour Party, the Conservative Party is constituency-based with local branches. In the Conservative Party, individual membership is the sole category available and, at the time of the 1976

Houghton Report on *Financial Aid to Political Parties*, this was given as just under 1,495,000. Even though it may have fallen, the individual Conservative membership is considerably in excess of that of Labour. None the less, ironically, in technical terms the Conservative Party is not a mass party. By that we mean that the Conservatives have not seen the mass, that is, the membership, as the policy-making source. The Conservatives have some 300 full-time staff working in London, Edinburgh and in their eleven provincial offices. There are also 300 full-time constituency agents who are trained by Central Office, but are employed by the local constituencies in which they operate.

As R. McKenzie puts it (1967, p. 636), the parties which face each other in the Commons are (a) the Conservative Party, and (b) the Parliamentary Labour Party. They are aided by extra-parliamentary bodies. In Labour's case the extra-parliamentary body *is* 'The Labour Party', while the Conservative extra-parliamentary organization is the 'National Union of Conservative and Unionist Associations'. The rather technical-sounding distinction is significant in underlining that the Conservative organization in the country is conceived of as being only supportive in its relationship to the parliamentary party. McKenzie (1967, p. 637) points out that until well into the nineteenth century, the Conservative Party was no more than a grouping of a few hundred Members of Parliament and Peers who were associated together for sustaining a Conservative Cabinet. The mass organization resulted from the expansion of the electorate and the curtailment of corrupt practices (see Table 5.4).

ELECTION OF THE LEADER

The Conservative leader (since 1965) is elected by the Conservatives in the House of Commons. Thus while the introduction of an election was advocated as a modernization of the party, it ironically was a step away from extra-parliamentary influence. In the former 'magic circle' consultations, the views of the Executive Committee of the National Union were canvassed. (In theory, the individual MPs are still meant to take into account the views of the party in the country. The 1922 Committee is informed collectively of the views of the peers and party members, after a survey by the leader of the party in the Lords and by the chief officers of the constituency organizations.) Under the current arrangement, the leader *can* be challenged each year within twenty-eight days of the opening of each new session of Parliament (and between three and six months from the date of Assembly of Parliament after an election), but, politically, this challenge is unlikely unless the opinion polls show no other hope for the party

Table 5.4   *Growth in Electorate*

Year	Increase by	Electorate
1833	(1832 Act)	717,224
1868	(1867 Act)	2,225,692
1886	(1884 Act)	4,937,204
1918	(1918 Act some women over 30)	21,392,322
1945	(1920 Act women over 21)	33,240,000
1983	(1969 Act – 18 plus)	c. 42,700,000

Source: Based on Mackintosh, 1982, p. 24.

than a change at the top. The Conservatives proceed by secret ballot (not even names of proposers and seconders are published). To win on the first ballot an overall majority *and* 15 per cent more votes of those entitled to vote than any other candidate are required. If a second ballot is required, new nominations are required (encouraging lowly placed candidates to drop out), and an absolute majority of votes is needed. At a third ballot, if needed, the three top-placed candidates are listed and voters must make their preferred candidate '1' and second choice '2'. The candidate with the lowest number of first choices is eliminated and his or her votes redistributed among the two remaining candidates. The result of this final counting produces the leader. Normally, of course, such an extenuated process is avoided by withdrawals, 'in the name of the party unity'.

PARTY ORGANIZATION

The Conservative Party, like Labour, has a system of area and provincial bodies between national and constituency level – but, as in the Labour case, these are not of prime importance. The arrrangement at national level is complex, but even that is arguably of limited importance. The Conservative MP Nigel Forman, recently observed (1984, p. 65) that: 'The extra-Parliamentary figures in the hierarchy of the National Union are frequently soothed with Knighthoods rather than consulted on matters of policy and on the whole the voluntary side of the party knows its place in the scheme of things.'

The main national level institutions are:

(1)   *The Executive Committee of the National Union.*   This has about 200 members, mainly representatives of the areas, but also including the party leader and other principal officers and officials. It is the Executive Committee which has the (rarely required) power of recognition or discipline of constituency associations. It meets about

every two months. Much of the detailed work is done by a General Purposes Sub-Committee which meets monthly (R. McKenzie, 1967, p. 207).

(2) *The Central Council* meets once a year and is the governing body of the National Union. It includes the leader of the party, Conservative MPs and peers, prospective candidates (although it is commonplace to refer to 'candidates', the law on funding on campaigns makes a rather artificial distinction necessary, and, until the campaign officially opens, they are *prospective* candidates) principal officials of Central Office, members of the Executive Committee, and representatives of constituencies. In total about 4,000 party members are eligible to attend.

(3) *The Annual Conference* is only slightly larger in size than the Central Council, but meets for a number of days and receives more publicity. The annual conference has no constitutional (in party terms) claims to make policy. R. McKenzie (1967, p. 82) quotes Balfour's celebrated remark that as leader he would as soon take the advice from his valet as from a Conservative annual conference. However, McKenzie goes on to say that Balfour 'could not ignore entirely the mounting evidence of impatience with his cautious tactics which was reflected in the debates at the annual conference of the National Union ... when the Leader loses the confidence of any considerable body of his followers, then the formal possession of these powers in no way ensured his continued authority within the party'. It is this political advisability of not alienating support that gives a Conservative conference its importance.

Moreover, political balance demands that the media – and television in particular – give as full coverage to the Conservative as Labour conferences. This has meant that the deliberations of the conference have a greater prominence in the policy-making of the party than once was allowed. The party leader now attends and is conspicuously seen to be listening – prior to Edward Heath in 1965, the leader arrived only at the end of formal business to give a message of encouragement to the troops before they left to carry on the constituency battle. There seemed to be a definite period in the 1960s and 1970s when the conference became more controversial. Whether this was deliberate – to provide good television and show that there was genuine debate in the party – or whether issues such as immigration, Rhodesia and law and order could not be successfully kept low key is not clear. Our impression is that the motions have slipped back to the congratulatory and uncontroversial. Television coverage also puts a premium on avoiding open conflict.

If the Conservative conference is not the opportunity for public battles between the constituencies and the elected leader, it is not because of the constitutional place of the conference in the scheme of things, but because of the loyalty, not to say deference, of the Tory Party. Indeed, the personal following of the leader poses a problem of adjustment when non-voluntary change at the top takes place. Constituency opinion broadly backed Edward Heath at the time of the Thatcher challenge. It was the MPs in the election who suddenly forced constituency members to transfer loyalty to a new regime. The traditional unity of the party is conspiciously strained when this takes place.

The emergence of the Centre Forward group in May 1985 was only the most recent of a number of factions reacting to the particular Conservative theology of the Prime Minister (see Forman, 1985, p. 52). A pamphlet, *Changing Gear*, produced by the leftish 'Blue Chip' group of the 1979 vintage of Tory MPs, began with a quotation which was from a 1981 speech by Harold Macmillan in honour of Disraeli (thus neatly managing to invoke both these symbolically important names):

> We have at least the most important thing of all at the head of our Government, a Prime Minister of courage, who I hope will not be led away from the old tradition of consensus. People can be governed in two ways, either by tyranny ... or they can be governed by persuasion ... [Disraeli] taught us to make our Party, wide, comprehensive, progressive ...

The organization within Parliament is based on the 1922 Committee, named after the meeting in 1922 of Conservative back-benchers in the Carlton Club which led to the replacement of Austen Chamberlain by Bonar Law when the parliamentary rank and file rejected Chamberlain's wish for a coalition government. The 1922 is an organization of back-benchers: when the party is in Government, the elected officers are senior back-benchers not of the party leadership. There are elected posts in the party committees which cover most Whitehall departments – for example, finance, education, employment, and so on.

To a Conservative government, the election to the 1922 Executive Committee and its committees can be signals to the leadership of its popularity. Ministers are expected to brief the 1922 on their programmes, and meetings are an opportunity for back-bench concern to be signalled. In Opposition, the Shadow ministers appointed by the leader automatically become chairman of the party committees, and this gives interested back-benchers a continuing opportunity to influence the Shadow minister. As an extra channel of influence from the committee, a Whip attends each meeting – and the subject specialist from the Conservative Central Office services the committee. William Deedes, himself a former Conservative MP and minister, has legitimately pointed out that the volume of political business now conducted in private party meetings rather than on the floor of the House has increased. He notes: 'It is a bi-partisan failing. The Tory 1922 Committee share every bit as much blame for this development as the Parliamentary Labour Party. Private laundries have become the vogue' (in Mackintosh, ed., 1978, p. 156).

CANDIDATE SELECTION

As in the Labour Party, the principal constituency influence is through candidate selection. The process is broadly similar to that in the Labour Party. The constituency selection committee will produce a short list of from sixteen to twenty applicants who will be invited to address the committee and answer questions. When a shorter list of three is required to appear before the executive council of the association, it is recommended by Central Office that separate ballots are held – the name of the successful candidate on the first ballot not being included in the second, and so on. In the executive council, if an overall majority supports one candidate, then that candidate is recommended to a general meeting of the association for adoption. If there is no overall majority, or at the discretion of the executive, more than one candidate is put to a subsequent general meeting. Balloting at the general meeting takes the form of the elimination of the lowest-placed candidate to allow redistribution of that support among the better-placed challengers. Sitting Members have a right to an automatic place on the short list of candidates interviewed by the executive council.

Within the Conservative arrangement there is no need for branch nomination, and safe seats – particularly in by-elections – will produce a flood of self-selected candidates. A constituency *can* select someone not on the Central Office list of vetted candidates, but this is considered to be unusual. Any candidate not on the Standing Advisory Committee list of approved candidates needs approval *before* the meeting of the Constituency Executive Council to consider his or her name on a short list. Central Office can, if need be, recommend candidates, and Conservative associations are unlikely to prove recalcitrant if a particular candidate is steered towards them. However, the problems that some senior MPs (including Leon Brittan) had in finding a seat after the boundary changes in the early 1980s show that Central Office is reluctant to intervene locally. Indeed, the Treasury Minister, Jock Bruce-Gardyne, failed to find a seat. Centrally, the party would like a wider range of candidates in terms of sex, colour and class – but the machinery to arrange this is absent and the party has to live with the aggregate of the various constituency choices.

Readoption of Conservative MPs has not always been a formality. After the Suez invasion, four of the seven left-wing rebel MPs were subsequently refused readoption, while all eight right-wing rebels were readopted. The most interesting case was Nigel Nicolson at Bournemouth East. Ultimately, Nicolson took his case to members of the constituency association in a postal ballot. Of 9,724 members, 7,433 voted. Nicolson lost with 3,671 votes to 3,762. This is one of several Conservative flirtations with a 'primary' system. Other Conservatives refused readoption include John Henderson at Cathcart before the 1964 election, R. Reader Harris at Heston and Isleworth in 1970, and Sir Charles Taylor at Eastbourne in 1971 (Rush, in Mackintosh, ed. 1978, pp. 16–17).

After the Report of the Chelmer Committee, which was set up in 1969 to investigate ways of making the party more democratic, Conservative Central Office published, in 1972, new model rules for constituency associations. These included a rule that: 'The sitting Member of Parliament shall be required to submit himself for readoption if he wishes to stand again for Parliament . . .'

The Labour Party's new mandatory reselection is not therefore much out of line with Conservative practice. However, the spirit of the Member of Parliament/Association relationship in the Conservative Party seldom departs from the advice from Central Office to constituencies that they must be careful not to seek to turn their representative into a delegate.

Our general interpretation of who dominates policy-making in the Labour and Conservative parties still sides with R. McKenzie's *British Political Parties* (1967, p. 635) – though his thesis dates back to its first edition in 1955. His central argument may have been overdrawn even then, but there *is* a gap between the constitutional nostrums of the parties and the power accorded the leader . . . 'whatever the role granted in theory to the extra-parliamentary wings of the parties, in practice the final authority rests in both parties with the parliamentary party and its leadership'. Dennis Kavanagh (1985) has attempted to undermine the McKenzie thesis as being faulty in 1955 and even less satisfactory since.

Kavanagh holds the view that more recent changes in the Labour Party have 'smashed the old rules of the game', but nevertheless concedes that:

In practice, of course, Labour prime ministers have been as free as Conservative ones in deciding to form a government, selecting a Cabinet, dissolving Parliament, defying annual party conference resolutions, and insisting on collective Cabinet responsibility.

Constitutionally, the parties, therefore, appear very similar when they are in government.

He goes on to argue that McKenzie's thesis ignores the important differences between the parties when they are in Opposition and argues that reforms have 'used the language of party democracy and constitutionalism to shift the party's policies to the left and to achieve a radical re-distribution of power between the different institutions of the party'. This kind of argument looked much stronger before the 1985 conference, when Kinnock reasserted the power of the leader.

The Organization of the Liberal Party/SDP Alliance

Opinion poll data of the 1980s, and percentage votes in the 1983 general election (25·4 per cent), mean that the Liberal Party and its SDP partner deserve attention as a major element in the party landscape. As a consequence of tactical and regional voting, the Alliance lost only 13 deposits in 1983, while Labour lost 119 (Conservative lost 5). Yet there is an air of unreality about the discussion of its structure, as the experience of governmental office is still lacking.

The major partner after the 1983 election in terms of seats (17) and party members (up to 200,000) is the Liberal Party. The major organizational phenomenon on the Liberal side is the Liberal Assembly which has representatives from constituencies, the parliamentary party and the party bureaucracy. This elects a Council (about 200 representatives) which runs the party – meeting four times a year – between Assemblies, but it also has a National Executive Committee (about 50 members) which has similar responsibilities and meets eight times a year. Norton (1984, p. 128) writes: 'According to the party constitution, the Assembly decides Party policy. However, decisions are not binding on Liberal MPs.' Forman (1985, p. 63), on the other hand, writes: 'The process of party policy-making remains ultimately in the hands of the Leader of the party and his principal colleagues in Parliament.' From these two comments we can see a potential for conflict.

What has been of interest organizationally is the change, instituted in 1976, of the party-wide election of the Liberal leader. Initially, this choice was made by mandated constituency representatives who voted in different bloc votes depending on Liberal electoral success in the area. In 1981 a change to 'one member, one vote' was made.

The Social Democratic Party was launched on 26 March 1981, after the Limehouse Declaration of 26 January 1981 signed by the

Gang of Four – Shirley Williams, Roy Jenkins, Bill Rodgers and David Owen – who were all former Labour Cabinet ministers. In large part, the breakaway was a reaction to charges within the Labour party, such as the electoral college for the Labour leader. Although as a device it might be thought neutral, and at least as defensible as election solely by the PLP, it was thought that the change was a symptom of the growth of the non-social democratic forces within the party.

Some twenty-eight MPs (twenty-seven Labour and one Conservative) joined the new party – though only six SDP candidates won in the 1983 general election. Its membership quickly built up to 70,000, but this has probably not been sustained. The SDP organization – because of its initial weakness – is based on area parties, which can cover more than one constituency. Each area party elects representatives to the Council for Social Democracy which is the party's policy-making body, but policy issues can also go to a postal ballot of all members. This extra-parliamentary power is, of course, greater than that which drove the Gang of Four from the Labour Party – but it is saved, in their eyes, by its one member – one vote nature, and by the fact that MPs are not mandated by party policy. Selecting the leader (who must be an MP and nominated by 15 per cent of SDP MPs) is by 'one member – one vote' ballot.

A postal ballot provision also extends to the election of the President – all party members can vote. Candidate selection, too, is conducted by postal ballot of all members of the constituency. As well as the SDP Council, there is also a National Committee which is responsible for managing the party and an annual Consultative Assembly which meets to 'provide a forum for discussion'. All members of the Council, the National Committee, the Parliamentary Committee, adopted candidates, SDP peers, MEPs and chairmen of area parties attend, but otherwise attendance is self-selected.

Electorally, the Liberals were the more successful party of the Alliance in 1983, but this appears to reflect the distribution of seats to fight within the Alliance (and the SDP's organizational weakness at the time) rather than any discrimination by the electorate. Joint policy commissions have been set up between the SDP and the Liberals, but the issues of formal amalgamation and even joint selection of candidates are still controversial, as is the question of who 'leads' the Alliance at election time.

Financing the Parties

While remarkably varied figures relating to party finances have been published, it is probable that neither of the two main parties get the greater part of their money from individual membership. Broadly, Labour gets three-quarters of its funds from trade unions, while the Conservatives get three-fifths from companies. A study by *The Economist* (6 October 1984) put company contributions to the Conservatives as high as Labour's trade union dependency. In the year to the June 1983 election, it reckoned that the Conservatives (and associated bodies) received £4 million from registered companies and just over £1 million from the constituencies: Michael Pinto-Duschinsky (1985, p. 330) puts the figure for 1983/4 at £8·7 million in donations and £1·1 million from the constituencies. Data published by the Conservative Party in 1985 attempted to counter the claim that the Conservatives rely heavily on big business. They showed £3 million in centrally collected finance and £7·8 million from constituency subscriptions, functions and interest. It is possible to, in part, reconcile this with *The Economist*'s data. There is a difference between money gathered and spent centrally, and the total flow of money (including constituency spending). However, there is also a problem caused by 'a highly uninformative set of accounts,' in the words of *The Times*, 7 October 1985.

The Economist also observes that:

> Of the top 10 companies in the list of the largest donors that gave directly to the Conservative party, seven include among their leading personalities people who have received a title since Mrs. Thatcher took office in 1979. These seven gave £429,000 to the Conservative party. All those listed are outstanding private businessmen who probably would have got an honour anyway; several have done public service too. But who will say confidently that their company's political donation did not also play a part. (6 October 1984)

In 1983 it was calculated (*Sunday Times*, 13 January 1983) that the trade unions had given Labour about £5 million. Pinto-Duschinsky, (1985, p. 333) gives the trade union *affiliation* total in 1983 as £3 million and constituency affiliation fees as £0·6 million. (The 1984 figures were broadly similar, see *The Times*, 30 September 1985.) This dependence on union cash has risen in past decades – but was threatened by the Trade Union Act of 1984 which stipulated that all unions with a political fund must ballot on the issue every ten years – which meant unions had to ballot their members by 31 March 1986 – unless they had voted on the issue in the previous ten years. The money can be passed on to the Labour Party as subscriptions for affiliated members – or can be used for special election funds, sponsoring MPs, or campaigns such as against privatization – this is especially likely in election years. The main contributors for 1983 and

Table 5.5   Company Contributions to Conservative Party

These companies gave the Tories £30,000, or more, in the election year.

Company	Chairman	Year-end	£	Previous year
Allied-Lyons	Sir Derrick Holden-Brown	3/3/84	82,000	82,000
AGB Research	Bernard Audley	30/4/83	50,000	50,000
Beecham Group	Sir Graham Wilkins	31/3/84	35,000	21,000
Bowring Services	Peter Bowring	31/12/83	41,974	16,870
British & Commonwealth Shipping	Lord Cayzer	31/12/83	97,942	43,889
Brooke Bond	Sir John Cuckney	30/6/83	42,630	8,630
Consolidated Goldfields	Rudolph Agnew	30/6/83	50,000	25,000
Distillers	John Connell	31/3/84	50,000	Nil
European Ferries	Ken Siddle	31/12/83	61,000	27,000
General Accident	Gordon Simpson	31/12/83	40,000	20,000
Glaxo	Sir Austin Bide	30/6/83	32,000	32,000
Guardian Royal Exchange	John Collins	31/12/83	79,234	53,080
Hambros	Charles Hambro	31/3/84	36,000	21,000
Hanson Trust	Lord Hanson	30/9/83	82,000	42,000
Hawker Siddeley	Sir Arnold Hall	31/12/83	33,380	7,600
Kleinwort, Benson, Lonsdale	Robert Henderson	31/12/83	30,000	20,000
London & Northern	John Mackenzie	31/12/83	54,000	40,000
Marks & Spencer	Lord Rayner	31/3/84	50,000	25,000
Morgan Grenfell	Lord Catto	31/12/83	31,200	21,150
Newarthill	Sir John Greenborough	31/10/83	33,000	35,000
Northern Engineering	Sir Duncan McDonald	31/12/83	45,000	45,000
Plessey	Sir John Clark	30/3/84	57,000	25,000
Racal	Sir Ernest Harrison	31/3/83	75,000	30,000
Rank Organisation	Sir Patrick Meaney	31/10/83	48,500	33,500
Rank Hovis McDougall	Peter Reynolds	3/9/83	30,000	20,000
Royal Insurance	Daniel Meinertzhagen	31/12/83	35,000	32,933
Sedgwick Group	Carl Mosselmans	31/12/83	40,000	10,000
Sun Alliance and London Insurance	Lord Aldington	31/12/83	39,116	33,920
Taylor Woodrow	Richard Puttick	31/12/83	79,035	53,950
Trafalgar House	Sir Nigel Broackes	30/9/83	50,000	40,000
Trusthouse Forte	Lord Forte	31/10/83	41,100	35,700
United Biscuits	Sir Hector Laing	31/12/83	43,000	33,500
Willis Faber	David Palmer	31/12/83	41,850	27,500
Wimpey	Clifford Chetwood	31/12/83	34,000	26,000

Source: The Economist, 6 October 1984.

Table 5.6   *Trade Union Political Levies, 1983*

Union	Members	% Paying Levy	Money to Labour £
Transport and General	1,547,443	98	625,000
Public employees	689,046	97	300,000
Railwaymen	143,404	97	75,000
Miners	208,051	96	118,000
Communication workers	196,426	93	93,500
Shopworkers	403,446	92	192,500
Health Service employees	222,869	91	100,000
General and Municipal	875,187	87	325,000
Post Office engineers	129,950	76	47,500
Electricians	401,092	74	90,000
Apex (clerks)	100,000	69	42,500
Building workers	259,873	66	85,500
Engineers	943,548	58	425,000
Sogat (print)	216,639	56	38,000
Draughtsmen	215,052	53	50,500
NGA (print)	133,949	44	15,500
Steelworkers	93,175	43	35,000
ASTMS (white collar)	410,000	32	65,000

Source: Sunday Times, 13 January 1985.

those major unions which have less than 60 per cent of their members paying the so-called political levy are listed in Table 5.6

Since 1913 union political funds had required a vote in favour before they could be created. The 1984 Act means that the decision has to be consciously confirmed every ten years. The funds are contributed not by all members, but only by a levy on those who do not take the deliberate step of 'contracting out'. This contracting out means that as many as one-third of trade unionists in unions with political funds do not contribute – and some other unions do not have such funds at all (for example, NALGO and the CPSA) (*Sunday Times*, 13 January 1985). Pinto-Duschinsky (1985, p. 334) reports that 'some [unions] affiliate on the basis of a number exceeding their total levy-paying membership and others on a far smaller number. In 1982, for example, the Engineering Section of the AUEW had 655,894 levy-paying members, but affiliated on the basis of 850,000; the Transport and General Workers' Union had 1,604,230 levy-paying members and paid an affiliation fee entitling it to 1,250,000 votes.' Unions also contribute directly to local constituencies – some of which sums are passed on to the Labour Party headquarters at Walworth Road. To the surprise of most commentators, the matter of ballots does not seem to have been a major difficulty, and by early 1986 over thirty unions had conducted their ballots, with no decisions to stop the funds. The unions do, however, have a separate problem of falling membership. At the end of 1979 membership of unions affiliated to the TUC (not to the Labour Party) stood at 12·2 million. By the end of 1983 the equivalent figure was 10·1 million – a decrease of 17 per cent. This fall is particularly acute in unions with memberships in manufacturing industry – for example, the TGWU and AUEW (see *Social Trends*, 1985, p. 164).

The Conservatives have also complained of lack of funds in recent years, and in the pre-election year of 1982 the Conservatives launched a special £1 million campaign. However, the Conservatives still (or as a consequence) managed to spend a reputed £5 million in the 1983 campaign – compared with £2·5 million by Labour and £1·5 million by the Alliance (Norton, 1984, p. 118). Other estimates, though, put the Conservative spending as high as £15–20 million see the *Scotsman* 28 September 1985.) One reason for some conflict in reported figures is again the difference between what is raised by and spent by constituencies, and what is raised and spent centrally.

As the 1984 Trade Union Act has not seriously affected trade union cash to the Labour Party, the pattern of heavy business funding for the Conservative Party and trade union funding for Labour remains. One rapidly developing option in British politics is the direct mail soliciting that is so well developed in the USA. One attempt is described in Cockerell, Hennessy and Walker (1984, p. 200). In 1982, while Cecil Parkinson was Chairman of the Conservative Party, three-quarters of a million voters who had been canvassed as possible supporters in key marginal seats received 'a friendly personalised letter' (via a computer) from Mr Parkinson. The letter went on to ask the recipient to join the Tory Party. The response rate was apparently close to American levels (5 per cent), but while door-to-door members gave 50p or £1 each, the average postal donation was £8. The SDP also uses direct-mail approach, and Labour have now entered the world of 'credit card politics' by renting lists of suitable Labour prospects.

The first impression of the finances of the Alliance is of a qualitatively different level from that of the big two parties. Pinto-Duschinsky (1985, p. 336) gives a figure of £383,000 for central Liberal organization routine income – but that, he says, is not strictly comparable to Conservative and Labour accounts because of the Liberal Party's decentralized structure. The Liberals have, however, been recipients of large sums from the Joseph Rowntree Social Service Trust (in 1983, £322,663 spread between the central organization and constituencies). The SDP, on the other hand, is a

Table 5.7   *Estimated Total Conservative, Labour and Alliance Campaign Spending, 1983*

	Conservative	Labour	Alliance
	(£ million)		
Central campaign expenditures (excluding grants to candidates	3·8	1·8	1·0
Local spending (including grants from central party organs)	2·1	1·9	1·6
Total	5·9	3·7	2·6

Source: Pinto-Duschinsky (1985, p. 339).

larger-scale operation with £424,000 in membership income in 1983/4. While the figure was considerably less than the £760,000 received in the first burst of enthusiasm in 1981/2, other large donations gave the SDP a total income in 1983/4 of £1,602,000.

While Table 5.7 shows clear differences in levels of party spending, Pinto-Duschinsky (1985, p. 339) goes on to take into account the value of subsidies-in-kind – free postage, free use of halls, free broadcasting time, and so on. Given the broad equality of the three 'parties' in this regard, if total campaign costs (actual and subsidized) are examined, the Alliance expenditure looks more on a par with the competition. (Conservative £10·7 million, Labour £8·5 million, Alliance £6·6 million.)

Figures published in September 1985 by the Conservative Party superficially seem at odds with Pinto-Duschinsky's data. These showed spending of nearly £12 million in 1984. However, £7·9 million was spent on the constituency agents and regionally based staff. While nothing should be simpler than reporting on the financial affairs of open membership organizations, in fact, the political parties discovered creative accounting before the local authorities.

CHAPTER SIX

The Cabinet Arena

Introduction

It is a cliché to say that British government is based on a system of departments. Some of these are more or less permanent (with the gradual addition, or loss, of specific functions); others have recently been created, or divided, or combined. Each of the departments has its own hierarchy of civil servants and its own small team of politicians. It is to the minister in charge of the department – not to government as a whole – that legal powers are given. Each of the heads of main departments with executive responsibilities requires funds. They are, in the jargon, spending ministers. Sticking to the jargon, the traditional role of the spending minister is to 'fight his own corner', that is defend his departmental budget. Newspaper head-lines of the style, 'Fowler fights in Cabinet over mortgage aid cut' (*The Times*, 12 May 1985) are the characteristic demonstration of this tendency. When the Cabinet met at Chequers in June 1985 for a Sunday meeting to discuss long-term trends in public expenditure – and, in theory, to confirm Mrs Thatcher's intentions to cut expendi-ture to allow tax cuts – most ministers apparently put the case for rises in *their* own departmental budgets. Given responsibilities to deal with, the departmental minister generally finds that he or she has more problems than resources.

To state this is to state the obvious, but it is also often claimed that British government is Cabinet government where ministers *col-lectively* determine priorities. Although they are not irreconcilable, there is some conflict between these propositions about a collective, collegiate Cabinet and about a continuous contest among spending ministers. Furthermore, there is a well-developed argument in the literature that Britain is increasingly run on presidential lines and that, accordingly, government is 'prime ministerial' rather than Cabinet or departmental. This argument also has some obvious virtues. No doubt other conceptions of the governmental system can be advanced, but these are the principal versions in currency.

The debate in the literature (mainly between Cabinet government and prime ministerial protagonists) has reached no conclusion. This is partly because of the restricted amount of data available (though this problem can be exaggerated), and partly because the proponents of each interpretation have been willing to concede that the picture is complicated. For example, in 1965 Professor Jones – the most powerful *critic* of the prime ministerial power argument – acknowledged the political strengths of the prime minister because, 'The Prime Minister is the one minister who stands on the peaks of both politics and administration' (in Jones, 1976, p. 14).

Professor Mackintosh, one of the prime ministerial proponents, was equally ready to concede that, 'Cabinet Ministers still have a great advantage over non-Cabinet Ministers. Ultimately they will be told what has happened and they have the right to express their views.' Mackintosh explicitly denied exaggerated notions of the Prime Minister's powers and claimed: 'The country is governed by the Prime Minister who leads, co-ordinates and maintains a series of Ministers, . . . Some decisions are taken by the Prime Minister alone, some in consultation between him and the Senior Ministers, while others are left to the heads of departments, the Cabinet, Cabinet Committees or permanent officials . . .' (1977, p. 541). Making policy is discovering and adapting to constraints: the usual perspective in the prime ministerial power debate of 'who dominates' fits reality poorly.

This chapter reviews the extensive range of political memoirs published in the past twenty years to support a conclusion that what is commonly termed prime ministerial power is, in reality, an attempt to impose some cohesion on government. As Jones (1985, p. 73) puts it: 'The prime minister is . . . faced with the major task of how to keep this very fragmented system together. He has to engineer a consensus among this disparate group and to steer it in a consistent direction.'

If one looks at 'insider' descriptions of how Cabinet business was conducted by, say, Douglas Jay, one finds that events can be readily reconciled with different interpretations. For example, Jay writes (1980, p. 323): 'One . . . evening . . . Wilson very reasonably gathered at No. 10 for a general talk with himself, Callaghan (Chancellor), Brown (Secretary of State at the D.E.A.), myself (Board of Trade) . . . In the end, Wilson's proposals were agreed; the Cabinet confirmed them; and they were generally well received.' It is difficult to say whether effective control in this small case lay with the Prime Minister, the inner Cabinet, a partial Cabinet, or the formal Cabinet.

While this elasticity of arrangements is frustrating for discussants, it has practical benefits for those involved. It allows different formulations in different political circumstances. For example, had there been no ambiguity over responsibilities, the Opposition might have had more success with their argument that, as minister with charge of security, Mrs Thatcher should have been forewarned of the Argentinian invasion of the Falklands. On that occasion, the indeterminate responsibilities allowed the Foreign Office to take the blame. Thus it is not the case that ambiguity is always undesirable in political argument and organization.

This chapter will comment only obliquely on interpretations of prime ministerial v. Cabinet government. It is about the *Cabinet system* rather than the Cabinet. To put matters more precisely, our chapter heading, 'Cabinet Arena', is a short version of the unwieldy 'Cabinet and other central institutions arena'. The distinction is made to attempt to put the Cabinet in a context of being one of the mechanisms for co-ordinating the policies at the centre of British government.

Co-ordination or Fragmentation?

As developed further in Chapter 7, there are, in the Whitehall world inhabited by ministers and civil servants, tendencies to sectorization and departmental pluralism. For example, Lord Butler acknowledged: 'Most of my work when I was Minister of Education was done outside the Cabinet and I hardly referred to the Cabinet at all, and that was a major reform in our social affairs'. (Herman and Alt, eds, 1975, p. 193). Thus, one interpretation of British government is that there is, characteristically, departmental pluralism. Examples of departmental defence of its territory and clients proliferate. In the original version of the 'enterprise zone' idea developed by Sir Geoffrey Howe while the Conservatives were in Opposition, the zones were to be managed by *ad hoc* authorities because local government was seen to be part of the problem being addressed. However, in office, after straight and predictable departmental politics the Department of the Environment (DoE), then headed by Michael Heseltine, managed to retain administration of the zones by 'its' local authorities. Other elements of Howe's original package were also trimmed back in the intra-Whitehall discussions. 'Rolling back' of wage-controls, employment protection legislation, and health and safety requirements, all failed to be implemented after objections from the relevant departments (see Jordan, 1984a). Another minor but typical case is a proposal discussed in 1984 when the Department of Education (DES) wished to allocate specific education grants to local authorities, rather than allowing the individual local authority discretion over how much to spend on education from its general block grant. The *Sunday Times* (10 December 1984) reported that while this DES plan 'has some support from the Treasury, it is likely to be opposed by the Department of the Environment which blocked a similar plan two years ago'. Again it seemed, the DoE was assuming a 'sponsor' role for defending its local authorities.

Richard Crossman (1972, p. 70) observed: [Ministers] . . . have to win the battle in the Cabinet. The Cabinet Minister goes to the Cabinet as the champion of his Department and, therefore, goes supplied with a departmental brief . . . He is there to fight the battle of the Department in the absence of the Department.' For the department, the effective minister is vital. Crossman continued: 'Nothing [the department] can do can reverse the disaster of an incompetent Minister failing to fight for them in a Cabinet committee or in the Cabinet, fight for their legislation, fight for their money.'

Part of the minister's tactic in promoting his own department is to avoid interfering in other departments – which might encourage their interest in his own area. Crossman argued (1972, p. 75): 'Why wasn't I in fighting for the right of X or Y or Z? Because I couldn't afford to make too many enemies by exposing causes I wasn't vitally concerned in, when I needed the support of these colleagues in my own departmental offices.' Another former Labour minister, Edmund Dell (1980, p. 25), has similarly argued:

> It is very difficult for a Minister in charge of a great public spending Department to do other than fight for his Department's programmes. If he fails to do so, if he is unable to claim victories in his battles with the Treasury, he will find himself written off by all the interest groups that look to his Ministry for satisfaction of their demands . . . Even when the country faces such a crisis as that in the autumn of 1976 it can be an exhausting battle crowned only with limited success to secure recognition from a Cabinet of Spending Ministers that the party is over.

Bruce Headey interviewed fifty ministers in the early 1970s and asked: 'What are the most important tasks a Minister has to perform? In other words, what is a good Minister actually good at doing?' Only five ministers gave answers along the lines, 'Contribute to Cabinet decisions on a wide range of issues'. This compared with, for example, forty-four who saw the main role as departmental policy-making. One Conservative minister volunteered: 'The main thing is the department. This absorbs all your energies. There is not enough time to read cabinet papers . . .' Headey concludes (1974, p. 60):

> This tends to confirm the view, endorsed by some academics and politicians, that in Britain we have departmental government rather than cabinet or parliamentary government. Ministers pre-

sumably regard their departmental work as the most important side of their job because they believe that most policy proposals are put into near final form within departments rather than in Cabinet. In so far as the Cabinet is important to Ministers, it is seen as an inter-departmental battleground (by nineteen Ministers) rather than a forum for collective deliberation on policy (by five Ministers).

In the literature, this interpretation that focuses upon policy-making in almost private worlds of departments and their client interests is variously styled policy community model, sub-government model, sectorized or segmented policy-making, and so on; the different labels capture the same point of decentralized policy-making.

The institutionalized conflict between departments and between their ministers is a basic factor of governmental organization – departmental competition has led to a Balkanized Whitehall. The former Minister of Health, Kenneth Robinson, has been quoted as saying: 'There's an unspoken conflict between Ministers of Health and Treasury Ministers ... One was just aware that if, by some miracle, one cut smoking down by fifty per cent, the economy would be in a dicky position. My job was not to look after the economy but to try to do something about public health'. (Taylor, 1984, p. 81). Pursuing the same anti-tobacco line as Minister of Health in 1974, Dr David Owen found the Department of Trade 'routinely' against, as was the Department of Industry, 'because of jobs' and the Minister of Sport, because of sponsorship. The Treasury had 'customary departmental objections' but, in this case, the Treasury ministers were personally sympathetic and so the Treasury was not wholly hostile. But, in any case, the Treasury view was now that the demand for cigarettes was not particularly price sensitive – and so the health argument could be used as a basis for a tax increase.

Processes to counter this fragmentation certainly exist. However, confusingly perhaps, two of the principal forms of central co-ordination are often presented as competing propositions – viz. Cabinet government and prime ministerial government. *It is useful to emphasize that these are essentially both arrangements to provide central co-ordination.* Richard Rose (in Rose and Suleiman, eds, 1980) uses the neat phrase, when contrasting European and American systems, that: 'In the Cabinet system, there is government as well as sub-governments.' The neat contrast, however, obscures two points. First, in the USA, too, there must be government: in both systems it is a matter of degree and not of either/or. Secondly, the 'government' in a Cabinet system need not come only from the formal Cabinet. In Rose's discussion (ibid., p. 292) one can often substitute prime minister for Cabinet; for example, 'The pattern of Cabinet [or Prime Ministerial] policy establishes guidelines for what is and is not acceptable action by individual ministers'. As it happens, our judgement is fairly close to that of Rose: American government is less aggregated than British. However, the fact of a Cabinet is no guarantee that it will act collectively. All modern governments appear to be infected by fragmentation.

There are, in fact, two styles under which Cabinet government could be the central co-ordinating mechanism. The first – what could be termed the *collective consensus* style – is, however, not much supported by the weight of memoir evidence. Barbara Castle (1973) confessed that before experiencing office she had the naïve (mis)understanding that

> cabinets were groups of politicians who met together and said, these are the policies that we are elected on, now what will be our political priorities? And they would reach certain political decisions and then would refer those to an official committee to work out the administrative implications of what they had decided. I suddenly found I wasn't in a political caucus at all. I was faced by departmental enemies.

She was echoing Beatrice Webb's description of the MacDonald Cabinet:

> ... [at Cabinet] meetings only routine daily business is transacted – very few big questions of policy are discussed. The Prime Minister carries on his foreign policy without discussion. Meanwhile each of the Ministers goes on in his own way in his own department without consulting his chief. I could not have imagined a body which has less *corporate* responsibility than MacDonald's Cabinet. Are all Cabinets congeries of little autocrats with a super-autocrat brooding over them? (quoted in Mackintosh, 1977, p. 477).

Richard Marsh (1978, p. 87) begins his discussion of his experience as a Cabinet minister by observing: 'The most unwelcome revelation of being a member of the Cabinet is the sense of isolation from one's colleagues, and the lack of solidarity, whatever might be said about collective responsibility.' Crossman often complained of this lack of involvement in the full range of issues. For example, he claimed that in the press he had read daily of the proposed cancellation of the TSR 2 aircraft project, 'but as a member of the Cabinet I know *absolutely nothing* about it ... So much for Cabinet responsibility ...' (1975, Vol. 1, p. 132).

However, even if the Cabinet is only a forum for *conflict and contestation*, it could still be a co-ordinating mechanism in resolving disputes. But those who favour a prime ministerial power interpretation of central policy-making point out that whether or not the Cabinet *should* be the effective centre of government, there is considerable evidence that it does not play this putative role – even in the latter conflict and contesting Cabinet style. In fact, there is not a great deal of time for Cabinet to act as a forum for reflective discussion and agreement. Cabinets normally meet on Thursdays from 10.30 to 1 p.m., but can meet earlier or on a second day (usually Tuesday) if business is heavy. Even so, once routine matters (Parliamentary Business and Foreign and Commonwealth Affairs) have been disposed of, there is little time for general debate. Crossman makes the point, 'Now I realise how rarely great issues are discussed in Cabinet as issues of principle, and how one moves normally through a series of *ad hoc* decisions on narrow issues which don't seem to raise the great moral principles' (1976, Vol. 2, p. 499). Lord Boyle observed that, 'any Minister who tried to get real interest in something that didn't involve a decision on expenditure, was a long-term issue . . . would be more likely to meet bored acquiescence from his colleagues'. Tony Crosland noted that, 'There isn't much correlation between how important an issue is and how much time is spent on this in Cabinet' (both quoted in Kogan, ed., 1971, p. 37). R. A. B. Butler (in Herman and Alt, 1975, p. 193), while deploring the fact, accepted that Cabinet ministers arrived at Cabinet overburdened with briefs – but only in their own field. While he wanted Cabinet to be a place where greater issues were decided and discussed, he observed that this was less and less the case. Butler partly ascribes this to the fact that departments are so very big and busy. Richard Marsh (1978, p. 98), again, recalled:

> most Ministers tended to find that they were out of the picture on the major issues. The method of handling Cabinet business was such that there was normally no way of becoming involved in issues outside your Department brief. If you were Minister of Agriculture for example, your knowledge of important negotiations on say, Rhodesia would be confined to a twice weekly mention among a whole string of other things at the main Cabinet . . .

Pliatzky (1985, p. 59) has also noted that: 'The timetable pressures on Ministers, the deadlines they are expected to keep, and the sheer volume of ministerial business are among the enemies of rational and considered collective decision-making.' He quotes the former minister, Edmund Dell, commenting on this 'system of government which plunges Ministers into Cabinet after Cabinet, Cabinet Committee after Cabinet Committee . . . Because of the burdens Ministers carry, including the burden of frequent attendance at Cabinet Committees, they may not have had time to study their colleagues papers properly. They may have received them only the previous evening and may have had time merely to skip through them, possibly after midnight' (Dell, 1980b, pp. 35–7). He also quotes Joel Barnett who described how 'not only would I be working seven days [a week] but also much of the evenings and nights too . . . Even with that amount of time spent working, it was often extremely difficult to read the papers adequately to brief myself for the host of meetings I had to attend' (Barnett, 1982, pp. 16–17).

This time pressure contributes to the lack of interest in general issues reported by most insiders. Crossman observed that '[Cabinet] . . . is not a coherent effective policy-making body; it is a collection of departmental Ministers' (1975, Vol. 1, p. 201). This was, in his turn, only updating the Conservative, Leo Amery, who had written in 1935: 'There is very little Cabinet policy, as such, on any subject . . . There are only departmental policies. The "normal" Cabinet is really little more than a standing conference of departmental heads where departmental policies come up . . . to be submitted to a cursory criticism . . .' (1935, p. 444).

In the Reith lectures in 1983, Sir Douglas Wass gave several examples of Cabinet failing to be the central arena. He noted (lecture 2) that 'Cabinet does not behave like a high command issuing orders to its field officers' (Wass, 1984). He claimed that the Cabinet is not briefed on the overall implications of proposals. Wass argued that the Cabinet can be too easily rail-roaded by the strong departmental brief (lecture 2). He argued that ministers rarely look at the totality of their responsibilities, at the balance of policy, or at the progress of the government towards its responsibilities. Joel Barnett (1982, p. 59) also argued, on the basis of his Treasury experience, that there was a lack of relative priority of decisions in social, socialist, industrial, or economic terms: 'More often they were decided on the strength of a particular spending minister, and the extent of the support he or she could get from the Prime Minister.' As we have seen, ministers will regularly adopt the role of departmental defender; they are incapacitated in acting as a central co-ordinating mechanism.

Boyd-Carpenter (1980, p. 146) notes that although Lord Thorneycroft and Enoch Powell had resigned from the Treasury team in 1958 over excessive public expenditure, when Thorneycroft returned to the Ministry of Defence he had to be restrained from spending and 'Powell, as Minister of Health was to show no undue concern at the levels of expenditure incurred by the National Health Service'. Barbara Castle recorded (1980, p. 43) how, as Chancellor, Denis

Healey was all for withdrawal from military commitments East of Suez – which he opposed at the Ministry of Defence. She commented, 'How history reverses the roles!' These kind of arguments about the weakness of Cabinet government do not necessarily imply prime ministerial power, but they certainly suggest that the Cabinet is not the central forum for co-ordination.

Ministers seem disinclined to take a broader view of governmental as opposed to departmental, needs. Even Gordon Walker, who resists the prime ministerial thesis, concedes that there may well be a tendency for Cabinets to be dominated by departmental interests. But he did cite his own case as an exception and claimed that his own attitude as a minister was to advance Cabinet policy as a whole, rather than his departmental position. He cites a case when, in 1951 as Commonwealth Secretary, he argued in favour of ending the subsidy of the sea passages of British emigrants to Australia. Similarly, when he was Secretary of State for Education in 1968, Gordon Walker 'did not conceive it as my sole or prime duty to fight all out and at all costs in defence of any departmental estimates as they stood' (1972, p. 26). While he may have felt that accepting the postponement of raising the school-leaving age was 'responsible', his colleague, Crossman, reckoned that this was 'pathetic weakness' (1976, Vol. 2, p. 637). Walker's estimate that about half the ministers in charge of spending departments took similarly broad 'governmental' views seemed on the generous side. Lord Boyle (1980, p. 6), reflecting on Gordon Walker's position, countered 'That a Minister . . . [who] becomes too impressed by the concept of "Cabinet policy as a whole" may be storing up pretty desperate problems for his successor, his department and even his Cabinet colleagues who later on have to sort out the mess'. By this he meant that if one minister foregoes resources for his or her sector, or the pursuit of a pay award for those employed in it, anomalies grow which have to be dealt with eventually.

Ironically, Gordon Walker and Crossman shared an emphasis on the need for co-ordinated, coherent policies. But Gordon Walker obviously felt that it was possible that departmental views and concerns could be 'woven into a unified and dominant Government policy and that Ministers consider their major duty to be to partake in the formulation of this policy'. Crossman repeatedly argued on the need for the emergence of central strategy – but generally thought this mainly the Prime Minister's responsibility (for example, 1976, Vol. 2, p. 627). (See Jordan, 1978.)

There seems little difference between the protagonists of the prime ministerial/Cabinet government debate on the need for co-ordinated decisions. But, interestingly, Douglas Jay complained that the workload by the 1960s on senior ministers had been greatly increased (compared with his experience in 1944–50) because 'co-ordination', which had been lacking in the early years of the war, was seriously overdone by the 1960s. He claimed: 'What took three hours to decide in 1944 and three days in 1950, too often took three months in 1965. There was always one more committee to placate' (Jay, 1980, p. 315). Although Jay's complaint has a ring of authenticity, there are, in fact, more complaints about the lack of co-ordination. Jay, however, usefully points to the fact that too much co-ordination can be itself a problem.

Co-ordination by a Prime Minister's Department?

There has been much speculation in Mrs Thatcher's terms of office that she was moving towards the creation of a Prime Minister's Department. While the term 'Prime Minister's Department' is politically taboo, the increase in prime ministerial support at the centre leads to that *function* being performed none the less. However, such talk needs to be put in context when, a century ago, G. C. Thompson was noting 'tendencies' that could cause the constitution 'of its own accord to slide involuntarily, almost imperceptibly towards a Caesarism'. He drew attention to the 'Presidential character' of the office and speculated that, more and more, the Prime Minister's tenure and power would depend on the acclaim of the multitude (quoted in Waltz, 1968 edn, p. 37). Lord Morley, in *Walpole* (1889), said that the flexibility of the Cabinet system allowed the Prime Minister to take upon himself a power not inferior to that of a dictator, provided always that the House of Commons would stand by him.

However, it can be argued that the need for a formal Prime Minister's Department is undermined precisely because the existing arrangement supplies most of the putative benefits. As Harold Wilson (1976, p. 82) put it: 'Everything [a Prime Minister] could expect to create [by a Prime Minister's Department] is there already to hand in the Cabinet Office.' With Mrs Thatcher's incremental build-up of advisers at the centre, this is even more true.

The argument for a Prime Minister's Department is the argument for central co-ordination – to overcome the excessive departmentalism that is widely depicted. (Pliatzky [1985, p. 53] portrays the Prime Minister as 'beleaguered by the surrounding Departmental barons with their tier upon tier of supporting troops'.) As we outline in Chapter 9, the PESC system was designed to permit collective central decision-making, but one indication of its failure is James Prior's call in 1984 that, 'It is perhaps time that the "Star Chamber" was replaced by a more permanent management system, intended to operate through the year, to set priorities and examine individual spending programmes, and to prepare proposals for reasoned collective decision in Cabinet' (*The Times*, 8 March 1985). That was precisely the original PESC aim.

The former head of the Central Policy Review Staff (CPRS), Sir Kenneth Berrill, explicitly called for a Prime Minister's Department in his 1980 Stamp Memorial Lecture. Berrill confirms the tendency of a departmental head to 'fight his own corner', 'so that after a year or two's experience at the centre one can predict with a high degree of certainty each department's arguments and views on any topic on the agenda'. He argues that the longer a particular portfolio is held by ministers, the more likely they are to see the country's problems increasingly through the eyes of their department and less in terms of the strategy of the government as a whole. He accounts for this identification of ministerial goals with departmental priorities as the result of 'very long hours ... immersed in the details of their department's affairs', and the continual battering of ministers on these affairs in the media, Parliament and from the 'ever more professional organised pressure groups'.

Berrill goes on to claim that the 'sum of spending departments' interests can be a long way from adding up to a coherent strategy'. Hence he sees the need for strength at the centre to 'hold the balance in any decision between the requirements of the strategy and the crosspulls of the interest of the different spending departments'. Berrill quotes Crossman's statement that 'perhaps the biggest task of a Prime Minister is to stop the fragmentation of the Cabinet into a mere collection of departmental heads'.

Sir John Hoskyns, formerly head of Mrs Thatcher's policy unit, has similarly characterized Whitehall unflatteringly as, for example, 'a headless chicken'. He argued that there is no central group for the goal-seeking synthesis of the work done by departments into a single strategy. He sought 'a small new department, responsible for the development and over-seeing of the government's total strategy, across all departments, integrating policy and politics into a single whole' (1983, p. 147). Marcia Williams (now Lady Falkender), formerly research and political secretary to Harold Wilson, also endorses the idea of a Prime Minister's Department (see 1983, p. 264). Hector Hawkins, who served in the CPRS, has argued for the Think Tank to become the Prime Minister's personal *cabinet* (in the French style): 'We suffer at the moment [because] each ministry is an independent satrap ... There is no way of co-ordinating these different policies that emerge from the different ministries except Cabinet committees and Cabinet which are dealing with the day-to-

day issues as they come up, sorting them out on an *ad hoc* basis . . .
not a strategic basis' (Hennessy, Morrison and Townsend 1985,
p. 102). In his Reith lectures, Sir Douglas Wass called for stronger
staff support for the Cabinet as a whole.

While all these 'stronger centre' analyses share a theme, differences
in prescription are apparent. In his 1980 Stamp Memorial Lecture
Berrill talked of the need for a Prime Minister's Department and
Hoskyns for a reconstructed Cabinet Office. Despite their differing
terminologies, they were each seeking to reinforce a capacity for
central capability. In other words, these were to be mechanisms to
combat excessive departmentalism. Arguably, however, any attempt
at central co-ordination ends up as being dominated by the Prime
Minister – whether that is the intention or not.

Although his label for his suggested reform was a 'Prime Minister's
Department', Berrill saw the role of strategic direction extending
beyond the Prime Minister to what he termed the troika – the Prime
Minister, the Chancellor of the Exchequer and the Foreign Secretary. Even this unity was seen to be in danger of departmentalism
but, in general, he saw a 'centre and the centre has to hold'. In
summary, Berrill was not talking about a more interventionist Prime
Minister. He specifically rejects prime ministerial involvement in
more detailed decisions, but he seeks a degree of parallel competence
in the centre, 'not all industry issues can be left to the Department of
Industry or agriculture to M.A.F.F.'. Berrill's call for a Prime
Minister's Department was not to erode Cabinet government but to
provide the central co-ordination which classically has been ascribed
to the Cabinet.

From 1970 to June 1983 the CPRS attempted to fill the central
capability role. It was small scale – thirteen to twenty members,
about half of whom were civil servants – but tackled a wide range of
issues. Peter Hennessy and his colleagues (1985, p. 21) list thirty-six
topics which were investigated. They quote an internal CPRS paper
setting out its functions as:

'Sabotaging' the over-smooth functioning of the machinery of
Government.

Providing a Central Department which has no departmental axe
to grind but does have overt policy status and which can attempt a
synoptic view of policy.

Providing a central reinforcement for those Civil Servants in
Whitehall who are trying to retain their creativity and not be totally
submerged in the bureaucracy.

Trying to devise a more rational system of decision making
between competing programmes.

Advising the Cabinet collectively, and the Prime Minister [note ambiguity], on major issues of policy relating to the Government's Strategy.
Focussing the attention of Ministers on the right questions to ask about their own colleagues' business.
Bringing in ideas from the outside world.

One of the predictable features of CPRS life was that while the principle of 'second-guessing' could be accepted by almost all, ministers and departmental civil servants felt that *their* patch was special, and that decision-making there required the benefit of long-term experience and expertise. There was the well-publicized Foreign Office campaign against the critical CPRS *Review of Overseas Representation*. Hennessy and his colleagues quote a Home Office official who seemed to approve of the CPRS in general terms but went on: 'When they turned their attention to prisons it was not very good. It seemed to us that their paper rehearsed the problems, which were only too familiar to us, without being very helpful.' Sir Frank Cooper, former Permanent Secretary at the Northern Ireland Office, expressed the same scepticism of outside analysis: 'We didn't have any great hopes that it would bring some blinding flash of new insight . . . simply because the people who were working in the office were totally immersed in it.'

Hennessy, Morrison and Townsend (1985, p. 91) quote two of the Think Tank's own members conceding the mismatch between staff and issues: 'They were thinly spread over a lot of areas. The staff was not very good . . . The members of the Tank were very ordinary. They had no real experts.' Another reckoned that 'Apart from the odd occasion where one was genuinely an expert, we ranged over a tremendously wide field. We were interfering a lot on a fairly superficial plane. I always felt frustrated at second guessing without the depth of knowledge that made it fully justified.'

The experience of the CPRS suggests that there are some perennial problems of central assessment. Can the 'second-guess' organization match the detailed knowledge of the 'first'? If the centre is kept small it is spread too thin, while if it is large it is accused of duplication . . . Strategic analysis can, and will, be seen as meddling in departmental business. However, Mrs Thatcher's reasons for shutting down the CPRS in July 1983 do not seem to have been along these lines, but probably reflect her reaction to the political embarrassment in the 1983 election campaign when a CPRS report on public-spending options was leaked. Moreover, the decision can perhaps be seen as *relocating* the central capability even more firmly under the Prime Minister: shutting down the CPRS allowed Mrs Thatcher to make more personal appointments (see below) while still controlling numbers at the centre.

In this debate there is an apparent acceptance of the need for a direct hierarchical style of co-ordination – that co-ordination was from an authoritative centre knocking heads together. Wildavsky (in Calden and Wildavsky, 1974) has argued that co-ordination is often just another word for coercion. It certainly has this flavour in many prescriptions on British government. It is now a conventional wisdom that some central machinery or unit is needed. One source runs:

> Less and less can it be presumed that the negative process of piecemeal review, rejection and modification of individual proposals flowing up from departments to the centre, will eventuate in the sort of integrated programme of objectives that conditions seem certain to require. Thus it may be expected that the need for positive initiations at the centre . . . will become more pressing.

The quotation is slightly disguised as, in fact, it dates back to 1942 and concerns the USA (V. O. Key, quoted in Heclo and Salaman, eds, 1981, p. 127). This kind of diagnosis of the need for hierarchical 'command' is recurrent in terms of times and systems.

However, it is possible that indirect approaches to co-ordination are at least as defensible – though many of those currently advocating reform at the centre are included to discount informal co-ordination. Lindblom has provided the intellectual justification for the process of co-ordination without a co-ordinator:

> In the synoptic ideal, the integration of parts remains an intellectual task for the analyst and whatever closure is accomplished is attributable to and therefore limited by, his capacities to understand the relationship of the parts. In the strategy of 'disjointed incrementalism', however, integration of parts is not entirely . . . an intellectual accomplishment, but a result of a set of specialised social or political processes. In other words there is a possibility of co-ordination through a 'hidden hand' of interaction.

In the language of policy-making, it is easy to assume that governments have policies for all problems and spend their time evolving policies. This is often to impute too rational an image to the process. The language of policy-making is a convenient shorthand, but it can mislead. For one thing, a government can have a policy which cannot be implemented. Thus no doubt the policy of the Labour government in 1974–9 was not to increase unemployment. For other problems there may well be no policy (in the sense of a set of means to bring about desired change) as, arguably, for Northern

Ireland or, more clearly, towards the Falklands before the Argentinian invasion. What passes for a policy is the status quo and a series of reactions to tendencies to disturb the status quo. Or there can be a policy, but it can be recognized that there are no resources to match the policy – as with the 1964–6 Labour government's 'policy' on poverty. Was the policy the intention or the inaction? Or policies can be contradictory. Britain (and other countries) appear to have a 'policy' to encourage free trade and yet have a 'policy' to encourage domestic industry by preferential purchasing.

These comments on policies are made to make the point that Cabinet and the Prime Minister often must discriminate between lesser evils rather than attempting to implement desired policy. 'Making policy', then, often implies reactions to crises, or disputes over priorities as much as developing machinery to serenely implement party values and priorities.

Co-ordination through the Prime Minister

To the extent that there *is* co-ordination in this process of crisis management in British government (notwithstanding the lack of a formal Prime Minister's Department), it effectively takes place through the Prime Minister's Office and the Cabinet Office, with its penumbra of supplementary institutions. The complex administrative geography at the centre is set out by Jones (1985). It includes the Efficiency Unit, the Prime Minister's Policy Unit under Professor Brian Griffiths, Mrs Thatcher's personal advisers such as Sir Percy Cradock (foreign affairs), Sir Alan Walters (economics), Sir Robin Ibbs (efficiency). Francis Pym, after his dismissal from the government in 1984, complained of the Prime Minister's steps 'to expand the Downing Street staff to include experts in every major area, thus establishing a government within a government' (quoted in Pliatzky, 1985, p. 54). While some might be critical of these developments, we see the expansion as telling us something about the nature of the co-ordination problem – it is not likely to occur at formal Cabinet without extensive orchestration.

Above, Berrill used the term 'troika' to establish that the centre is not solely the Prime Minister, but extends to the Chancellor and the Foreign Secretary. These 'three' are seen as the centre for (at least) two reasons. First, their departmental responsibilities are wider than that of the single functional ministry – the Chancellor must balance priorities, unlike the spending minister who can 'argue his corner'. Secondly, these three are usually first, second and third in any ranking of political seniority and to say that 'the troika decides' is simply to say that when the 'heavyweights' agree, things are likely to happen. However, the Prime Minister decides who is to hold the important offices.

(i)   APPOINTMENT AND PATRONAGE

In explaining how the Prime Minister (with central support) co-ordinates Whitehall – and attempts to mitigate the well-developed tendencies to departmentalism, his or her right to make the important appointments is one of the resources he or she has available. Thus the list of factors which has been developed to account for prime ministerial power overlaps considerably with the list that is needed to explain prime ministerial co-ordination. Our argument, however, is not whether prime ministerial power is good or bad, but that some central co-ordination capacity is needed with Whitehall. Where else, but the Prime Minister, is it to come from?

'Appointment' is one of six factors which we discuss as relevant to explaining *how* co-ordination emerges. While prime ministers may be obliged to appoint major party opponents, if only to preserve party unity, there is still considerable power in the allocation of particular posts to individuals. When Richard Marsh attempted to resist a move from the Ministry of Power to Transport, the Prime Minister, Harold Wilson, firmly told him that 'if the captain asked a fielder to move from square leg to cover point then that was exactly where he had to move'. To a degree, however, this is negotiable; thus, for example, Sir Alec Douglas-Home wanted Boyd-Carpenter to go to the Ministry of Health, but he held out and retained his position as No. 2 in the Treasury. Likewise, Reginald Maudling refused the Ministry of Supply and Ministry of Health in 1957 before accepting the post of Paymaster-General, and Roy Jenkins reportedly turned down a Cabinet place at DES in 1964. However, in 1982 Jim Prior found that his transfer to the Northern Ireland Office was not negotiable – and he was then luckier than colleagues such as Sir Ian Gilmour, Lord Soames, Francis Pym, Norman St John Stevas and Patrick Jenkin, who found their appointments to the back-benches similarly non-negotiable. Where the Prime Minister might not feel free to dismiss some figures from the Cabinet, he or she can keep them off key Cabinet Committees – as happened to Jim Callaghan after he was active in stopping Harold Wilson's trade union reform proposals – or the Prime Minister can transfer a minister away from the department (and policies) which give the Prime Minister concern. This happened to Tony Benn when Harold Wilson transferred him from the Department of Industry to the Department of Energy. In appointing individuals to posts, the Prime Minister can thus advance certain policies – as in Mrs Thatcher's appointment of so-called monetarists to key economic posts – keeping critics of this approach away from the Treasury.

In his memoirs, Crossman (1975, Vol. 1, p. 23) admitted his ignorance of the matters for which he had been made officially responsible:

> ... all through [the first weeks] I've had an underlying anxiety caused by my complete lack of contact (thank God they can't quite realise it) with the subjects. For years I've been a specialist on social security and I know enough about it. Science and education I had picked up in the months when I was Shadow Minister. But I've always left out of account this field of town and country planning ... all this is utterly remote to me.

With Crossman in Housing and Local Government, Wilson had more influence over the pensions issue than would have been the case if Crossman had been allowed that field.

The Prime Minister's patronage goes beyond that of appointing the twenty or so places of full Cabinet rank that we have discussed. About sixty ministers of state and under secretaries (usually collectively termed junior ministers) need to be appointed. Posts as parliamentary private secretary (about forty in number) are unpaid, but are a form of patronage in that they carry the possibility of further promotion at a later date. At any time, nearly a third of the governing party will have posts in the government (see Rose and Suleiman, 1980, p. 6) – forming the so-called 'payroll vote'. Added to this career incentive for loyalty, Mrs Thatcher has been liberal with knighthoods for senior back-benchers – ensuring some loyalty by non-ministers, by the award of titles – and probably more by the prospect of further distribution.

Another, perhaps more direct and obvious way in which the patronage of the Prime Minister can steer individual decisions in his or her preferred direction, is encapsulated in Douglas Jay's claim about Harold Wilson and the Common Market. As Jay noted – without it being a great issue for him – the Prime Minister's opinion is likely to swing quite a number of ministers. On the Common Market, he said (1980, p. 389), 'The issue was decided by those who, having no firm views of their own, voted with the P.M. ... In modern conditions, where the Prime Minister has the sole power of appointment and dismissal ... this is probably unavoidable'.

Crossman used to tell a rather similar story of how there were three types of minister in the Cabinet. He said that there was, first, the rivals who were too powerful and too much of a potential nuisance to be left out, then there were those with useful expertise who were good at the job and, thirdly, he would claim, there were the other five votes. When someone failed to resist the temptation to ask, 'What other five?', Crossman would say, 'Oh, the five are placed in the Cabinet to support the Prime Minister . . .'.

Another form of patronage of some topicality is the 1980s civil service promotions. Mrs Thatcher has been accused of politicization of the civil service in consequence of her active participation in the appointment of senior officials, such as Sir Clive Whitmore (her former principal private secretary at the Cabinet Office) to be head of the Ministry of Defence and Sir Peter Middleton to be head of the Treasury. Although previous prime ministers had an undoubted right to question the recommendations of the civil service's own Senior Appointments Selection Committee, Mrs Thatcher has been unusual in making use of this opportunity. She also abolished the Civil Service Department which prompted the early retiral of the then Head of the Civil Service, Sir Ian Bancroft.

Ironically, she actively intervened to secure a good posting for Clive Ponting who had impressed her in his efficiency work for Lord Rayner – though Ponting (1986, p. 9) subsequently complained of her 'politicization' of the civil service.

Some of her advisers – most notably Sir John Hoskyns and Norman Strauss – have canvassed the case for much greater politicization. Sir John has said: 'We need to replace a large number of senior civil servants with politically appointed officials on contracts, at proper market rates, so that experienced top quality people would be available' (quoted in Fry, 1985, p. 25).

However, the few significant promotions (and non-promotions) made by Mrs Thatcher that have attracted controversy are, as yet, a long way from a politicized civil service – politicization of public officials can perhaps become credibly identified in some local authorities. A civil servant has written that 'the present Administration has certainly exercised vigorously its undoubted right to vet new senior appointments to satisfy itself that candidates will not reopen its firmly established policies . . . These developments are a long way from wholesale politicization . . . ' (quoted in Fry, 1985, pp. 24–5).

There is a temptation to assume that nothing is possible other than the extremes of complete politicization or a complete neglect of the area by the Prime Minister but, as the above quotation makes clear, the civil service can live with a Prime Minister – Mrs Thatcher – who is particular about the people in her immediate entourage. As in other areas, Britain is likely to continue not to make a clear choice of one system or another, but will continue its fudge. Patronage of civil servants is thus still more a potential than an actual power.

(ii)   AGENDA CONTROL

Another clear strength of the Prime Minister in imposing his or her wishes on the Cabinet is how the meeting is handled – from the setting of the agenda, to the discussion and summing up. Boyd-Carpenter (1980, p. 75) relates how when Attlee was opposed by the whole of the Cabinet, he let discussion go on and then said: 'I see the Cabinet is fairly evenly divided on this. We'll put it to another meeting.' Apparently, it never appeared on the agenda and was settled as he wished. Such stories may be apocryphal, but the fact that such tales circulate reflect prime ministerial dominance. (One anecdote that regularly emerges is how the Prime Minister sums up a discussion which he or she favours by, saving 'The "ayes" four, the "noes" sixteen. The "ayes" have it.') The examples of agenda control are many – though, as usual, many are subject to controversy. One example (from the Shadow Cabinet) can be taken from Reginald Maudling's experiences (1978, p. 209). He notes that, as a former Chancellor, he circulated to his Cabinet colleagues a memorandum summing up his views in favour of incomes policies and against reduction in the money supply. He observed, with some bitterness: 'I do not recall that this memorandum was ever discussed by the Shadow Cabinet. Our agenda was not in my hands.'

Bruce-Gardyne and Lawson's account of the Labour government's decision not to devalue in 1964 and 1966 is an apparent instance of the importance of the ability to control the agenda. Indeed, it appears that Harold Wilson was so obsessed with avoiding discussion of the topic that any paper mentioning devaluation was ordered to be destroyed. Civil servants – who felt obliged to consider the contingency – used the code word 'British Railways', so as not to attract the Prime Minister's attention (1976, p. 127). It is likely that dissidents within a Cabinet can eventually force a matter on to the agenda, but the Prime Minister can certainly delay and, in some cases, can more or less veto discussion through control of the agenda.

The most recent and spectacular controversy over agenda control has been hinted at already – when Michael Heseltine resigned as Secretary of State for Defence in January 1986. He claimed in his resignation statement that Mrs Thatcher attempted to stop discussion of the European option for rescuing Westland, and that when he protested this went unrecorded in the minutes – and that when the Prime Minister feared losing a vote in a Cabinet sub-committee she crudely cancelled the meeting. Heseltine claimed:

> I sought on a number of occasions to have the issues properly addressed ... The first attempt had been at the Cabinet on

Thursday December 12. The Prime Minister refused to allow a discussion in Cabinet that day. I insisted that the Cabinet Secretary should record my protest in the Cabinet minutes.

When the minutes were circulated there was no reference to any discussion about Westland and consequently no record of my protest. Before the next Cabinet meeting I complained to the Secretary of the Cabinet. He explained that the item had been omitted from the minutes as the result of an error . . . The minutes as finally issued still did not record any protest.

Opinion on whether or not Cabinets vote is divided, but Barnett (1982, p. 77) puns that prime ministers count, indeed their counting is all that matters. Again, Barnett (1982, p. 111) describes how one can get a paper through Cabinet in thirty seconds when there are other politically contentious items on the agenda, but notes that 'It cannot be done wihout the cooperation of the Prime Minister'. Many of Crossman's descriptions confirm Jay's point (p. 135 above) that formal votes are unnecessary because positions in Cabinet had a habit of crumbling if the Prime Minister gave a clear lead. For example, when Michael Stewart put in a paper suggesting the introduction of comprehensive schooling by legislation, Harold Wilson sought to achieve that goal while avoiding compulsion and legislation. Crossman (1975, Vol. 1, p. 133) describes how 'Even the other members of the [Cabinet] Social Services Committee immediately withdrew [support] when the Prime Minister made his point of view clear'. At the same time, it is worth noting *how* Harold Wilson proceeded. He started by 'describing Michael Stewart's paper as the model of what a Cabinet paper should be – something he approved in every way'. In other words, while the Prime Minister may be dominant, it is good political sense to proceed by building consensus and allowing colleagues the chance to back down with their reputation intact. Brian Sedgemore similarly records (1980, p. 67) how wide Cabinet support to channel North Sea oil revenues to a special development fund disappeared when the Prime Minister summed up against such a move.

A former member of Mrs Thatcher's Cabinet, David Howell, remarked that Mrs Thatcher's style was to show her preference and let others talk her out of it. The invitation to challenge her appears to be often resisted – especially, as Howell notes, 'tremendous battle lines will be drawn up and everyone who doesn't fall in line will be hit on the head' (*The Times*, 10 January 1986).

Partly this dominance over colleagues is *because* the Prime Minister is the *Prime Minister*; partly it is the dominance that makes someone Prime Minister. There is some significance in the fact that one cannot think of many jokes at a Prime Minister's expense, but Prime Ministers can afford to make fun of their ministers. When Maudling, as Chancellor, appeared at No. 10 in a new light-blue dinner jacket, Macmillan welcomed him with the line, 'Ah Reggie, playing the drums at the 400 club again tonight, I see'. Not surprisingly, Maudling did not wear it again (Maudling, 1978, p. 103). When Wilson was Prime Minister, he sent urgently for his new Postmaster-General, Tony Benn. Marcia Williams describes how Benn shouted, 'Right, I'm coming at once', and pounded along the corridor full of excitement and anticipation. She continues:

> I knocked on Harold Wilson's door and said; 'Postmaster General for you, Prime Minister'. Upon which, Tony literally bounded into the room eyes shining, and beaming away in his enthusiastic way. 'So glad you could come, Tony', said the Prime Minister. 'Want to see you, Postmaster-General, rather urgently.' By this time Benn was hanging on every word so that he was all attentiveness when the Prime Minister continued, completely dead pan. 'It's my father's eightieth birthday – and I want to make absolutely sure that the telegram I send gets there . . .' (Williams, 1983, p. 214)

(iii) BILATERAL DEALS

One major device by the Prime Minister to impose his or her views is by arranging policy in advance of Cabinet with the relevant minister in a bilateral deal. The Prime Minister and the departmental minister together are a potent combination. Kenneth Robinson (in Taylor 1984, p. 86) claimed that his proposal to legislate on smoking was killed in 1968 by the new Secretary of State, Dick Crossman, going to the Prime Minister and persuading him that it was a vote loser: 'It was a decision reached between Dick Crossman as Secretary of State and Harold Wilson as Prime Minister.' Sir Douglas Wass made the point in his 1983 Reith lectures that 'every Chancellor I have worked for has obtained the Prime Minister's agreement to changes, even quite trivial ones, in the way the economy is run. The pure doctrine of collective responsibility should surely have required the Chancellor to consult the Cabinet as a whole if he felt he needed backing, but this they did not do' (Wass, 1984, p. 23). In the arithmetic of the Cabinet, the Prime Minister and the departmental minister together are likely to outweigh other combinations.

The bilateral deal between the Prime Minister and the departmental minister is a double-edged tool, however. It can be an arrangement for prime ministerial 'back-seat driving', but it also means that if the minister can get prime ministerial backing – or even non-involvement – he or she can run his or her policy sector in a fairly autonomous fashion. (See Hennessy, 1986, chapter 5.)

(iv) MANIPULATING 'THE LOBBY'

In 1984 controversy over the book by Michael Cockerell, Peter Hennessy and David Walker, *Sources Close to the Prime Minister*, addressed attention to Mrs Thatcher's influence over the press and hence the use of this device to augment her standing in the Cabinet. The main technique for news manipulation is the non-attributable story delivered to the specialist Lobby-status journalists. This is another debate marred by doctoring of the views of the opposition. The real argument is not about press control. It is more subtle – that 'Downing Street guidance' is an important way of defining issues in terms which suit the Prime Minister. Cabinet reports, predictions of future decisions, character assassinations of colleagues, all appear from 'Whitehall' sources. The conclusion of Cockerell and his colleagues (1984, p. 11) was that the current arrangements are the 'culmination of a hundred years of political news management' and that Mrs Thatcher 'has become presidential in her use of American techniques of presentation and news management'.

Though the press might not be controlled, it is certainly influenced by the flow of material which comes from the Prime Minister's press secretary, in recent years Mr Bernard Ingham. For example, at one point when Mrs Thatcher was assuring the House of Commons that Jim Prior had her full confidence, her press officer – Bernard Ingham – was giving a less enthusiastic version. In 1969 in a classic episode, Harold Wilson's press secretary indicated to the Lobby journalists that Jim Callaghan had been reprimanded in Cabinet for a breach of collective responsibility: no such reprimand was heard by ministers attending that meeting. However, by being reported, the non-reprimand had the same effect as an actual dressing down. When the Lords amended the 'Paving Bill' for the abolition of the Metropolitan Authorities in June 1984, the press was quickly running stories of how, in the relevant Cabinet committee (MISC 95), Mrs Thatcher's instinct was against having interim nominated authorities to run the GLC before it disappeared.

Judge (1984, p. 24) notes how pre-Budget leaks in March 1983 revealed Mrs Thatcher's desire to raise tax relief on larger mortgages. This was seen as an attempt to ensure that credit fell to the Prime Minister. Similarly, before the publication of the Franks Report on the Falklands, selective leaks ensured that a pro-governmental interpretation found its way into the press. The image of the reality that is presented from the No. 10 Office is that favoured by the Prime Minister. Rose (in Rose and Suleiman, eds, 1980, p. 20) showed how the press attention to the Prime Minister *vis-à-vis* his or her senior colleagues had soared in recent years. Attlee had only one-third of *The Times* references to his Chancellor/Foreign Secretary/Leader of the House. Churchill and Eden had less than the totals of their colleagues, but from Macmillan to Callaghan the Prime Minister had considerably more attention than the men in these three main offices. Rose also cites Martin Harrison's convincing data in the Nuffield election studies on the increase in mentions of the Prime Minister on election campaign television – and a remarkable lead over the number of mentions of his or her next most cited colleague.

The final two prime ministerial strengths we discuss here – individual ministerial responsibility and collective responsibility – are usually discussed in constitutional terms. Low (1904, p. 136), for example, dramatically discussed individual ministerial responsibility as 'the main shaft and supporting pillar of the political edifice'. They are examined at some length because of some important resignations in recent years, but we discuss both terms in the context of providing particular advantages for the Prime Minister.

(v) INDIVIDUAL MINISTERIAL RESPONSIBILITY (IMR)

Individual ministerial responsibility (IMR) is a topic where the prime ministerial dimension is almost all-important. For example, Mrs Thatcher refused the resignation of John Nott after the Argentinian invasion of the Falklands. Lord Carrington had his offer of resignation turned down over the Crichel Down (agriculture) affair in 1954 and, similarly, his resignation over the Portland (security) affair in 1961. Whether a matter is considered as ministerial responsibility or not very much hinges on whether the Prime Minister wishes to throw a blanket of defence around the minister concerned or not. Pimlott's study of Hugh Dalton, in discussing the resignation of the then Chancellor over the budget leak in 1947, concludes that 'the simplest answer is the best one. The Prime Minister accepted Dalton's resignation because he wanted to be rid of him'. (*The Times*, 9 March 1985). Nicholas Fairbairn's resignation from the (non-Cabinet) post of Solicitor-General for Scotland in 1982 was again a case where the resignation was encouraged, not because of his department's handling of a notorious rape case in Glasgow, but because of Fairbairn's consistent unpopularity with a succession of Chief Whips (Jordan, 1982).

Individual ministerial responsibility was defined by Jennings (1961) as having two elements:

Each Minister is responsible to Parliament for the conduct of his Department. The act of every Civil Servant is by convention regarded as the act of his Minister. A weak version of the principle is sometimes advanced that the Minister's responsibility is satisfied if he answers personally to Parliament and promises remedial action. That is not the classical version, which implies the sanction of loss of office on the Minister. The *Economist* in 1954, proposed, if Ministers fail to take early and effective action to counter potential miscarriages of justice or policy within their departments, they must step down from office.

That strict IMR was given the *coup de grâce* by Professor Finer as long ago as 1956 is one of the few academic certainties. He pointed out (1956, p. 386) how the number of possible cases between 1855 and 1954 were 'a tiny number compared with the known instances of mismanagement and blunderings'. Ministers do *not* as a rule or convention resign – for example, over the man in the Queen's bedroom, or the escape of Gerard Tuite from Brixton prison, or over the Vehicle and General Insurance crash in 1971, or the Sachenhausen concentration camp compensation row in 1968, or the Ferranti excess profits episode of 1964. When the grand constitutional principle of IMR is invoked it is time to look at the expedient short term – for the convenience of the Prime Minister in deflecting general criticism with a scapegoat, or some particular reason why the minister, personally, wished to go.

Ministers do resign, but not under the formula of IMR which suggests that they are taking responsibility for policy or administrative misadventure in their department. Personal misadventures, such as those of Lord Lambton or John Profumo, lack the departmental aspect of IMR. Even the Dalton case, where the error was political, was a personal rather than a departmental error of judgement. Michael Hesletine's resignation in 1986 was over policy and Mrs Thatcher's style of decision-making – not in relation to his 'responsibility'. Resignations such as Sir Ian Gilmour's from Mrs Thatcher's Cabinet had nothing to do with IMR. Indeed, it was a 'resignation' in name only. His letter of resignation made it clear that it was not voluntary and had been 'requested' by the Prime Minister.

The strongest postwar candidate examples of IMR are the resignations of Sir Thomas Dugdale, Minister for Agriculture, over the Crichel Down land affair in 1954, Leon Brittan over Westland in 1986 and the three Foreign Office ministers (Carrington, Atkins and Luce) over the invasion of the Falklands in 1982. The Argentinian and Westland resignations have revitalized discussion of a subject that appeared to be settled.

Although Dugdale's case is almost invariably cited as an example of IMR, it imperfectly fits any reasonably strict definition. The episode concerned the disposal of land originally acquired by the Air Ministry in 1937. Promises to allow various farmers to bid for the tenancy were not honoured by the Ministry of Agriculture after 1949.

A Public Inquiry was held into the affair (published as Cmd 9176), and when it subsequently reported in a critical fashion, Sir Thomas Dugdale took responsibility for the actions of his staff – but as he found no corruption, did not resign. In the report, the individual civil servants were 'named and blamed' – which erodes one of the principles of IMR. Moreover, when Sir Thomas Dugdate eventually resigned on 20 July, he still did not accept that any serious maladministration had taken place. As K. C. Wheare (1975, pp. 268–86) has suggested, the minister was towards the end of his career and seems to have become disillusioned by the criticism. That a minister gets fed up hardly endorses a convention of the constitution.

When Leon Brittan resigned in January 1986, the timing came after 'more than half the 20 speakers' at a 1922 (back-bench) Committee called on him to stand down. *The Times* (24 January 1986) noted negligible support for Mr Brittan in the Parliamentary Party and reported 'anger that Mr Brittan had failed his colleagues by not offering a prompt and protective resignation in spite of Cabinet-level pressure'.

His letter to Mrs Thatcher on 24 January stated: '. . . it has become clear to me that I no longer command the full confidence of my colleagues. In these circumstances my continued membership of your Government would be a source of weakness rather than strength and . . . it is for this reason that I have tendered my resignation.' It was several days later that the concept of resignation for errors by his staff became established. On 27 January Mr Brittan said: 'I made clear to my officials . . . that, subject to the agreement of No. 10, I was giving authority for the disclosure of the Solicitor-General's letter to be made. I therefore accept full responsibility for the fact and form of that disclosure . . . His officials had acted in accordance with his wishes and instructions, at all times and they were not to be blamed . . .'

The Prime Minister did not seem to consider the leaking of a letter from one of her Law Officers to be a very serious matter. Her reluctant acceptance of Leon Brittan's resignation stated: 'I am very sorry . . . I was unable to dissuade you . . . from resigning . . . I hope it will not be long before you return to high office to continue your Ministerial career.'

Finer's key point has to be remembered – that even if occasional examples did fit the IMR definition, they could not be said to represent *a convention*. This resignation seems to fit Finer's predictions remarkably closely – that resignations occur where the minister's act has not so much offended Parliament, but where it has alienated his own party, or a substantial part of it.

The most convincing resignations in terms of IMR are undoubtedly those in 1982 following the Argentinian invasion – but even they fail the test. Lord Carrington's resignation letter said: 'I have been responsible for the conduct of [Foreign Office] . . . policy and I think I should resign.' Several factors undermine the textbook clarity of the cases, however. For one thing, Lord Carrington's letter noted the strong criticism in Parliament and in the press of the government's policy. Left unexplicit was the strong opinion in the Conservative Party 1922 Committee, again confirming Finer's point about alienating the party. The resignations were in the face of lack of support from party colleagues, as much as in pursuit of some constitutional convention. As Richard Luce put it in his letter to the PM, his resignation was to 'help you [by having] . . . a new minister'. This was political assistance, not constitutional necessity. Moreover, all three ministers defended past Foreign Office policy – unlike the usual concept of accepting blame.

Individual ministerial responsibility in the textbook fashion was a rigorous matter. Low (1914, p. 146) made it clear that the minister did not have to be directly involved to be 'responsible'. He said: 'If a butler, after being told that he is responsible for the plate chest, carelessly allows the spoons to be stolen, he may be discharged without a character and may never again get a good place . . . Disgrace, poverty, even starvation, are the sanctions by which the sacredness of responsibility is everywhere enforced.'

This sort of resignation in accepting responsibility for others is what Finer terms 'vicarious' punishment. This argument was developed as a means of ensuring parliamentary control of the anonymous civil servant, but it is no longer seriously advocated.

After the Crichel Down affair, there was a major redefinition of IMR. The Home Secretary, Sir Maxwell Fyfe, set out four categories of cases – only the first two of which foresaw ministerial resignation:

(1) Where a civil servant carries out an explicit order by a Minister, the Minister must protect the civil servant concerned.

(2) Where a civil servant acts properly in accordance with the policy laid down by the Minister, his Minister must equally protect and defend him.

(3) Where 'civil servant', makes a mistake or causes some delay, but not on an important issue of policy or where a claim to individual rights is seriously involved, the Minister acknowledges the mistake and he accepts the responsibility, although he is not personally involved. He states that he will take corrective action in the Department.

(4) Finally where a civil servant acts in a manner in which the Minister disapproves and of which the Minister had no prior knowledge, the Minister is answerable to Parliament but is not expected to endorse, or suffer loss of Office for the errors of his civil servants. (*Hansard*, vol. 530, 20 July 1954, col. 1286)

Effectively, these rules pension-off the concept of vicarious error. Ministers do not resign for the mistakes of their staff – unless they themselves have been party to the error. After Lord Carrington offered his resignation following the Romer Committee's criticism of security at the Portland Underwater Detection Establishment, Opposition minister, George Brown, pressed that, 'In the light . . . of flat and frank criticism, does it not make nonsense of Ministerial Responsibility if no Ministers accept the corollary of that and resigns?' (*Hansard*, vol. 642, 22 June 1961, col. 1685). The Prime Minister, Harold Macmillan, repeated the Maxwell Fyfe realistic (that is, castrated) doctrine: 'The doctrine of Ministerial Responsibility is well known – it is the ultimate responsibility. But in modern conditions it must be recognised that the Minister's duty is to carry out his task as efficiently as it is possible' (*Hansard*, vol. 642, 22 June 1961, col. 1685). Macmillan thus defended Carrington because he was not directly involved in the circumstances. Such a defence has been used in numerous other cases, such as the 1964 Ferranti affair over excess profits. By the 1960s it was widely accepted that ministers could not be held punishable for the full scale of departmental business – particularly when (as in the Portland, Ferranti and other cases, such as the Vehicle and General Insurance collapse of 1971, the Sachenhausen concentration camp compensation case of 1968) a succession of ministers were responsible over a number of years. As George Brown put it over the Foreign Office's inadequate and poor treatment of the Sachenhausen claimants: 'It happens that I am the last of a series of Ministers who have looked at this matter and I am the one who got caught with the ball when the lights went up' (*Hansard*, vol. 758, 5 February 1968, col. 112).

When Mr Whitelaw, as Home Secretary, announced the inquiry into the escape of Tuite from Brixton Prison he said, 'In the circumstances, the governor, Mr Selby, must himself accept, and very properly does accept, the primary responsibility' (*Hansard*, vol. 998, 2 February 1981, col. 21). After the mass breakout from the Maze in 1983, the Hennessy Report (House of Commons 203, 1983–4) found matters 'for which the Governor must be held accountable' and that a civil servant in the Prison Department 'must be held responsible for the short comings'. The governor resigned, but no minister did so.

A further retreat from the Victorian principles has been appearing with some regularity. When things have gone wrong in departments, and where *ministers themselves have been fully aware of the circumstances*, resignation has not followed, but ministers have suggested, 'I acted on the best advice available'. When the Court of Appeal decided that the Home Office had acted improperly in preventing early purchases of TV licences to avoid a price increase, the Home Secretary, Roy Jenkins, argued, 'what is done in my department is my responsibility', but also claimed, 'it would have been better to take the advice of someone who would have given the right advice' (*Hansard*, vol. 902, col. 237–8.) This new defence means that ministers shield themselves by using their civil servants, whereas the tradition was that civil servants were shielded by ministers.

The discussion might confirm that there is no convention that links loss of office to departmental error. Also implicit, however, is an argument that IMR is a convenience for a Prime Minister. In circumstances such as the Westland leaking or the Falklands' invasion, Mrs Thatcher or her staff were – to some uncertain degree – involved. It is useful for a Prime Minister that blame can be attached to particular departments – a scapegoat principle. For example, over the Falklands, it is certainly not the case that the Foreign Office was pursuing a policy on its own. It appears that the withdrawal of the *Endurance* – which was interpreted by Argentina as lack of commitment – from the South Atlantic was a cost-cutting exercise by the Ministry of Defence which was opposed by the Foreign Office. It appears that the intelligence reports were ultimately assessed by the Joint Intelligence Committee chaired by the Prime Minister. It appears that a Foreign Office proposal to send hunter-killer submarines to the area as a preventative measure was turned down by a committee including Mrs Thatcher.

In the multitude of cases when things go wrong in departments there is no convention of resignation. Whether a resignation is accepted is a decision for the Prime Minister. And even when a resignation is pressed against the advice of the Prime Minister there can – as in the Westland and Falklands cases – be clear political advantages for him or her. Not so much a convention, as a prime ministerial convenience.

(vi) COLLECTIVE RESPONSIBILITY

Although Michael Heseltine resigned from Mrs Thatcher's Cabinet on the grounds of a breach of collective responsibility by the Prime Minister, we would argue that collective responsibility is another convention which is of more use to the Prime Minister than to his or her colleagues. Mr Heseltine's resignation statement argued that Mrs Thatcher had cancelled a pre-arranged meeting because, 'Having lost three times [at earlier meetings] there was to be no question of risking a fourth discussion'. However, the collective responsibility argument was used by the Prime Minister on 15 January 1986 in her counter-attack. She developed the claim – first made on 10 January – that Mr Heseltine was 'in a minority of one'. Every other person in the Cabinet agreed to her requirement for all governmental statements on the Westland affair to be cleared by the Cabinet Office, save Mr Heseltine who found himself unable to accept that procedure. (It is, of course, worth noting that the rule only really affected one minister – Heseltine.) Mrs Thatcher defined collective responsibility as follows: 'Decisions reached by the Cabinet or Cabinet committee are binding on all members of the Government.' Mr Heseltine claimed that there was no decision for him to breach, but prime ministerial power is such that Mrs Thatcher could effectively decide what was the relevant 'collective' line. Clearly, under certain circumstances, the faithful maintenance of collective responsibility which holds the government collectively responsible to Parliament, will frustrate the execution of individual responsibility. For example, replying to an Opposition attack, Mr Callaghan, reminded the House: 'The task of the Chancellor of the Exchequer is central to that of the whole Government's economic and financial policy ... therefore ... the House should make up its mind on the whole record of the Government and that, if the House cannot support us this evening, I would ask for a dissolution of Parliament and go to the country' (*Hansard*, vol. 951, 14 June 1978, col. 1129). In such cases, the collective Cabinet supports and defends the single minister, but, more usually, the convention is turned on the minister – he or she must support the decisions of Cabinet in public, or resign.

One of the main rationales for the existence of collective responsibility is that if it did not exist ministers would break ranks on unpopular (but perhaps necessary) measures. Gilmour (1969, p. 214) wrote that, 'The spectacle of ministers currying favour in their own party by dissenting from unpopular decisions would be more than their colleagues could bear'. However, as a 'wet' minister in Mrs Thatcher's government, Gilmour managed to distance himself from the Prime Minister's ideological imprint on the Cabinet.

For example, he said: 'The interventionist state and the welfare state are not going to go away . . . Those who believe otherwise have, in my view, fallen into the trap of ideology and dogma – which is, or should be, to Conservatives the unpardonable sin' (*The Times*, 12 February 1981).

Collective responsibility is, however, above all a convenience for the Prime Minister, as it reinforces dominant opinion, usually defined by the PM, in the Cabinet. Harold Wilson, for example, used the collective responsibility argument to Tony Benn, Judith Hart and Joan Lestor to ensure that the government representatives on the Labour Party's NEC did not cause him any political embarrassment by breaking ranks: 'I must ask you to send to me in reply to this minute an unqualified assurance that you accept the principle of collective responsibility and that you will from now on comply with its requirements and the rules which follow from it in the National Executive Committee and in all circumstances' (Sedgemore, 1980, p. 75). Judge's (1984, p. 21) proposition that a convention of collective responsibility serves to constrain precipitate action by the Prime Minister is not sustained by many examples. We would argue to the contrary that the doctrine allows the Prime Minister to stifle dissent. This requirement of silence extends to decisions made in Cabinet committee, where any minister tempted to dissent has no opportunity to voice his or her opinion – and even to junior ministers and parliamentary private secretaries who have no part in the decision process which collectively binds them. Of course, the 'leak' is the response to this, and so well developed is this defence mechanism, it is difficult to see that the convention still pertains. Patrick Gordon Walker (1972, p. 32) realistically noted that the leak is the mechanism by which the doctrine of collective responsibility is reconciled with political reality. Therefore the doctrine of collective responsibility is that ministers must not *openly* disagree.

Judge (1984) has attempted to rescue the 'responsibility' conventions from the academic dustbin. However, he does not, in fact, seriously propose that individual or collective responsibility operates in legal textbook fashion, but that the conventions have changed in the 'flexible, malleable core of the constitution'. What is difficult to square with this argument is that our interviews with Members of Parliament do not produce an articulation of a contemporary interpretation of the conventions, but garbled versions of the constitutional lawyer versions which Judge seeks to dismiss. And is there not something peculiar about a convention that is so flexible that it can totally change in character and remain the same convention?

Our general position on this undoubted phenomenon of prime ministerial dominance can be indicated by quoting one of Crossman's many valuable (if contradictory) points. In *Inside View* (1972, p. 76) he remarks that it is the job of the Prime Minister to stop the Cabinet fragmenting into a collection of departmental heads. In other words, the position is not one of a united Cabinet continually being outflanked by a cunning Prime Minister, but a Prime Minister attempting to stimulate non-departmental views.

The list of prime ministerial strengths above is intended to make the point that the Prime Minister is well placed to advance options which he or she likes and to quash those which he or she does not like. Tony Benn has claimed: 'The Prime Minister is thus able to use the Government to bring forward the policies which he favours and to stop those to which he is opposed, including policies deriving from Labour policy or the Manifesto'. (1980, p. 13). In *Inside View* Crossman (1972, p. 48) observed that 'sometimes as a member of Cabinet you didn't realise you lost the battle; it was not your impression of what happened. But once it is there, written in the minutes (technically termed – conclusions) it *has* been decided against you.' This does *not* mean – as Harold Wilson claimed – that prime ministerial government means 'whatever the Cabinet argued or decided, the Prime Minister could reverse the entire discussion, and impose his idiosyncratic doctrine, by sitting down the following day with the secretary of the Cabinet to cook the Minutes' (*Listener*, 5 January 1978).

Roy Jenkins recollected that, while pushing through public expenditure reductions in 1968, he as Chancellor and Wilson as Prime Minister carried through the cuts in seven Cabinets, lasting three to four hours, in eleven days (with preparatory meetings). He confirms that Wilson 'counted noses', and recorded that on the various controversial elements, 'on none of the issues did we have more than a narrow majority and that majority was each time made up of different people. So it was a close run thing' (*Observer*, 4 November 1984). As with much of the evidence, this both proves that prime ministers get their way – and that some political skill is needed to ensure this. Prime ministers do lose out – most notably when Harold Wilson failed to push through the *In Place of Strife* union reform proposal in the face of Cabinet (and parliamentary party) opposition. But – though it is perhaps trite to say it – there is no great record of prime ministers intriguing to become Chancellor or Foreign Secretary, and plenty of evidence of the reverse.

At the same time, there is scope for departmental power as the Prime Minister literally cannot become involved in everything. And the amount of freedom for the Minister depends on each individual Prime Minister – their temperaments vary. Thus Boyd-Carpenter (1980, p. 152) records that Macmillan's attitude to his ministers was ideal: 'He did not fuss at them; he expected them to bring him in when they thought it was necessary, and otherwise to get on with their jobs.' This compares with his recollection (p. 124) of Eden who, as Prime Minister, 'nagged at his Ministers, ringing them up with enquiries about matters which either were not ready for submission to him or indeed were not of sufficient importance to bother a Prime Minister'.

Even Sir Douglas Wass, who clearly would have preferred a system of Cabinet government, recognized that, 'I believe the power and authority of the Prime Minister has grown at the expense of other Cabinet colleagues', and 'the Prime Minister has at his call the Cabinet office and the Treasury in effect, and that gives the Prime Minister an immensely strong position, whether he exercises that power is a matter of choice' (*Listener*, February 1984).

The growth of central intervention has certainly not diminished under Mrs Thatcher, and her Secretary of State Francis Pym (1984, p. 17) claims that 'the style of [governmental] operation has steadily become less flexible and more centralised. This process stems from the Prime Minister's tendency to think she is always right . . . within the Government the Prime Minister exercises direct control over more and more Departments . . . She would like to run the major Departments herself and tries her best to do so . . . she cannot know enough to dictate the policy of each Department . . . Her response has been to expand the Downing Street staff to include experts in every major area, thus establishing a government within a government.'

Co-ordination takes place in different ways, and the argument so far is that much of the force of the prime ministerial tendencies stems from the need for co-ordination rather than prime ministerial hyper-activity. But, as Jones argues, there is necessarily a limit on the activity of the Prime Minister as an individual, and high-level co-ordination comes from the other central institutions. However, the bulk of co-ordination probably comes from the recognized interdepartmental practices – the Prime Minister's time is too limited to be the sole source of co-ordination. There is, for example, the private secretary network. Each minister's Private Office is directly linked to the switchboard of the Prime Minister's private secretaries. (In 1985 Mrs Thatcher had seven – a principal private secretary, four with subject specialisms, and two assistant secretaries.) Despite the present Conservative government's hi-tech exhortations, British government is perhaps principally co-ordinated by the rather old-fashioned xerox machine. Pliatzky (1984, p. 33) has described how it is, in fact, unusual for one individual minister to write to another and, almost always, his letter is copied to, say, half-a-dozen ministers who make up a Cabinet committee, or to all the members of the Cabinet –

'the photocopier is nowadays both literally and figuratively an essential element in the machinery of government'.

Two observers of the Wilson Cabinets, Joel Barnett and Joe Haines, have underlined the importance of another co-ordinating mechanism – the 'Cabinet of Permanent Secretaries'. Haines (1977, p. 161) says: 'This committee of [civil servant] heads of departments ... meets each week to discuss the business which will come before Cabinet and whether – and if so, how – Ministers will be advised on that business. If the Whitehall machine has a collective "line" on policy, and it often does, it is at these meetings that it will emerge.' Barnett (1982, p. 188) claimed: 'Plotting is too strong a word but there is no doubt that officials at these meetings plan how to "steer" Cabinet and Cabinet Committees.'

Cabinet Committees

Pliatzky (1984, p. 32) notes that the multiplicity of policy decisions which require inter-Departmental clearance is vastly greater than could be handled in actual Cabinet – or even in 'the endless series of meetings of Ministerial Cabinet committees.' He says the system also needs a 'technocratic backup' of committees of officials or the informal contacts between officials. He says (1984, p. 33), 'If Heclo and Wildavsky were to take a look at the way Whitehall handles almost any major subject ... they would find a "village community" similar to that on the public expenditure front ...'

The circulation of documents to interested departments is supplemented – as Pliatzky hints – by meetings of Cabinet committees. These are the most *systematic* arrangements for co-ordination. These meetings are of five different types:

(1) Standing committees of ministers.

(2) Standing committees of civil servants.

(3) *Ad hoc* committees of ministers.

(4) *Ad hoc* committees of civil servants.

(5) Mixed committees of ministers and civil servants.

Although all this Cabinet committee machinery is officially secret, this was breached in the Falklands War when the composition of the inner Cabinet OD (SA), was revealed, and in 1979 the Prime Minister had announced to Parliament, the title and chairman of four of the main standing committees:

Defence and Overseas Policy	Prime Minister
Economic Strategy	Prime Minister

| Home and Social Affairs | Home Secretary |
| Legislation | Lord Chancellor |

The announcement of the creation of these committees was not a matter of revelation, but of confirmation. Evidently, since their existence was so well known, it was thought that there was no harm in giving the appearance of openness. As usual, the major contributions to public knowledge came not from Parliament, but the press – in articles in *New Society* in 1978, *The Economist* in 1982, and in other work mainly by journalists. The tendency for the government to leak the existence of Cabinet committees – such as that on football hooliganism in March 1985 (Mrs Thatcher, the Home Secretary, the Secretary of State for the Environment, and the Sports Minister) – is again less a contribution to open government, than an opportunistic attempt to link the government with public condemnation of hooliganism and to display symbolic action.

Our main point about the Cabinet committee system is that it is an extra prime ministerial power – perhaps *the* prime ministerial power. The drift of decision-making from Cabinet to Cabinet committee is to relocate decision-making on to ground even more favourable to the Prime Minister. This line was recently endorsed by Sir Frank Cooper in his Suntory–Toyota lecture at the London School of Economics in March 1986. He argued that secrecy over the existence and membership of Cabinet committees, 'which often decide on vital issues that never come before the full Cabinet, was – to conceal the full power of the Prime Minister' (*The Times*, 13 March 1986).

STANDING COMMITTEES (OF THE CABINET)

At the core of the Cabinet committee system are the standing ministerial committees, of which there are probably about twenty-five. The main committee is called 'Economic Strategy' – or some variant of that title. The main economic committee has a series of sub-committees on the economy which cover more specific topics.

Cockerell, Hennessy and Walker list the main economic affairs (political) committees in spring 1984 as shown in Table 6.1

Their list can be contrasted with one in *The Economist* in 1982 to show that the broad pattern is stable, but has minor alterations of interest. By autumn 1985, for example, a committee on 'the rates' issue was part of the economic committee system.

There is also a system of related committees on foreign affairs. The parent committee, as it were, is OD (Overseas and Defence) under the Prime Minister, but there is also OD(E) on Europe (chaired by the Foreign Secretary), OD(FOF) on the future of the Falklands

Table 6.1   *Cabinet Committees on Economic Affairs*

Committee Initials	Chairman	Function
EA	Prime Minister	Economic Strategy
E (NI)	Prime Minister	Public sector
E (NF)	Chancellor (Lawson)	Nationalised industry finance
E (PSP)	Chancellor (Lawson)	Public sector pay
E (DL)	Chancellor (Lawson)	Privatisation (i.e. disposal)
E (CS)	Chief Secretary (Rees)	Civil service pay

Source: Cockerell, Hennessy and Walker, 1984, p. 84.

under the Prime Minister, the Northern Ireland group under Lord Whitelaw, and so on. The well-recorded Falklands 'War Cabinet' was technically a sub-committee within this system – OD(SA).

In the area of home affairs and legislation, there are permanent committees on Future Legislation under the Leader of the House; Home Affairs, currently under Lord Whitelaw; the Civil Contingencies Unit, again chaired by Lord Whitelaw; and Home (Civil) Defence under the Home Secretary. There are also specific sub-committees, such as H(HC) on reform of the House of Lords.

These committes of politicians are shadowed by committees of civil servants. These 'official' committees will broadly represent the same departments as the ministers on the 'political committees'. As Crossman puts it (1972, p. 73): 'Whitehall likes to reach compromise at an official level first so that Ministers are all briefed the same way.' In his *Diaries* (1975, Vol. 1, p. 198) he noted that the importance of the network of official committees was the 'really big thing' that he had failed to recognize in his academic work before taking office. He continued, 'there is a full network of official committees; and the work of the Ministers is therefore strictly and completely paralleled at the official level. This means that very often the whole job is pre-cooked in the official committee to a point from which it is extremely difficult to reach any other conclusion than that already determined by the officials in advance ...' Barbara Castle (1973) made the same point:

> The official net is terrific, the political net is non-existent ... I suddenly discovered that I was never allowed to take anything to cabinet unless it had been processed by the official committee. In the official committee the departments had all their inter-departmental battles, and probably made their concessions to each other. The departments did the horse-trading and having struck their

bargains they then briefed their Ministers on it, and so at cabinet meetings I suddenly found I wasn't in a political caucus at all. I was faced by departmental enemies.

Brian Sedgemore (1980, p. 27) cites his own experience as a civil servant and junior minister to claim that by the 1970s, 'The effectiveness of inter-departmental committees had grown enormously. In particular, the inter-departmental civil service committees which now parallel each cabinet sub-committee were exercising great power. Often these official committees were being used to foreclose options for ministers rather than open them up.'

The bulk of work on an issue is done by the civil service – perhaps six interdepartmental meetings to prepare the ground for a single political 'decision'. Seidman (1976, p. 197) writing on co-ordination problems in the USA, observes: 'Intra-agency committees are the crab grass in the garden of Government institutions. Nobody wants them, but everybody has them.' In Britain, too, interdepartmental committees proliferate, with departments with very marginal interests being obliged to attend – just in case the marginal becomes important. The basic purpose is to *avoid* conflict at ministerial level: to remove unnecessary dispute from the overloaded political tier. Naturally, in such cases, the minister's role is often legitimation rather than decision, but it is not just overload that stops the ministers from taking a more active role in shaping choices.

Ministers are so accustomed to their role as advocate for the department that the committees are poor arenas for compromise. Barnett claims that on complex issues Cabinet committees are just about the worst possible way of arriving at sensible decisions. Ministers come briefed by officials who were members of the official committee which shadowed the ministerial one. He says that shadowed is an inappropriate term for the Official Committee. After carrying out the detailed analytical work intended only to set out the options for Ministers, the Official Committee usually left their Ministers in no doubt whatsoever as to which was the best option – the one it recommended. Another example he gives of the attempted pre-orchestration of the Cabinet was when he had been told that a senior colleague had been briefed to support him (as Chief Secretary to the Treasury) at a Cabinet committee. At the last moment, Barnett spoke for the opposite side: this did not stop his fellow minister from reading his brief out – 'I agree with the Chief Secretary' (1982, p. 17). Crossman (1977, Vol. 3, p. 737) also claims: 'the Committee [on local government reform] has clearly been briefed by the civil servants to deal with departmental interests ... Even I am only concerned to get a structure which helps the Health Service reorganization. It's staggering how little serious discussion there has been of the basic principles.'

Another Crossman (1975, Vol. 1, p. 59) illustration was from one of the first meetings of the Legislation Committee that he attended: 'The meeting was a bit ludicrous: we were supposed to consider priorities, but couldn't, since it was obvious that everyone there was deeply committed to his own particular measure whether it was a minor piece of legal reform ... or a really major piece of our programme.'

Gerald Kaufman (1980, p. 71) in his chapter, 'How to get on in Cabinet committee', describes the departmental briefing for such committees as works of art:

> They will analyse the issue in question ... not from the standpoint of the Government as a whole but purely from the Departmental point of view. They will advise you on the 'Line to Take' ... the sentences beginning with masterly injunctions such as, 'The Minister will wish to say ...' ... They will even include speaking notes, which the Minister can read out without having taken the trouble to study the actual Cabinet papers at all ... At one meeting, dealing with an exceptionally complicated subject, all those gathered together simply read out their briefs to each other; it seemed the most sensible thing to do.

Later, Kaufman (p. 72) records how the Cabinet Office provides the chairman of the committee with a steering brief and, 'if he strays too much from it, the member of the Cabinet staff who is sitting beside him ... will murmur in his ear.'

The official committees accordingly exist to attempt to reconcile conflicting departmental objectives – and to brief ministers to avoid conflict. Crossman reveals an example of the relationship of the official 'ground-clearing' when he sought to introduce local government reform. His Permanent Secretary at Housing and Local Government, Dame Evelyn Sharp, circulated a paper to the other interested departments – Home Office, Education, Health, Transport, Scotland and Wales. He says, 'So the officials got together and began to work towards an agreed official policy'. However, when Crossman discussed what was agreed, he wanted a mass of changes. He imposed changes, but he had later to agree that his Permanent Secretary had been tactically correct in wanting to stick to the carefully formulated official package. This package allowed all the departments to brief their ministers in favour – 'As a result of her work on the official committee, unanimity was achieved ... each of the Ministers concerned received a brief telling him or her to accept my proposals without suggesting any amendment' (Crossman, 1975, Vol. 1, p. 441).

Table 6.2   *Official Committees*

Chairman	Ministerial Committees Title	Topic	Equivalent Official Committee
Prime Minister	E(NI)	Public sector/Nationalized industries	NIP
Chief Secretary, Treasury	E(CS)	Civil service pay/strikes	E(OCS)
Prime Minister	OD	Overseas and Defence	OD(O)
Foreign Secretary	OD(E)	EEC	EQ(S) steering EQ(O) routine
Home Secretary	HD	Home (Civil) Defence	HD(O) HD(P) (plans)
Prime Minister	MIS	Intelligence	PSIS

Official committees thus shadow or steer almost all permanent political committees. Some of the most important examples of the parallel committees are set out in Table 6.2.

AD HOC AND MIXED COMMITTEES

The above examples are standing committees. On the one hand, politicians and, on the other, officials. In the Whitehall classification they differ from *ad hoc* committees – which again come in political and official flavours. In practice, the line between, say, a sub-committee of E Committee set up for one particular crisis, and an *ad hoc* committee on something, such as that on football hooliganism in March 1985, is blurred, but in terms of the referencing system the initials of the supposedly permanent committees distinguish them from the serial numbering of the *ad hoc* committees. Similarly, some *ad hoc* committees deal with pretty perennial topics. Another area of blurring is between the *ad hoc* meetings within the officially recognized Cabinet Office 'net', and other meetings which might, nevertheless, be involved in co-ordination. The line between Cabinet Office committees and other committees might be clear in terms of official status – but unclear in functional terms. Thus, a minute from a William Armstrong (who much later became Cabinet Secretary) in 1946 noted that among the seventy-odd committees which were then labelled 'Cabinet committees' some had less right to the title than some of the 700 other interdepartmental committees (cited in Hennessy, 1985, p. 20). In the *ad hoc* system, the committees are numbered from 1 upwards for each government. The numbers have the prefixes GEN (general) or MISC (miscellaneous). Those prefixes alternate with each change of government. Thus Harold Wilson in 1974–6 created 118 MISCs. James Callaghan reached at least GEN 158 in his three years and, by the time of discussions about the abolition of the GLC, Mrs Thatcher had reached MISC 95 (*The Economist*, 6 February 1982). Obviously, not all these MISCs are operational at one time.

The numbering system includes official and political committees. Thus Mrs Thatcher's MISC 14, chaired by the Chancellor (on innovations in policy), was shadowed by a civil service briefing group – MISC 15. Some committees appear in the MISC series, although their work-load is annual – for example, each year there is likely to be a committee on the rate support grant (MISC 21 in 1981) and the 'Star Chamber' committee to decide on public expenditure bids from the departments (MISC 62 in 1981). There is, finally, a fifth category of committee – mixed ministers and officials: the Civil Contingencies Unit (CCU) of the Cabinet Office is one of these.

If Cabinet committees are *where* the bulk of decisions get taken, the capacity of the Prime Minister to determine *who* participates is crucial. Patronage and appointment considerations are as important in the subterranean world of Whitehall committees as in full Cabinet. Patrick Gordon Walker (1972, p. 87) attempts to salvage Cabinet government from the proposition that most business is done in committee, by portraying the committees as 'partial Cabinets' – the 'relevant Minister's meeting'. Gordon Walker says: 'A partial Cabinet is the very opposite of Prime Ministerial government: it presupposes that the Prime Minister carries influential colleagues with him'. To our mind, this is unhelpful to the debate in suggesting that prime ministers have any option but to carry influential colleagues with them. This is not at issue, but what is worth discussing is the regularity with which this happens, and the balance of political resources between the Prime Minister and his or her colleagues.

While the Cabinet committee system can be used to broaden the range of participants in a decision and to co-ordinate the parts of Whitehall, it can also be used to *narrow* participation. One account of Britain's decision to buy the Trident missile system asks, 'how could a Labour [Callaghan] cabinet justify even exploring a policy so contrary to its party manifesto?' Callaghan resolved this by confining discussions to an inner quartet of ministers, code-named 'Misc.' Its members, in addition to Callaghan, were Denis Healey, the Chancellor; David Owen, the Foreign Secretary; and Fred Mulley, the Defence Secretary. Callaghan also *personally* gave the Ministry of Defence clearance to work on the project, so that Mulley could say truthfully that he had authorized no such thing (*Sunday Times*, 7 April 1985). Cockerell, Hennessy and Walker (1984, p. 86) suggest that this 'committee of four' was outside the official Cabinet committee system.

It is also worth noting that the work-load in the committee system is so high that often a high percentage of ministers on the committees are actually 'second-eleven' junior ministers, attending as substitutes. Given the importance of pre-meeting briefing and interdepartmental briefing, this does not seem a major issue.

The composition of Cabinet committees appears to be rarely challenged – and, in this way, the Prime Minister can build-in a majority to reflect his or her preference (assuming, of course, that he or she has a preference – which is far from always being the case). Bruce Page's article in the *New Statesman* in 1979 (21 July) describes how Jim Callaghan, as Prime Minister, did not like the Home Office's proposal on the fourth TV channel. He, accordingly, did not follow the Home Office's own draft list for a suitable committee to discuss the matter, but brought in Messrs Hattersley, Rodgers and Benn and put himself in the chair to push through his own inclination. The Castle *Diaries* (1980, p. 53) record Michael Foot's view that Harold Wilson had 'packed the Europe Committee . . . with pro-marketeers'. Brian Sedgemore (1980, p. 76) claimed that Harold Wilson and James Callaghan chaired the Energy Committee specifically to exclude Tony Benn from the post.

Hennessy and Arends (1983, p. 21) have convincingly developed the running battle in the footnotes about whether the decision for Britain to develop an atomic bomb was prime ministerial or Cabinet? They show that, while the matter went to GEN 163 (Atomic Energy) under Attlee in January 1947, the decision was shaped by earlier decisions in GEN 75. The composition of GEN 163 also made it unlikely that the atomic option would be rejected. The minutes make it clear that the main ministers included Ernest Bevin (as Foreign Secretary) and Alexander (as Minister of Defence) who were in favour. Likely opponents, such as Dalton (Chancellor) and Cripps (President of the Board of Trade), were not invited to attend. At GEN 75 Dalton and Cripps had objected to the atomic bomb project – and hence GEN 163 was GEN 75, minus Dalton and Cripps. As Hennessy and Arends observe (p. 21), 'Attlee, clearly, was determined that the decision should go through on the nod'. Discussing this same case, Crossman (1963, p. 55) says that the decision:

> was settled in the Defence Sub Committee without any prior discussion in the full Cabinet.

Nor was there any Cabinet discussion *after* the decision. When the minutes of the particular meeting of the Defence Committee came before full Cabinet, the Prime Minister did not feel it necessary to call attention to this item . . . it became Cabinet policy without a word being said . . . So completely had the reality of collective Cabinet responsibility been transformed by this date into a myth, that no member of Mr Attlee's Government either noticed anything unusual about this procedure or felt aggrieved that he had not been consulted.

In the light of these examples of prime ministers 'weighting' committees, arguably Cecil Parkinson's position in the Falklands War Cabinet was to ensure an extra voice for Mrs Thatcher – who perhaps suspected that neither Mr Pym at the Foreign Office nor Mr Whitelaw was as robust on the issue as herself and John Nott at the Ministry of Defence. Similarly, while John Biffen (as a non-spending minister and with useful Treasury experience) had regularly participated in the Public Expenditure Star Chamber exercise, by June 1985 it was rumoured that, as he had become something of a 'consolidator' (the new jargon for dissent), he was to be dropped in the 1985/6 cycle. This kind of prime ministerial scope for change allows the Prime Minister to keep broad control over the balance of the committees.

If Mrs Thatcher has changed the pattern of activity at the centre, it is to de-formalize the Cabinet committee system where Cabinet decisions are pre-formed. Thus it was claimed in 1985 – when the top civil servants, armed forces chiefs and judges were given salary increases of up to 46 per cent – that opposition within the Cabinet did not emerge because of the feeling that the Prime Minister had already 'cleared' the policy with a small hand-picked group. The *Sunday Times* (28 July 1985) suggested:

> There were some around the table who knew the whole thing would end in tears. But they excused themselves from the perils of confronting the prime minister on the basis that the fight had been lost when Plowden had been let loose on the Whitehall pay structure in the first place. That, plus her stitching-up operation with Armstrong and a few cronies before the cabinet met, was more than enough for them.

One point that perhaps detracts from Michael Heseltine's claim that he left the Thatcher Cabinet because of a concern at the method of decision-making, is that two of the famous ministerial meetings on the Westland issue (that is, 4 and 5 December) were *ad hoc* groups. Only on 9 December did the matter go to the Economic Strategy Sub-Committee. Such *ad hoc* meetings may be mutually convenient when Mrs Thatcher and her invited ministers agree, but they are difficult to reconcile – when happening systematically – with collective Cabinet government.

Peter Hennessy (1985, p. 39) has convincingly argued that this use of *ad hoc*, informal committees is *the* Thatcher style:

> Mrs Thatcher will ask a particular Cabinet colleague to prepare a paper on a particular issue just for her, not for the Cabinet or a Cabinet committee ... The Minister is summoned to Number Ten with his back up team. He sits across the table from Mrs. Thatcher and her team which can be a blend of people from the Downing Street Private Office, the Policy Unit, the Cabinet Office and one or two personal advisers.

Hennessy then quotes inside observers who claim that in such sessions Mrs Thatcher proceeds to act as 'judge and jury in her own cause' and that such practices lead to 'a devaluation' of Cabinet government and a 'presidential style'.

Hennessy supports these impressions with data which show that both full Cabinet meetings *and* Cabinet committees are fewer in number than under previous prime ministers. Only about 60–70 papers each year are now submitted to the Cabinet for discussion. This compares with over 300 per year in the early 1950s.

Cockerell, Hennessy and Walker (1984, p. 86) claim that Callaghan, too, would avoid the official committee system:

> ... in the last two years of Mr. Callaghan's premiership all important decisions on monetary policy and international economic affairs were taken by a cabal, a small group in which ministers were out numbered by permanent civil servants (i.e. the 'Economic Seminar'). To keep the group's existence secret from the members of the Cabinet, it was not given the status of a Cabinet committee ... The existence of this group made nonsense of 'collective Cabinet responsibility' ... It represented the government of Britain not by a Labour Cabinet but by the likes of ... Lord Richardson, governor of the Bank of England, Sir Douglas Wass, permanent secretary to the Treasury, and a clique of Labour Ministers.

Even the secret Cabinet committee system is in danger of becoming a 'dignified' rather than an 'efficient' part of the constitution.

There is no such thing as a debate on prime ministerial government – in the sense that both sides are remarkably close in their positions – once they have qualified, reserved and glossed their starting-points. Crossman (1972, p. 7) admitted that 'No sane man would pretend that a British Prime Minister *cannot* by mismanagement or continuous lack of success undermine his position'. There is no Yes/No answer. The debate on the Labour government's negotiations with the International Monetary Fund in 1976 ran through twenty-six full Cabinet meetings. Peter Hennessy has called this the 'highwater mark of Cabinet government'. Yet he continues, 'once the loan was secured strategic policy making was removed to a tiny gathering of ministers and officials' (*The Times*, 16 May 1983).

At the same time, former junior minister, Brian Sedgemore (1980), can record a meeting in 1977 between the Prime Minister (James Callaghan), the Chancellor (Denis Healey), the Chancellor of the Duchy of Lancaster (Harold Lever), the Head of the Treasury (Sir Douglas Wass) and the Governor of the Bank of England (Gordon Richardson) which decided to have a policy of letting the pound appreciate. This big meeting and decision were apparently not reported to the full Cabinet.

Inevitably, the empirical pattern is going to be patchy. One newspaper article (*Observer*, 9 June 1985) presented a 'victory' for 'Mrs Thatcher and her allies' (the hawks) over the Cabinet 'consolidators' over the abolition of wage councils (which regulate minimum wages in certain trades). The same article recorded a defeat for the same coalition at Cabinet in the matter of abolishing rent control for private house lets. Hennessy, who makes a convincing case on the 'presidential' character of Mrs Thatcher, also quoted material to the contrary. One Cabinet minister – not a member of the Falklands War Cabinet – claimed: 'She had to carry us on every major decision. That Task Force would never have sailed without Cabinet approval.' And certainly – post-Westland – the decision to call off the talks with Ford about the sale of Austin Rover which excited public criticism was interpreted as a restoration of a collective centre. Mrs Thatcher's 'tough it out' instincts were apparently defeated by ministers such as Norman Fowler (with a constituency interest) and others.

But beneath the ebb and flow of the battle between those with radical political temperaments and those who would proceed more cautiously, is the different contest between the political centre and the departments straining for autonomy. The outcome of these battles is recorded at Cabinet rather than resolved by Cabinet. It is this need for co-ordination that required prime ministerial control. An analytical weakness in Crossman's invaluable descriptive contribution is perhaps the failure to recognize that the *lack* of co-ordination developed from its own logic of specialization and sectorization. Co-ordination problems are not the failure of one individual or the lack of one particular organizational device, like an inner Cabinet, but follow from the success of sub-governments in meeting their own objectives and pursuing their own departmental rationality.

The emphasis in this chapter is, therefore, not whether Crossman is half-right in seeing prime ministerial government or Gordon Walker half-wrong in seeing Cabinet government, but that within the system there is a need for central co-ordination. The co-ordination that is available via the Prime Minister, the Cabinet Office and the other No. 10 staff is conceivably inadequate – but the divided Cabinet is not the institution to provide for such a need.

CHAPTER SEVEN

The Bureaucratic Arena

Introduction

Brian Sedgemore, MP, formerly a junior minister under Mr Tony Benn at the Department of Energy, has written: 'Two things only can be said about Parliamentary democracy in Britain today. First, effective power does not reside in Parliament. Secondly, there is little that is democratic about the exercise of that power' (Sedgemore, 1980, p. 11). He identifies the civil service as one of the areas where power can be found. Thus he suggests that 'The civil service in Britain today is an elite abrogating to itself political power in a manner which betokens trouble for democracy' (Sedgemore, 1980, p. 26). In evidence, he cites the *Eleventh Report* of the Select Committee on Expenditure which expressed concern about the relationship between ministers and civil servants (House of Commons, 1976–7, paras 137–42). The Select Committee noted that ministers often had difficulty in changing departmental views when they came into office and that, when policies are changed, the department would often try and reinstate its own policies through the passage of time and the erosion of the minister's will.

Sedgemore quotes civil service friends who appear to hold a view of the policy-making system rather close to our own. Thus he says that they admit privately to the existence of independent bureaucratic power, but try to qualify this by suggesting that a 'dualism' has developed in which there is both bureaucratic power and political power. Sometimes these two types of power are in agreement and sometimes they are in conflict. When conflicts arise, sometimes there is compromise, sometimes the bureaucracy wins, and sometimes the politicians win (Sedgemore, 1980, p. 31). Sedgemore does not accept this version of the system, though he concedes that it has the merit of being nearer to the truth than the conventional model of parliamentary democracy. We shall return to specific questions of civil service power in later sections of this chapter, but for the moment we wish to turn to that 'dual' model rejected by Sedgemore. It is a rather useful way of capturing the complex process by which decisions and policies emerge. We take this view because we believe that there is a necessary depoliticization and simplification in the way in which most decisions in complex industrial societies are made. There are a number of features of this 'logic', the first of which is the sectorization of policy-making.

Sectorization of Policy-making

As we noted in our discussion of Cabinet government, there is a strong tendency for ministers to behave not as a united team, committed to a coherent and integrated governmental programme, but as a collection of twenty or so individuals, each determined to defend (or expand) his or her policy area. Thus Heclo and Wildavsky (1981, p. 137) quote the case of a minister who was reasonably co-operative in trying to control his department's expenditure. When the Chancellor proposed a substantial cut in his departmental budget, the minister accepted a cut of half the initial proposal. When this was approved in Cabinet, without the minister objecting, word leaked out that he was a soft minister, unable to defend his department. Heclo and Wildavsky note that 'the man had crippled his reputation. Departmental officials considered him weak. His Cabinet colleagues believed that they could easily run over him. The interests affected no longer wanted him to deal with their subject. Other interests who wanted a strong minister to look after their affairs would be upset if he came to an office affecting them.' Thus there are strong political and psychological pressures causing the policy-making system to disintegrate into relatively autonomous sectors or segments. Moreover, there are good practical and intellectual reasons for the decoupling of issues and consequent sectorization of policy-making. This sectorization of policy-making is possibly the only practical way of governing, as it is quite impossible to take account of all possible linkages across all policy areas.

There is also the matter of political acceptance. In any policy area it is thought preferable by those involved to avoid rather than precipitate conflict. Avoiding 'noise' is one of the unrecorded dimensions of the civil servant's job description. Truman (1951, p. 444) returned several times to the premise of 'the web of established relationships in the administrative process' – webs used to convert the controversial into the routine. The rough-and-ready coalitions between spending departments and 'their' groups are now part of the assumptive world of those operating in central government.

True, there is much co-ordination and a ready recognition that what happens in one policy area is of relevance to another. This is why there are so many interdepartmental committees in Whitehall. Civil servants in Department A know full well that for a new policy to be accepted they must consult their colleagues in Departments B and C. However, our starting-point is to view Whitehall as a collection of separate fiefdoms – which we have elsewhere termed 'departmental pluralism' (Richardson and Jordan, 1979). This rather factionalized aspect of Whitehall can sometimes become public. For example, in October 1985 *The Times* reported a 'furious ministerial dispute' over a Home Office plan to ensure that government contractors do not discriminate against black workers. David Waddington, the Home Office minister, had announced that he and his colleagues were likely to support and introduce 'contract legislation' in an attempt to force companies to follow equal opportunity legislation. Mr Alan Clark, the junior Employment minister publicly denounced (with the backing of his Secretary of State, Lord Young) the scheme as hypocritical and totally contrary to the government's policy of reducing burdens on businesses, and so on. It was reported that Whitehall was in complete disarray over the issue and that Downing Street was attempting to 'knock some heads together' in order to unscramble the chaos (*The Times*, 15 October, 1985).

Other recent examples of interdepartmental conflict include that between Michael Jopling at the Ministry of Agriculture, Fisheries and Food (MAFF) and William Waldegrave, a Minister of State (that is, non-Cabinet minister) at the Department of the Environment (DoE). As Minister for Environment, Countryside and Local Government, Waldegrave was becoming the government's most prominent spokesman on conservation. This prompted Mr Jopling to issue a statement claiming: 'The interests of agriculture, conservation and the people who live and work in the countryside are now embedded in the policies of the Ministry of Agriculture, Fisheries and Food.' A few days later Mr Waldegrave asserted his responsibilities in the area in a speech emphasizing that *he* was responsible for the countryside and claiming that legislation might be needed if farmers did not put their own house in order (*The Times*, 8 January 1986).

This statement was the public expression of an interdepartmental battle which was particularly serious from MAFF's point of view. Periodically it is argued that farming no more deserves a separate department than any other industry. The Ministry of Agriculture, Fisheries and Food thus fears a 'domino theory' in which it will lose control of one aspect of agricultural policy after another and be left with a rump department to be merged with some other.

A *Financial Times* article on a new policy statement on the inner cities in early February 1986 claimed that 'it was more important for what it shows about the state of inter departmental rivalries in

Whitehall than for initiatives on deprived urban areas'. It continued: 'The key to yesterday's announcement by Mr Clark [one of the Department of Employment's two Ministers in the Cabinet] is the power struggle ... over control of inner-city policies. In this struggle, the Environment Department, until now responsible for most of the inner-city programmes has lost comprehensively ... Lord Young, Employment Secretary, will be the lead minister and Mr Clarke will be in day-to-day charge ...' Other departments were given only junior minister representation on the interdepartmental committee responsible for the programme.

The best (or worst) example of interdepartmental conflict in 1985/6 was, however, the difference of view over the future of Westland Helicopters. The episode cost both Mr Heseltine at the Ministry of Defence (MoD) and Mr Brittan at the Department of Trade and Industry (DTI) their posts, but the conflict was departmental rather than personal. The MoD view was that the Westland problem should be defined and solved as an issue about enhancing the European defence industry, whereas the DTI perspective was concerned at European protectionism and the possibility of American retaliation against UK sales in the USA.

We should not be surprised by the fact that departments which are supposed to be serving the same government take what is a parochial view of policy. This is in line with arguments about bureaucratic self-interest. As James Q. Wilson (1973, p. 13) suggests, 'it is reasonable to assume that the behaviour of persons occupying organizational roles ... is principally, though not uniquely, determined by the requirements of organizational maintenance and enhancement'. That is to say, where the loyalty is to a department rather than the bureaucracy as a whole, the civil servant will primarily advance departmental goals. Though Wilson was writing about such political organizations as unions, parties and pressure groups, this view of organizational behaviour has been more generally applied. Thus Anthony Downs (1967, pp. 262–3) has suggested that public bureaucracies behave according to certain 'laws'. For example, he believes that 'all organisations tend to become more conservative as they become older, unless they experience periods of rapid growth and internal turnover'; 'the larger an organisation becomes, the poorer the coordination of its actions'; 'every large organisation is in partial conflict with every other social agent it deals with'.

Of particular relevance to our view that policy-making is sectorized, is Downs's concept of 'policy space'. He notes that the boundaries between organizations are not always easy to define – there are many possibilities for overlapping and intertwining relations. Downs (1967, p. 212) cites the example of eliminating poverty in society.

If we imagine that a given social function (such as eliminating poverty) is located somewhere in a dimensional space, we can conceive of its relationship to other functions in terms of relative proximity. The basic measure of distance along any dimension of this space is *degree of interdependence* ... Each social function by a bureau has a certain location in policy space in relation to the functions of other bureaus.

Related to the concept of 'policy space' is the concept of 'territory' – each organization or bureau has a notion of its own 'territory', rather as an animal or bird in the wild has his own territory, and it will resist invasion of this territory by other agencies. There is not a precise definition of exactly where the territory ends. For example, there is territory which is at the *periphery* of the bureau influence and where it has some, but not great, influence and there is territory which is quite *alien* to the bureau and where it has no influence. On the other hand, it has its *heartland* which is quite alien to any other bureau and which it will defend with great vigour and determination.

Downs (1967, p. 215) notes the 'extreme jurisdiction sensitivity of most bureaus'. We have seen good examples of this sensitivity over conservation, Westland and the inner cities. Similarly, Richard Crossman noted that one of the first issues he faced as the incoming Minister of Housing and Local Government in 1964 was the threat to the MHLG's 'territory' posed by his Labour government's new Land Bill. He reports (1975, Vol. 1, pp. 24–5) that his Permanent Secretary, Dame Evelyn Sharp, warned him that he had made a serious error in agreeing that Fred Willey should have charge of land planning, in a new ministry, leaving Crossman with housing responsibilities at the MHLG. 'As soon as she realised this she got down to a Whitehall battle to save her Department from my stupidity and ignorance.'

Similarly, MAFF successfully resisted the potential invasion of its policy space in the early 1970s when the DoE made another attempt to take over responsibility for land drainage policy. There was considerable sensitivity within MAFF that if land drainage was lost, the rot would set in and other functions would be lost to other departments. For example, developments in the area of health and safety, and education and training also posed a threat to MAFF. As we have seen, in theory a number of MAFF's functions could quite logically be transferred to other departments, thereby undermining the rationale for MAFF's existence. Hence land drainage was as good a place as any to start the fight to retain its administrative territory (Richardson, Jordan and Kimber, 1978, p. 54).

A current important territorial issue is the attempt by the DTI to exercise more influence over education policy in England and Wales, based upon the belief that the education system is not 'delivering' the right type of manpower to meet industry's needs. These moves are being stoutly resisted by civil servants in the Department of Education and Science (DES). A department's attempt to defend its territory does, of course, depend upon ministerial support, as the Crossman example illustrates. In that case Crossman quickly accepted the view of his Permanent Secretary. In a more recent case, the introduction of the Technical and Vocational Education Initiative (TVEI) in 1983, Sir Keith Joseph, Secretary of State for Education and Science, agreed to the Manpower Services Commission (MSC) being the 'lead' agency for this policy (the policy was initiated by the MSC), notwithstanding that it was a clear invasion of his own department's territory. His department was not amused (Moon and Richardson, 1984b, p. 28). Ministers normally fight for their policy area. For example, Lord Young, Secretary of State for Employment, was reported as resisting Home Office intervention in the co-ordination of inner cities policy, after the riots in the summer of 1985.

Sometimes, of course, departments will be anxious to present a difficult problem as falling within another department's territory! For example, when the *Sunday Times* discovered 'slavery' within households of wealthy Arabs and Asians, there was a marked reluctance on the part of any government department to accept that the problem lay within its 'territory'. The Home Office disclaimed responsibility on the ground that providing the 'slaves' worked for the employer specified on the visa, then all was in order. The Department of Employment (DE) denied responsibility as they were not responsible for people who had entered the UK on a visitor's visa. On raising the issue with the two departments, the *Sunday Times* was told by the Home Office: 'We are only concerned with the grounds under which domestic servants are admitted. Work conditions are a matter for the Department of Employment.' The DE said, 'Really and truly these are matters for the Home Office' (*Sunday Times*, 10 February 1985). A similar phenomenon can be seen when expenditure cuts are being proposed. Bernard Donoughue, senior policy adviser to the Prime Minister from 1974 to 1979, has described how cuts will be off-loaded to the periphery of a department's activity: 'It's a process whereby the administrators deciding on the allocation of the cuts push the cuts to the periphery, as far away from themselves as possible'. (Young and Sloman, 1982, p. 34).

A less serious variant of Downs's theoretical perspective on bureau maximization is the 'law' devised by C. Northcote Parkinson and known as 'Parkinson's Law'. Northcote Parkinson suggests that work expands to fill the time available to do it and that the number of officials and the work to be done are not related to each other at all. Two factors are at work in public bureaucracies, he argues. (1) Officials want to multiply subordinates not rivals, (2) officials make work for each other. He came to his conclusions after studying the increase in the number of officials employed by the Admiralty between 1914 and 1918. The number of ships actually decreased by 67·7 per cent and the number of fighting men decreased by 31·5 per cent, yet the number of Admiralty officials increased by 78·45 per cent (Parkinson, 1978, pp. 39–45).

Clientelism and the Importance of Consultations and Negotiations

An important way to increase the size and importance of any given part of the state bureaucracy is for it to develop close relations with outside groups. As Downs (1967, p. 7) suggests: 'No bureau can survive unless it is continually able to demonstrate that its services are worthwhile to some group with influence over sufficient resources to keep it alive'. Where would MAFF be, in its Whitehall battles, for example, without the farmers being organized by the National Farmers' Union? In this sense, it is quite wrong to see a *clear* distinction between public and private organizations. If, as we believe, the dominant policy style is consultation and negotiation, then it is to be expected that the relationship between the bureaucracy (public) and pressure groups (private) will often be symbiotic. Departments and 'clients' often co-ordinate their activity in pressurizing the rest of government on behalf of 'their' sector. This is not to suggest that there is never disagreement and conflict between departments and their 'clients'. For example, the breakdown of relations between the DoE and the Local Authority Associations under Mrs Thatcher's second government is a good example, showing that the policy-making system is not always consensual. (Though it may be the case that the DoE is itself unhappy over the position it finds itself in between the Treasury and the local authorities). The gradual breakdown in relations, accelerated by the Conservatives since 1979, was caused by the adoption of a control strategy by central government rather than the old strategy of conciliation and recognition of the interdependence between central and local government. As Rhodes (1984, p. 34) suggests: '... when control is the preferred strategy, the outcome will be unintended consequences, recalcitrance, instability, ambiguity and confusion: in short, the *policy mess* that has become the defining characteristic of British central-local relations.'

At the time of writing (1986), the Conservatives appear to be in the early stages of moving towards a more conciliatory stance on local government finance, having begun to recognize the political cost of continued conflict. For most issues in most policy areas, however, public and private are mutually dependent, with important consequences for the type of policy change which is possible. Rhodes (1984, pp. 21–2) has gone on to argue that the Conservative government might wish to change its tactics because the central 'authority' or 'command' style simply produced unintended consequences. Thus while the government wanted to boost capital spending, local authorities have, for example, foregone increases in capital-building programmes rather than face the 'downstream' current costs of heating, staff and maintenance. Local authorities have 'massaged figures', discovered creative accounting, built up contingency funds, reclassified spending – all to avoid and frustrate the new style. Rhodes observes: 'It is tempting to conclude that the harder the Secretary of State for the Environment, Michael Heseltine tried, the more he got (of what he didn't want!).'

This interdependence between departments and their clients can, of course, work to the detriment of the public interest. As Habermas (1976, p. 62) notes, a 'rationality deficit' can develop as a result of this problem of very close department/group relations. This is because 'authorities, with little informational and planning capacity . . . are dependent on the flow of information from their clients. They are thus unable to preserve the distance from them necessary for independent decisions. Individual sectors can, as it were, privatize parts of the public administration.' In many cases, the sectorization of public policy-making can become 'the private management of public business' (Richardson and Jordan, 1979). This privatization of public policy-making is neatly captured by a former Conservative minister, Sir Edward (later Lord) Boyle, who reflected that 'overwhelmingly the biggest number [of policies] originated from what are broadly called 'the education world'. Boyle's view was echoed by another former education minister, Anthony Crosland, who suggested that two of the four limitations on his ministerial freedom of action were the high degree of autonomy of much of the educational world and the strong pressure groups acting in this field (both quoted in Kogan, ed., 1971, pp. 159–60).

Viewing central government as essentially pluralistic in nature, that is, a collection of separate policy sectors reflected in departmental boundaries, leads naturally to the clientelistic relationships suggested above, in which the essential nature of the relationship between departments and groups is negotiative. Again, a certain logic of policy-making appears to be at work. Consultation and negotiation takes place for two reasons. First, because there is a cultural bias which emphasizes the need to legitimate decisions through consultation. Secondly, there is also a *functional* necessity for governments to consult the 'affected interests'. As Finer (1956) noted over a quarter of a century ago, the whole system of public administration in Britain rests on the assumption that pressure groups will grant their co-operation in the implementation of policy.

In formulating policies, bureaucrats are the more likely, compared with politicians, to have some notion of feasibility. It may be closely related to their perceptions of what will be resisted at the implementation stage. As one of the conditions of successful implementation is the co-operation of those involved (see Chapter 10), then it is sensible, rather than necessarily sinister, that the affected groups are closely involved in the formulation of the policies. In any case, they have technical expertise which the bureaucracy lacks. As Britain has a bureaucracy based upon the concept of the generalist, rather than relying on specialized technocratic civil servants, it is no surprise that they themselves have rather strong leanings towards consultation.

This bias towards the accommodation of groups in policy-making was reflected in a comparative survey of the attitudes of civil servants, conducted by Eldersveld and his colleagues. Of five Western European countries surveyed, British civil servants were the least likely to view the clash of particularistic groups as a problem (quoted by Hayward and Berki, 1979). This willingness of civil servants to consult and negotiate (there being no clear distinction between consultation and negotiation in practice) need not be only based upon 'good' democratic values. C. D. Foster (1971, p. 63), an economist who spent a period in the Ministry of Transport, believes that lack of confidence is an important factor in weakening the power of the civil service when faced with powerful outside interests. When so many public policy decisions are concerned with specific, technical, complex managerial questions, then awareness of particular circumstances is all-important. Thus an interventionist state tends towards a functionally differentiated and fragmented bureaucracy, and the relations between department and sectional interests tend to become closer (see also Beer, 1967, p. 85). Expertise, knowledge and information, grant power just as much as the ability to disrupt the implementation of policies. Because British civil servants tend to be relatively weak on specialist expertise, it is not surprising that they are reluctant to develop an *authority* relationship with outside groups and agencies (see Hood, 1983).

The marked preference for a co-operative and consensual relationship is reflected in policy-making procedures, even where the state is supposed to be in a regulatory relationship towards groups. Thus

David Vogel (1983, p. 89) notes that if British and American pollution policies are compared, it is easy to detect a different regulatory style. He suggests that 'British regulatory authorities have pursued a consistent policy of close cooperation with industry. They continue to rely more on persuasion and voluntary agreements and less on legal coercion than any other industrial democracy'. The American system is, in contrast, much more adversarial and has created much antagonism on the part of business and much conflict between governments and environmental organizations. Vogel (1983, p. 101) links the British regulatory style in the pollution field to more general factors: 'Environmental regulation, like public policy in general, does not take place in a vacuum. Each nation's approach to regulating industry, like its policies for promoting industrial growth, is the product of distinctive political traditions and institutions.' He concludes that there is nothing unusual about environmental regulation – Britain regulates the environment in much the same way as it regulates health, insurance, banking, consumer protection – namely, by a reliance on flexible standards and voluntary compliance, including, in many cases, self-regulation.

Environmental policy, however, is a particularly interesting policy area because it has seen a proliferation of groups since the early 1970s, pressing new issues and demanding participation in well-established policy areas. In that sense, 'environmentalism' presented a significant challenge to the policy-making system. Britain seems to have absorbed the environmental challenge with more 'success' (in terms of conflict management) than, say, West Germany (Richardson and Watts, 1985). There, the rise of the Green Party has demonstrated that traditional policy-making processes have been less successful in 'accommodating' the new groups. In contrast, British environmental groups seem to have gained access to the policy-making process, sufficient for them to have remained well ordered and non-disruptive. Philip Lowe and Jane Goyder (1983, pp. 62–3) conducted a survey of seventy-seven environmental groups in Britain and found that only four of them were not regularly in touch with at least one government department or agency, 'the median number being six government organisations per group'. They suggest that 'Government has not been a passive recipient of pressure from environmental groups but an active agent, establishing new consultative procedures, funding environmental groups, even promoting the creation of such groups'. Indeed, a quarter of the groups had government observers on their executive committees enabling 'their decision-making to be in step with Departmental thinking and vice versa'.

Lowe and Goyder raise the crucial question of whether the involvement of environmental groups is effective or whether it is merely token. Here there are possibly grounds for concern that environmentalists are being rather too effectively 'managed' It is encouraging from the environmentalist's viewpoint that those statutory agencies with a specific environmental remit, for example, the Countryside Commission, the Historic Buildings Council and the Nature Conservancy Council, were regarded as very receptive. These are the areas where the environmental lobby has been 'institutionalized' (Lowe and Goyder, 1983, p. 64) But it was discovered that

> Among the organisations considered unreceptive are all the major development-orientated government departments. Environmental groups do not enjoy the sort of close symbiotic relationships with senior civil servants in those departments as do major interest groups such as the National Farmers' Union with the Ministry of Agriculture . . ., the Confederation of British Industry with the Department of Industry . . . and road haulage interests with the Department of Transport . . . the *inclusion of environmental groups in consultative relations with the developmental departments is largely a token justice.* (Italics added)

Thus it has to be recognized that consultation may be entirely cosmetic, but the Lowe and Goyder argument perhaps overestimates the influence of, say, the Confederation of British Industries with the DTI, or the National Farmers' Union with MAFF. [For the latter, see the description by Holbeche (1986).]

Civil servants and ministers have a working knowledge of who really matters in the consultative process – particularly of those groups who have the ability to exercise some kind of veto, for example, doctors in the National Health Service, teachers in the education system, the police in matters of law enforcement. In the environmental case, the environmental groups seem to have been effectively confined to 'their' sector, even though policies emanating from other sectors (such as energy and transport) have very significant environmental consequences. Sectorization of policy-making can, therefore, work to the detriment of those organizations espousing issues of a particularly cross-sectoral nature.

Clearly, some consultation exercises are primarily concerned with legitimation and are almost sham exercises. Thus in the departmental consultations following the publication of the Finniston Report, *Engineering Our Future* (Cmnd 7794), during the summer of 1980, over 500 groups and individuals were consulted. Yet most of these groups proved to be peripheral to the making of the final decision on what changes should be introduced within the engineering profession. But while the consultations which led to the formation of the new Engineering Council were cosmetic for most of the bodies involved, the DTI had to give serious attention to the sixteen chartered engineering institutions, the CBI, the Engineering Employers Federation and a few other bodies. Indeed, the final stages of the *negotiations* (ultimately there was no pretence that the final stages were merely 'consultative') were with the 'big four' chartered institutions, and the Fellowship of Engineers (Jordan and Richardson, 1984, p. 395).

The outcome of the negotiations was an Engineering Council which presented no really effective challenge to the established position of the main professional institutions and, indeed, granted them a key role in the practical affairs of the council, such as the accreditation of degree courses. As *The Times* commented on 31 July 1981, the government's response (to the avowedly radical Finniston Report) 'has confirmed precisely the complacency and institutional jockeying which the Report had set out to break ... Instead of treating the Report on its merits the Government set out to find a consensus among the very bodies and opinions which the Report sought to supersede. The result is a soggy set of compromises of the sort that always emerges from such exercises.' The Engineering Council case reveals two contrasting complaints. For some groups the consultation was sham, but in the case of other groups it is argued that they were too successful, that the national interest was sacrificed in the desire to create consensus.

A classic defence of the practice of consultation and negotiation came from one of the key participants in the Finniston negotiations – Lord Caldecote, President of the Fellowship of Engineers. He replied to *The Times* (10 August 1981) in the following terms: 'It would have been quite useless to set up a new Council ... without the support of the majority of engineers ... It was therefore well worth spending much time and effort to reach a workable consensus so that the new Council can be set up ... with wide support from the engineering profession, employers and the academic world.' In other words, his argument was that the government had little choice but to compromise when implementation was inevitably in the hands of the profession. There was no alternative professional leadership available that could provide radical new faces, ideas and talents. His argument seemed to be that since the world outside Whitehall and its powers cannot be wished away, it has to be manoeuvred. Ultimately, who can reveal the 'public interest' but the 'interested public'?

The Finniston case is a good example of inner-circle negotiation with what Wyn Grant has termed insider groups (see Chapter 8). Thus there is nearly always an 'inner core' of groups on whom the department relies. Quite often there may be no other groups to consult. For example, in the field of new technology policy there are relatively few bodies with whom to consult, added to which the government is especially weak on expertise of its own. Policies designed to arrest Britain's decline in its share of world markets and to reduce import penetration are heavily dependent upon established key actors in the field, such as GEC, Plessey, ICL, and so on. Thus the government appears to be dependent upon the very organizations which need to change, if Britain's position in this key industrial area is to improve (Richardson, Moon and Smart, 1986).

Where there is a strong inner circle or core of groups in existence, then policy change is difficult, and such change as does take place is usually incremental. The bureaucratic preoccupation tends to be the avoidance of disturbance, the securing of a stable environment or negotiated order (Richardson and Jordan, 1979). The emphasis in consultation and negotiation is not new – as we suggest in Chapter 8. However, the practice seems to have intensified over the last twenty years or so.

In practice, it is realistic to think of each policy sector as consisting of several, inter-related, policy communities – the sort of policy field covered by a civil service assistant secretary or under secretary (now termed grades 3–5 in the new unified grading structure). Many linkages exist (for example, between branches of medicine, social services and social policy, or between different 'divisions' in the DTI) and a system of overlapping memberships between policy communities develops. There will also be linkages between policy sectors – for example, the environmental impact of various agricultural policies and practices is now becoming a political issue, necessitating increased interaction between MAFF and the DoE. Similarly, Britain's membership of the EEC has increased the interaction between sectors, because concessions in one sector are made as a trade-off for gains in other sectors as part of the complex EEC bargaining procedure. As discussed in Chapter 8, it seems likely that Britain is, in part, experiencing the phenomenon identified in the USA by Heclo (1978) – namely, the development of extended and open 'issue networks' in which the number of participants is increasing and outcomes are rather unpredictable.

Developing with this tendency for more groups to demand (and get) participation is the tendency to link what were once disparate issues, but the policy system is not leaderless because, as we suggest above, there is usually an inner core of groups and individuals who really count in any one issue (Jordan, 1981, p. 106). The existence of these cores is a strong force preventing disintegration of policy communities and sectors into the ill-defined issue networks suggested by Heclo. There is, therefore, 'a counteracting trend towards simplification and limitation of centrifugal forces ... which seek to maintain a manageable polity' (Jordan, 1981, p. 116). Once a policy community has been established, then there are good reasons for the members of it to hang on to the benefits of mutual exchange which underpin the community (Mackenzie, 1975, p. 73).

In addition to cultural, psychological and practical reasons for the continuation of policy-making via policy communities, there are institutional and structural reasons for its continuation. Mrs Thatcher's government provides a good example of this. Thus despite her often-stated antipathy towards consensus politics (because consensus was said to be a polite word for 'fudge'), and despite the government's general antipathy towards quangos, the system of standing and *ad hoc* advisory committees continues to operate. Relatively few of the 1,561 advisory bodies identified in Sir Leo Pliatzky's review in 1980 (Cmnd 7797, p. 1) were abolished by the Conservative government, as they fulfil the important task of co-opting specialized knowledge into the system. As the Pliatzky Report suggested, the case in principle for the advisory bodies is that 'the Department's own staff cannot provide the necessary advice by themselves, or that it may be desirable to enlist the participation of outside interests in order to formulate publicly acceptable proposals'.

Britain's reliance on committees of various types is not at all unusual in Western Europe. For example a Dutch Study, conducted in 1975, identified some 368 permanent advisory bodies, 42 per cent of which had been created since 1962 (van Putten, 1982, pp. 180–1, in Richardson, ed., 1982). Norwegian observers have also noted the prevalence of advisory committees for those issues which are specific and limited in nature (Olsen *et al.*, 1981, p. 64, in Richardson, ed., 1982). The British attachment to the institutionalization of consultation and negotiation is seen by Henderson, in a highly critical essay, as a means of risk sharing. To Henderson, the habit has some serious consequences for the quality of decision-making. Officials, he argues, protect themselves 'by making sure that, at every stage of the policy process, the right chairs have been warmed at the right committee tables by the appropriate institutions, everything possible has been done and no one could possibly be blamed if things go wrong'. (Henderson, 1977, p. 189).

Politicians and Civil Servants

The processes and institutional arrangements outlined above, all implicitly grant the bureaucracy a central role in the policy process. For example, the Henderson quote cited above emphasizes the caution of officials. This links up with Foster's (1971) emphasis on the lack of confidence of officials when, say, faced with specialized and technical demands from nationalized industries.

Even if the strict doctrine of ministerial responsibility has been consigned to the history books – if not the dustbin – (see Chapter 6) the doctrine that the civil service *serves* the politician is still in good currency. For example, Sir Brian Hayes, Permanent Secretary at MAFF has expressed the classical view of the role of the civil servant as follows: 'Civil servants ought not to have power because we're not elected. Power stems from the people and flows through Parliament to the minister responsible to Parliament. The civil servant has no power of his own. He is there to help the minister and to be the minister's agent' (Young and Sloman, 1982, p. 20). This traditional notion – that the civil servant is there to serve his or her political master – received a severe jolt in 1985, when Clive Ponting, an assistant secretary in the Ministry of Defence was acquitted in an Old Bailey trial of breaking the Official Secrets Act. Ponting had leaked information on the sinking of the Argentinian warship, *General Belgrano*, during the Falklands War. Ponting's argument was that he acted out of duty in leaking the secret papers to Tam Dalyell, Labour MP for Linlithgow. Despite the judge's advice to the jury that the interests of the state could only mean the policies of the government of the day, the jury's verdict implied that Ponting, as a civil servant, had a wider duty than solely to the elected government of the day.

Other civil servants have increasingly taken the Ponting approach in leaking sensitive documents to the media, much to the embarrassment of their ministers (see Pyper, 1985). Sir Brian's description of the role of civil servants is in great contrast to the views of radical politicians. For example, Tony Benn, reflecting on his own ministerial experience, argued that the civil servants 'are always trying to steer incoming governments back to the policy of the outgoing government, minus the mistakes that the civil service thought that the outgoing government made'. (Young and Sloman, 1982, p. 2). Here we see the grey zone between civil service advice and civil service power. If, as we argue, the management of public policy – its formulation and implementation – is a task which of necessity involves much closer contact between government and other organizations (both public and private) involved in a particular policy area, then it is inevitable that much of the work must be handled by civil servants. Ministers are quite simply too busy to be involved in all but a tiny proportion of a department's business. Hence, while our civil servants are often criticized as policy amateurs, they are often likely to be much more expert than the ministers who, on average, spend only twenty months in any one post.

The subtlety of the relationship between ministers and civil servants is captured neatly by Sir Patrick Nairne, then Permanent Secretary at the Department of Health and Social Security (DHSS). Responding to Benn's argument that there is considerable resistance to policy change when a new government takes office, he suggests that:

> there is often a tendency on the part of the civil servant to say, "look, we've got these particular plans in hand. They were just, you know, coming to fruition. They do accord very closely with what you're after don't they?", and in effect to try to maximise continuity. Sometimes ministers accept that when they have a chance to know what the facts are, they sometimes think that the existing plans are exactly the plans they want (Young and Sloman, 1982, p. 25)

That plans need to be backed by consensus is seen as one possible point of conflict between civil servants and ministers. Shirley Williams, former Secretary of State for Education and Science, sees civil servants on the one side:

> generally preaching continuity and consensus and generally eschewing radical ideas whether of the right or left. And then you have the politicians exercising their muscles and increasingly trying to establish a kind of machismo image by beating the civil servants over the head and moving more and more to the extremes precisely to show who is boss (Young and Sloman, 1982, p. 86).

Lord Crowther-Hunt, an academic unusually writing with ministerial experience, has also noted the pivotal position of the civil service in the complex process by which policies emerge. Thus he notes that each policy proposal has to be processed through the government machine, necessitating discussions with other ministers and their departments, with the Treasury and with outside bodies who are interested in the new proposals or are affected by them. The process is 'messy' and 'In the web of pressures, policies are refined and modified, sometimes even rejected, compromises have to be made, public opinion satisfied. So when policies eventually emerge from the government machine, it is hardly ever possible to determine relative responsibilities for what has or has not happened' (Crowther-Hunt, 1980, p. 397). He goes on to emphasize the central role played by civil servants. In his view, 'besides being part of the pressures themselves, they are also the crucial channel through which most of the other pressures must eventually be canalised'.

This description of the part played by civil servants on the policy process is rather close to our policy/community concept with the assistant secretary or under-secretary in charge. If policy-making and its implementation takes place via networks of relationships, as we suggest, then there is little doubt that civil servants sit at the centre of the network – sometimes orchestrating and sometimes reflecting 'community politics' both within and outside Whitehall. Lord Crowther-Hunt quotes the example of the preparation of the White Paper on devolution in 1974. Over half-a-dozen interdepartmental committees of officials had been set to work under the previous government of Edward Heath in response to the Report of the Commission on the Constitution. They went on to complete their recommendations after Harold Wilson was elected in March 1974. The recommendations represented well over 1,000 man hours of interdepartmental meetings of civil servants compared with at most, two or three meetings, lasting altogether a mere handful of hours for the ministers (Lord Crowther-Hunt, 1980, p. 387).

In a world of specialization and increasing complexity – with its concomitant interdependency of organizations, groups and individuals – it is inevitable that public (and private) bureaucracies should be extremely powerful. Finer (1980a, p. 371) may be right in suggesting that 'the one impossible expectation is that the bureaucracy shall be at one and the same time both creative and controlled'. Indeed, he sees the bureaucracy as the essential core of the modern state, bringing incalculable benefits. Having obtained the benefits of bureaucratic organization, we must also pay the costs. Bureaucratic power brings with it a bureaucratic style of policy-making. As Finer suggests (quoting the late Levi Eshkol, though on a different matter), 'You've got the dowry – the trouble is you've got the bride as well'.

Alternative Policy Styles

We have described what appears to be the most common style of policy-making in Britain, namely, a system of bureaucratic accommodation designed to produce consensus and agreement amongst the relevant policy communities – albeit sometimes extended policy communities with increased numbers of actors. Thus if the mass of policy-making activity in any one year is akin to a massive iceberg floating in the sea, then our description probably fits the vast bulk of the iceberg which sits below the water line. But it is clear that policy is not always made in this way – certain issues, such as abortion law reform or constitutional change, are 'processed' in quite different decision-making areas such as Parliament, via referendums, or through electoral politics. Such issues are resolved in the full glare of publicity and sometimes with high degrees of political mobilization.

Other issues are processed in private, internally, within Whitehall, with little or no participation by outside groups. For example, the decision to purchase Trident can hardly be described as involving a policy community of groups. However, while the policy is not made with the integrated participation of group spokesmen, the decision *is* made in terms of affected interests. For example, on Trident there is the interest of the research bureaucracy at Aldermaston, there is a wish to aid British Shipbuilders, a job-creation aspect. There are arguments in favour from part of the military hierarchy – and arguments against from the parts of the forces 'squeezed' by the demands of the nuclear budget. This is not to suggest that the critical decision to build Trident was the outcome of pressure-group politics – merely that, even with Trident-type decisions, there is a group dimension. Thus groups do not have insider access to influence all kinds of policy – but even where policy is evolved internally, in the longer term it will only be tenable if it can be 'sold' to an influential constituency. Such policy-making is best described as internalized policy-making, but with some feedback mechanism after the initial decision. There may be leaks to the mass media and specialized press, and small numbers of 'professional policy-makers' (Heclo, 1978) may be drawn into considerations of foreign or defence policy (for example, academics and some specialist correspondents), but significant group participation of a consultative nature would be quite rare.

Similarly, another form of internalized policy-making – policy-making within parties – may totally exclude outside groups. A good example is Moran's study of the 1971 Industrial Relations Act (Moran, 1977). Edward Heath had, in 1965, instituted an almost unprecedented attempt to make detailed policy whilst in Opposition. A party committee (which included individual businessmen) made policy without a dialogue with major interest groups. Moran (1977, p. 60) describes how after 1969:

> when the Tories became worried about enforcing their proposals, more serious attempts were made at consultation: there was increased contact with the CBI, some private meetings were held with a number of trade union leaders ... This attempt to sell a policy which had already been effectively decided on was, however, very different from the practice of working it out in the first place in consultation with various groups.

Moran suggests that this relative lack of consultation was, in part, responsible for the failure of the policy when the Conservatives came to office. In our terms, they had ignored the 'logic of negotiation'.

Another example where external groups were less important than internal ones is suggested in Banting's study of social policy. The policy options which were considered owed more, he claimed, to the ideas of intellectuals and professionals than to the pressure from organized interests (Banting, 1979, p. 141). He notes that, while the influence of these professionals can somtimes flow through group action (for example, through the Child Poverty Action Group), the groups themselves have few, if any, sanctions which they can impose upon government. Even where groups might be thought to have sanctions, a government might decide to press ahead with policy change. For example, British Telecom was privatized notwithstanding the opposition of the unions and lack of support from industrialists (Moon, Richardson and Smart, 1986).

A more important exception to our description of the policy process is when governments come to office with what are obviously 'non-negotiable' policies. True, these policies may bear the marks of group influence when the party was in Opposition, but they are often firm commitments which can only be modified at the very margin. For example, the Wilson governments of 1964–6 and 1966–70 had a clear commitment to the nationalization of the shipbuilding and aircraft industries. Similarly, Edward Heath came to office in 1970 pledged to introduce radical trade union legislation. As we have noted, the government did so, but the legislation proved to be a near total failure.

The Heath government was, more than any government since the Second World War, determined to introduce a different style of policy-making – indeed, in Opposition the Conservatives had produced a pamphlet under the title, *A New Style of Government*. Its subsequent White Paper, *The Reorganisation of Central Government* (Cmnd 4506) was a clear attempt to produce a more 'rationalistic' approach to policy-making, but this, too, has had little impact in the long term.

Another determined attempt to change the style of policy-making has, of course, been made by Mrs Thatcher, after her election in 1979 and her re-election in 1983. No one can doubt Mrs Thatcher's intentions as a conviction politician, unhappy with consensus and determined to tackle what she perceives as Britain's long-neglected problems. None the less we have noted in Chapter 4 that the clear strategy set out in the Medium-Term Financial Strategy (though a policy of 'succession' in relation to the previous Labour government) has proved impossible to hold in practice. Moreover, there is other evidence that the determination to be innovative in traditional policy areas has had to be dropped – for example, the government's initial desire to see a much-reduced Department of Trade and Industry.

U-turns have taken place. For example, the government soon reversed its early decision to cut back on the scope and funding of anti-unemployment schemes (see Moon and Richardson, 1984a,

p. 31). Similarly, Mrs Thatcher, despite the earlier and much-publicized tough stand against increased EEC expenditure, agreed to a £252 million extra payment to Brussels in June 1985, and agreed to increase the percentage of VAT which Britain passes on to the EEC from 1 per cent to 1·4 per cent. Her government continued to provide hefty public subsidies to steel, coal, shipbuilding and to British Leyland. Big concessions were made on student grants, pension reform, regional policy, family allowances and the planned end to the solicitors' conveyancing monopoly. 'Soft' loans were provided to customers to allow British companies to compete for large international contracts.

Where radical policy change has been introduced it has often been in the face of resistance from organized groups, but it is possible to argue that there has been a decline of the trade unions as a veto group. Rod Hague (1984, p. 159) sees the Thatcher government as departing 'abruptly from its post 1945 predecessors, Labour and Conservative alike, in making plain its view that it saw no role for the unions in the framing of economic policy, and in challenging the legitimacy of union participation in state institutions'. A. King (1985, p. 487) also notes that 'The unions, in particular, were dismayed by their exclusion from power, but there was little they could do about it.' (However, notwithstanding such comments, the TUC's participation in a wide range of governmental bodies – including the National Economic Development Council [NEDC] – has continued.)

Despite an early and tentative attempt by Jim Prior, as Secretary of State for Employment, to achieve some kind of workable consensus with the unions over industrial relations reform, the Conservatives subsequently pressed ahead (under Norman Tebbit and then Tom King) with fundamental changes to the legal position of trade unions in Britain. The government's approach seems to have been to achieve radical ends by a series of legislative measures – rather than attempting everything in one Bill. Thus Employment Acts have been passed in 1980, 1982 and 1984. In total, the flow of legislation has introduced such changes as restriction of 'secondary picketing', ballots for union executives, pre-strike ballots, ballots on the political levy, ballots for closed-shop arrangements, the availability of public funds for union postal ballots, changes to the legal immunities of trade unions, and provision for unions to be sued for damages if their industrial action is unlawful. All of these provisions were opposed by the trade union movement and many of the changes have already had quite profound effects.

Yet, amidst the opposition, the unions did, on occasions, enter discussions with the government. For example, in February 1984 the TUC published its own guidelines on political funds, which had been agreed between the TUC and the Employment Secretary, Tom King. The agreement concerned the 'contracting out' provisions, thus avoiding legislation on this particular point. Earlier, Moss Evans, of the Transport and General Workers' Union (TGWU) had negotiated a 'deal' with the government which allowed the TGWU to continue with a workplace ballot. (It was this 'deal' that eventually went wrong, with accusations of ballot rigging in the TGWU resulting in a re-run of the elections for the new general secretary in 1985.)

Although government/union relations have continued to be bad – particularly after the banning of trade unions at GCHQ (the government's communications headquarters at Cheltenham) in 1984 – the TUC has remained on a whole range of advisory committees and has played a continuing and active role in such bodies as the Manpower Services Commission (MSC), the Advisory, Conciliation and Arbitration Service (ACAS), and the Health and Safety Executive. Even its withdrawal from the NEDC in protest at the GCHQ action was reversed after a few months, in a joint initiative with the CBI concerning the possible reform of NEDC procedures.

This confusing combination of co-operation and conflict is, of course, made possible by the sectorization of policy-making described earlier – that is, there can be a total breakdown of relations in one sector and the continuation of 'business as usual' in another. Because of this, it is wrong to see the unions as totally devoid of power under the Conservative governments after 1979. Thus the unions continued to exercise a veto within the key area of job creation and training schemes under the MSC (Moon and Richardson, 1985, pp. 109–11).

Another main area of extremely bitter conflict was in the field of central/local government relations. However, as suggested in Chapter 4, Rhodes (1984, p. 30) points out that the conflict is as much related to the needs of national economic management as it is to party dogma. Sharpe (1985) has also noted this tendency over a period, and under different governments, for the centre to exert greater control. While we acknowledge that the trend accelerated when the Conservatives came to office in 1979, its direction under Labour was clear. The Conservatives have taken increasingly tough powers to restrict local authority spending (via penalties for 'excessive' expenditure and 'rate capping') and have abolished the metropolitan counties and the Greater London Council (GLC) altogether. As with trade union reform, these changes have been carried out in the face of stiff resistance, and it is difficult to imagine other governments being so dogged when faced with such opposition.

Other policy areas have also provided evidence of radical change

Table 7.1   *Privatization in Britain 1979–85*

Company	Business	Date of sale	Means of sale	Remaining government holding†	Net proceeds £m‡
British	Aerospace	February 1981	offer 51·6%		43
Aerospace		May 1985	offer 48·4%	nil	346
Cable &	Telecoms	October 1981	offer 49·4%		182
Wireless		December 1983	tender 27·9%		263
		December 1985	offer 22·7%	nil	600
Amersham	Radio				
International	Chemicals	February 1982	offer 100%	nil	64
National	Road		management		
Freight Co	haulage	February 1982	buyout	nil	5
Britoil	Oil	November 1982	tender 51%		627
		August 1985	offer 48·9%	nil	425
Associated	Seaports	February 1983	offer 51·5%		46
British Ports		April 1984	tender 48·5%	nil	51
International	Aviation				
Aeradio	comms	March 1983	private sale	nil	60
BR Hotels	Hotels	March 1983	private sale	nil	51
British Gas					
Onshore Oil					
(Wytch Farm)	Oil	May 1984	private sale	nil	82
Enterprise Oil	Oil	June 1984	tender 100%	nil	380
Sealink	Ferries	July 1984	private sale	nil	66
Jaguar	Cars	July 1984	offers 100%	nil	297
British Telecom	Telecoms	November 1984	offer 50·2%	49·8%	3,916ᵃ
British Technology	Misc	—	private sales	—	
Group§ and other			and placings		716

Source: *The Economist*, 31 December 1985.
Note: ᵃGross proceeds. †Excluding special share held in some companies. ‡Including part payments not yet received. §Includes sale of 25% of ICL (1979), 100% of Fairey and 50% of Ferranti (1980) and 75% of Inmos (1984).

without much consultation. As suggested earlier, the massive privatization programme was not the product of policy community politics. By the end of 1985 some £8 billion has been raised by the Thatcher governments by selling off assets – over half from the sale of British Telecom (see Table 7.1).

Undoubtedly, privatization in its various forms – sale of public assets or contracting out of services by government to private contractors – accords with Conservative philosophy, but several points suggest that the financial attraction of using asset sales to limit public-sector borrowing has been important.

(1) The sale of assets was not a strong theme in the 1979 manifesto. It only specifically mentioned the resale of interests

affected by the 1977 Aircraft and Shipbuilding Act – and shares in the National Freight Corporation.

(2) The Public Sector Borrowing Requirement (PSBR) has exceeded intentions – and without asset sales this excess would have been even larger. Thus without asset sales in 1984, the 1984 Budget would have predicted a PSBR of £10·85 billion rather than £7·27 billion (£2 billion was to be raised from public corporation sales and £1·6 billion from council house sales). The White Paper of January 1985 revealed over-run in the 1984–5 spending – despite higher than expected receipts from privatization. As part of the attempt to constrain this over-spending in future years, the targets for asset sales were conveniently raised. Whatever ideological rationalization exists for privatization, the programme has allowed *more* public spending than would have been possible without the borrowing figures being totally discredited as monetarist policy.

(3) The dominant *form* of asset sale has left the government open to criticism precisely from the neo-liberals whom privatization is sometimes supposed to satisfy. As in the British Telecom and British Gas examples, the transfer of quasi-monopoly powers from the public to private sectors means that the benefits of privatization in improving service to the consumer cannot be assumed.

(4) The retention by the government of 49 or 51 per cent of the shares in privatized companies – or single special control shares ('golden shares') in others – is another reason to suspect that it is cash-raising rather than 'efficient market use of resources' which is pushing the programme. For these, and other reasons, there are grounds for attempting to explain the government's behaviour in terms of 'selling the family silver to pay the house-keeping' rather than some fulfilling of ideological commitment.

The government's general strategy towards the unemployment problem is possibly another example of a departure from the usual policy style – for example, it has so far resisted pressure from both the CBI and TUC for a special programme of expenditure on 'infra-structure'. As Anthony King (1985, p. 487) suggests, in reflecting on the experience of the Thatcher government as a whole, 'Ideology ruled in the general; pragmatism in the particular; each trampled over the other from time to time'. Once total levels of expenditure on anti-unemployment measures had been set, the way in which money was spent, and the design of implementation of schemes, was very much decided through consultation and negotiation with the relevant interest (Moon and Richardson, 1985). Just as the curate's egg was 'good in parts', then so Mrs Thatcher's government has been 'radical in parts'.

The 1984 miners' strike is, on the face of it, probably the best example of Mrs Thatcher's *dirigiste* style, far removed from our own consensual bargaining model. Thus it is quite possible to believe that this strike would not have started without the desire to embarrass Mrs Thatcher and without the provocation of the appointment of Mr MacGregor as chairman of the National Coal Board (NCB). Mrs Thatcher's 'conviction politics' and its echo by the NUM leadership probably made a negotiated settlement impossible. But the improvement in redundancy payments on offer, the guarantee that no miner would lose his job against his will, and the guaranteed investment programme in the industry all suggest that an adversarial portrait of the dispute, in party terms, does not look entirely realistic. As noted earlier (p. 88), Labour governments had found the economic implications as compelling as the Conservatives. As Secretary of State for Energy, Tony Benn was apparently not against closing pits which were 'out of line in economic terms'. (Hansard, 4 December, 1978, col. 1016)

The Thatcher government has proved to be an exception to the 'normal' British policy style only to a degree, and in some areas. At the same time, it has tried to maintain the usual bargaining style in most areas of policy-making. As Neustadt (1980) suggests, command decisions are politically expensive.

By 1985 the Conservative government was attempting – perhaps for electoral reasons – to stress spending on pensions and the NHS. It faced the difficult task of bringing its deliberately cultivated tough image into line with its actual behaviour over the bulk of governmental activity. As *The Economist* reminded its readers, the Thatcher government was best characterized as dry talk and wet action. The facts that characterize the bureaucratic arena, inhibit ideological consistency.

CHAPTER EIGHT

The Pressure Group Arena

Introduction

One of the themes of this particular book is that pressure groups are not an optional extra to the study of politics. The ties of this chapter to chapters on the parties, Parliament and, above all, the bureaucracy cannot be overemphasized – pressure groups operate in all arenas. This chapter focuses particularly on theories on the internal organization of the pressure groups. Pressure groups in action must be discovered and discussed in interaction in policy communities as in Chapter 7. The persuasive pressure-group literature has moved from presenting the group as articulating demands and making political inputs, to being, in Olsen's term (1981), 'integrated governmental participants'.

A starting-point for the discussion of groups has to be the difference between groups. Groups differ in goals, organizational cohesion, political clout, and so on. It is impractical to look for generalizations that cover major economic functional groups such as the Confederation of British Industry (CBI), respected campaigning groups like the Howard League for Penal Reform, and more controversial campaigning groups such as the Hunt Saboteurs Association.

If a definition is necessary, we prefer a wide version such as Lindblom's (1980, p. 85): 'We mean by interest group activities all interactions through which individuals and private groups not holding government authority seek to influence policy, together with those policy-influencing interactions of government officials that go well beyond the direct use of their authority.' As well as conventional organizational behaviour, the activities of a multinational company, or even wealthy individuals, could be subsumed under this definition. Such width can be seen as a disadvantage and we have been criticized for applying the label 'group' to everything that moves (Drucker et al., 1983, p. 262), but it is necessary to have a relaxed definition to capture the relevant actors in the policy process. Admittedly, there are special theoretical problems about the membership-based actors that constitute 'normal groups' – but it is likely that meaningful discussion has to disaggregate further – for example, trade unions have quite separate characteristics from local amenity associations or anti-nuclear movements, and so on.

Much of the literature divides the group world into two categories – along different axes according to the needs of the author in question. Clearly, any two-fold classification can be improved upon and made more sophisticated, but the basic divisions are a useful preliminary. Although various versions of the divisions exist there are links between many of them. There is a basic distinction between self-interested groups pursuing sectional, often economic, ends and those groups which seek to promote a change in social values or practices. In 1961 Allen Potter made the demarcation as follows: 'Organized groups are put here under two main heads: those organizing sectional interests; and those organizing shared attitudes' (p. 25). Sectional interests purport to speak in 'defence' of their members and groups organizing shared attitudes seek to 'promote' the causes which reflect the attitudes of their members.

Potter readily admits – and gives examples of – the existence of borderline cases, but the essential characteristics are clear enough. A group such as the CBI or the National Union of Mineworkers (NUM) is a sectional (or spokesman) group. The Child Poverty Action Group (CPAG) serves as an example of a promotional (or cause) group. Another approximate distinction is between groups 'of' and groups 'for': CPAG might be for the poor, but it is not necessarily an organization of the poor.

Borderline cases would include Alcoholics Anonymous, with an interest in the welfare of a particular group and a general education interest, or the Automobile Association which pursues members' interests and also motoring in general. The borderline case differs from the deliberately camouflaged case. For example, Finer (1966 p. 137) cited the promotional sounding London Foundation for Marriage Education, which far from promoting education in fact existed in support of the products of London Rubber Industries which were threatened by the new birth pill. A more recent example of the same pseudo-promotional group is the Hot Food Take Away Action Committee (HOTAC) which organized public petitions against the introduction of VAT on hot take-away meals – but was directed by the industry.

Moran (1985, p. 123) drawing on Cawson (1982), distinguishes between functional groups and preference groups. The former are groups 'created by the economic structure . . . the two most important kinds of functional groups [are] those representing business and those representing labour . . . By contrast, preference groups result from free associations between individuals suited by common tasks, attitudes or positions.' Such a categorization clearly overlaps with the sectional/cause type of language.

Although these classificatory problems exist, there is a value in the crude two-fold scheme. Stewart (1958, p. 25) made a very similar sectional/cause distinction to that adopted by Potter. He made the point that many of these cause groups 'are not admitted to [governmental] consultation'. This observation anticipated a frequently rediscovered dimension – the access of the group to the governmental system. Most commentators would grant that the sectional groups are the more influential – with regular, even bureaucratized, relations with government departments. A famous passage in an even more famous article by Professor Samuel Beer (1955, p. 39) states that he wanted to focus not on 'noisy threats and loud demanding claims' or 'mass demonstrations' but on 'the civil servants of the organised interest groups ... countless trade unions, trade associations and professional organisations ... [who] deal directly and continually with civil servants in government'. This private government of sectorized policy areas has been labelled 'silent politics' by Yates (1982, p. 87). Such interactions may not be the pressure-group activity of the newspaper headline but, arguably, they are the more important type. As part of the professionalization of relations there is now a steady trickle of civil servants into organizational posts 'on the other side of the table'. For example, the newly appointed (1985) director-general of the National Farmers' Union (NFU) is a former civil servant from the Ministry of Agriculture, Fisheries and Food.

Wyn Grant (1978) has used the terms 'outsider' and 'insider' to characterize the different strategies open to groups. Insiders are accepted as 'responsible' groups to be consulted on a regular basis. This concept of division by strategy was offered as an improvement on the conventional promotional/associational distinction but, in practice, the difference was partly anticipated in the earlier literature. Finer (1966, p. 36), for example, described how – what he called 'interest groups' – had more access to Whitehall (the bureaucracy) on the ground that the department and the interest groups could usefully exploit each other. He argued that it is part of the ministry's public duty to bring to sectional interests a sense of the long run and of the public interest, of which it peculiarly is the custodian, just as the interest group is the custodian of its members' interests. Nevertheless, he said, the connection between interest groups and the ministries is continuous, ubiquitous and close.

Grant bases his distinction on the strategy of the group, but a more important factor might be the view of the relevant government department. Some groups might *want* to be outsiders, as no doubt some motorists might *want* to drive a ten-year-old car, but it is more likely that they have no realistic chance of anything better. In large part, therefore, the outsider strategy is likely to be the consequence of non-acceptance by the department. One of the factors involved in acceptance as a legitimate interest is the credibility of recruitment figures. The National Housewives Register is palpably not of a kind with the National Union of Mineworkers in terms of recruitment success – quite apart from sanctions. In an industrial relations context, a group with much below half its potential membership would be suspect. Another factor which encourages recognition is realism in demands. In discussing a road lobby group recently, a civil servant argued to us that the group did not achieve maximum impact because 'their shopping list is so enormous that they have lost credibility'.

There are, then, economic limits to what can be pursued from the inside – no doubt there are also ideological limits. Ryan's study (1978) sets out to show how the group, Radical Alternatives to Prison (RAP), is given less access than the more establishment-oriented promotional group, the Howard League for Penal Reform. Undoubtedly, there was a difference in treatment by the Home Office – but it is difficult to see how RAP could be welcomed to 'frequent' contacts, as was the Howard League, when they set out to abolish prisons and disapproved of liberal reforms on the ground that 'reforms simply reinforced the system'.

Finer (1966, p. 99) wrote that there is clearly a relationship between access and good behaviour. The relationship does seem able to bear more publicity than Finer seemed to allow – the British Medical Association (BMA) was able to fight very publicly over the restricted list of NHS drugs proposed by the government in 1984, without fundamentally destabilizing relations. But there has to be some respect for confidentiality – and a group leadership with freedom to negotiate – before business can be done.

This categorization from the departmental view is well developed by Kogan (1975, p. 75) who used the terms 'legitimized' and 'non-legitimized' to discriminate between groups which 'have an accepted right to be consulted . . . before policies are authorized', and non-legitimized groups which have a different role which is to challenge accepted authority and institutions until policies are changed. Wolff (1965, p. 52) discusses interests 'outside the circle of the acceptable', and the sharp distinction in the public domain between legitimate interests and those which are beyond the pale. Dearlove (1973), in his work on politics at local government level, discusses helpful and unhelpful groups – a demarcation that corresponds to legitimate/illegitimate, in that helpfulness is seen from the viewpoint of the local authority. The helpful group is one which makes system-supportive demands. It is certainly true, as argued by Rhodes (1984), that in the interaction between groups and government, the power relation is 'asymmetric'. Central government has resources – of staff, finance, legitimacy – not available to other groups. However, the essence of the political community approach is that the fragmentation of government means that departmental loyalties are divided between their governmental 'hat' and their functional 'hat' – and links to their functionally related groups. The system-supportive group side-steps the implication of the asymmetry point. The group is not a supplicant at the door but a partner at the table.

Benewick (in Benewick, Berki and Parekh, 1973) also addressed himself to differential access as a means of categorizing the group world. His first category is of groups (sectional or promotional) 'whose access to the decision-makers is continuous, resources impressive, legitimacy established, and whose demands are considered to be mainly routine . . . when acting as pressure groups it is in their interest to maintain rather than disturb'. The TUC and CBI are outstanding examples. His third category consists of groups having no, or suspect, legitimacy. His second category is not clearly marked and seems to differ only by degree – the groups in the middle category have more limited resources than the first, and have intermittent access.

May and Nugent (1982) offer something that is superficially similar, in that they also feel it necessary to go beyond simple dichotomous classification and refer to 'insiders' and 'outsiders', and 'thresholders'. The thresholders 'are characterised by strategic ambiguity and oscillation between insider and outsider strategies'. In the previous chapter, we have noted that the TUC's current stance was characterized as 'a confusing combination of co-operation and conflict'. This was the sort of strategic ambiguity observed by May and Nugent. They differ from Benewick in establishing their central category more clearly – explaining why the pressures on certain groups make an unqualified insider role difficult. They also attempt to disaggregate the divisions of (1) group strategy from (2) group status (accorded by the decision-maker), from (3) the substance of group demands (that is, radical/moderate).

May and Nugent's concern to separate out dimensions and their observation that some groups cannot pursue an unreservedly insider strategy are useful points, but neither they nor the other authors reviewed, make a very convincing job of demolishing the sectional/ promotional starting-point. Nor does our own work encourage us that 'access' is as vital a dimension as some of the 'revisionists' suggest. In fact, our own interviews with civil servants convince us that groups must work pretty hard at ruling themselves out of consultative status: Civil servants – in their own words – 'prefer to shoot widely', or 'risk over-consulting'. While the key word in the language of the critics of pluralism is 'access', the fundamental issue is not who has access – which seems a rather devalued coin – but who has influence. In some exercises, we have counted very large numbers of participants, often hundreds, sometimes thousands of groups – but *who counts* is a much more vital matter.

There is ambiguity. Friends of the Earth (FoE) is a group which has perhaps consciously adopted outsider tactics. The FoE campaign director, Czech Conroy, recorded in a paper to the Royal Institute for Public Administration in 1981, how, when FoE was created in 1970, as a radical group it lacked what we can call 'insider resources'. It could not activate the 'old boy' network, numerical 'clout' and technical credibility. When FoE, in its early days, attempted to discuss the issue of non-returnable containers with Schweppes it did not receive a reply, but after 1,000 bottles were dumped outside Schweppes headquarters a meeting was arranged. This kind of deliberate 'event' attracts media attention; there is no news story when a small group meets a commercial company – but 1,500 bottles is a visual hook on which an environmental feature can be attached. In the ten years from 1971 to 1980 FoE organized more than thirty 'national demonstrations' and hundreds of local protests.

Friends of the Earth has continued to use this kind of open lobbying and have been suspicious of too close an embrace with government, but none the less 'the threshold' is more accurate a tag than simple outsider strategy. For example, when comments were not received from FoE on a consultation paper dealing with the labelling of appliances to show energy efficiency, it was telephoned and asked for its comments.

Friends of the Earth has also accepted invitations to sit on three departmental advisory committees – though it has declined other invitations. In 1974, through the intervention of the minister, Lord Melchett, it was invited on to the Waste Management Advisory Committee and they also serve on the Working Group on Land Wastes and the committee set up to review section 17 of the Control of Pollution Act. Friends of the Earth also has less formal dealings with civil servants, and several times a year will meet with groups of civil servants – at assistant secretary to deputy secretary level. Meetings with ministers have been less regular – depending on the bias and style of the individual minister.

Though, by the nature of their demands, FoE cannot expect

Type of group by goal

	SECTIONAL	PROMOTIONAL
LEGITIMATE or INSIDER	e.g. BMA NFU	e.g. Howard League for Penal Reform Disablement Income Group RSPCA
ILLEGITIMATE or OUTSIDER	e.g. National Union of Ratepayers' Association	e.g. CND Animal Liberation Front

Type of group by strategy

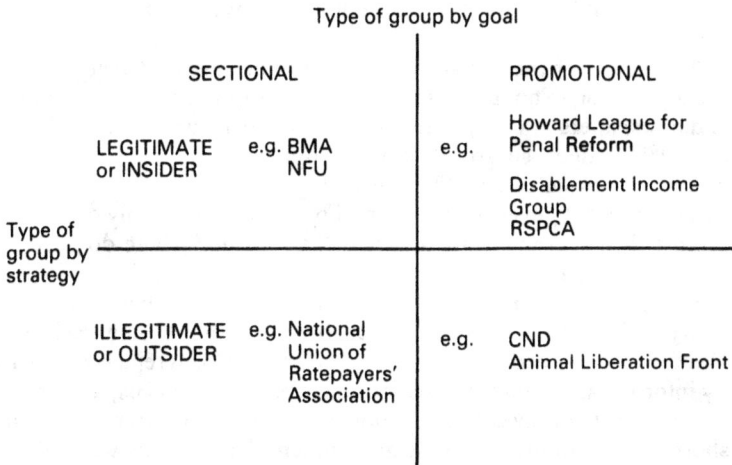

Figure 8.1   The goal/strategy mix.

clientele status – and nor have they sought it – there is still a choice between recognized spokesman status and outright outsiders. However, the fact that they have put some effort into lobbying and presenting evidence has apparently caused internal strains and produced some exits from the group in pursuit of more radical action (Ward in Marsh, 1984, p. 185).

The hunt by political scientists for methodological innovation has, arguably, refined rather than undermined the initial two-fold categorization. Our strongest working hypothesis is still that behaviour (strategy) will be linked to sectional or promotional type.

Just as some promotional groups are 'insiders', some representative bodies are 'outsiders' (especially when they lack economic clout or they fail to recruit a credible percentage of their potential membership – for example, the National Union of Ratepayers' Association, or various women's groups). Thus four main varieties of group are found as set out in Figure 8.1.

The usual non-technical understanding of the term 'pressure group' is probably something like CPAG, the Animal Liberation Front, or the Council for the Protection of Rural England. These would all count as being promotional groups and the fact is that most studies of pressure groups would see sectional groups as the significantly influential type. The instinctive response is to see pressure-group activities as the public protest, the petition, or the media event, whereas the most significant activities are probably insider consultation and negotiations – of the kind enjoyed by the sectional CBI,

NFU, or BMA – or even the promotional Howard League for Penal Reform.

The power of the pressure group is not usually to defeat governments – although on matters such as the imposition of VAT on books and newspapers in 1985, or the proposal to tax pension lump sums in the 1985 Budget, so great a political upheaval was caused that the Treasury was defeated. The 'normal' power, however, is often to determine what governments wish. To see the groups only operating against the government is to miss half the game. Where do governments find their ideas?

While 'pressure groups' suggests public, conflictual behaviour, the activity of most importance is probably quite the reverse. Eckstein (1960, p. 22) argued: 'The public campaign has been replaced largely by informal and unostentatious contacts between officials, and interest groups themselves have become increasingly bureaucratized (in short, more and more like the government departments with which they deal), for only bureaucratic structures are appropriate to the kinds of negotiations groups nowadays must carry on to realize their interests.'

If the British political process is one where 'elective dictatorship' (in Hailsham's phrase) is *not* practised and where rather (as the Head of the Civil Service, Sir Edward Bridges, observed in 1950), 'It is a cardinal feature of British administration that no attempt should be made to formulate a new policy in any matter without the fullest consultation with those who have practical experience in that field, and with those who will be called upon to carry it out', there is a difficulty with the expanding number of groups to be taken into account. The group density makes the formulation of policy that much more difficult.

As well as the problem of 'clutter' in consultation, the growing specialization of groups has, arguably, led to increased problems in settling conflict. The more specialized group (say, a single-commodity agriculture group) is less likely to take 'the broad view' than a group such as NFU which aggregates many aspects of the agriculture industry. Even more difficult to fit into consultative politics than the specialist group is perhaps the single-issue cause group that is now so prominent in American electoral politics. One US Congressman has been quoted as commenting in extreme fashion, 'Everyone who wants to get re-elected has to take 21 single issue groups worth 2·5 per cent each to build a majority'. As Obestar (1983, p. 618) has noted: 'If politics is the art of compromise, the single issue interest groups are often unwilling to play the game.' She quotes Hofstadter (1965), 'what is at stake [for such groups] is always a conflict between absolute good and absolute evil, and the quality needed is not a willingness to compromise but the will to fight things out to the finish'.

The growth of group numbers is difficult to prove empirically (it is difficult to count current examples – and almost impossible for earlier periods), but it is one of the few generalizations in politics that does not appear to have been challenged. In a limited number of cases, the groups can be seen to have been directly stimulated by the government – for example, the National Association for the Care and Re-settlement of Offenders (NACRO), MIND and the Royal Association for Disibility Rehabilitation (see Whiteley and Winyard, 1984, p. 41).

Sometimes the government produces a group complex without intending to. Eckstein (1960, p. 27) made the point that the development of interventionist government had generated groups in large numbers; that private associations now had much more to gain or lose from governmental decisions than in the past. He gave as examples: farmers with their incomes; doctors with the conditions in which they practise; businessmen with a host of matters, from capital issues to raw materials. He argues: 'In short we can usefully stand Bentley on his head to supplement Bentley right side up; if interaction among politically active groups produces policy, policy in turn creates politically active groups.' The former minister, Edmund Dell (1973, p. 30), has argued in a specific area, 'British governments have created not just aircraft and nuclear power plants but deeply entrenched interests that demand more and even more by way of resources if they are to be satisfied'. Extending the point, he later observed that governmental intervention distorted British commitments to aerospace and nuclear energy. It created vested interests 'which will employ highly articulate people who will lobby most effectively . . . when their usefulness in their present jobs has gone'.

The complexity that can rapidly develop in a policy area was exhibited when over 1,200 groups and organizations gave evidence to the Royal Commission on the National Health Service – many of these bodies were the product of the NHS itself and hence decisions on health matters in the 1970s were made in a more constraining group environment than the original decisions of the 1940s. In many circumstances, the issue is not of access by the group to departmental deliberations, but where the department might wish to steer, or at least support, the group activity. For example, the DHSS and DES send observers to the Cancer Education Co-ordination Group, and the Scottish Office is glad to have regular meetings with the Association of Building Control Officers to attempt to maintain consistency across the country and to pick up problems.

Some Theoretical Considerations

How groups are (or are not) in practice integrated into the British policy process is described more fully in Chapter 7. In this chapter we want to introduce some of the more important theoretical arguments which have emerged in the pressure-group literature.

Evidence of how decisions are made and the role of groups has accumulated. The aggregation has not, however, led to a consensus on how we should interpret the evidence of government/interest group relations. The main feature in the literature in recent years is the intellectual choice between pluralism and corporatism (see Chapter 1). If we see corporatism as the new paradigm in this area (as intended by Schmitter and Lehmbruch, 1979, p. 14), we are reminded of Ricci's summary of Kuhn's argument on paradigm shift – 'acceptance [of the paradigm] is a sociological event rather than a methodological step'. Ricci says (1984, p. 194): 'Thus, much as when individuals convert from one religious faith to another, a scientific "conversion experience" is not dependent upon "proof or error", ... at the moment of paradigm change, there can be no conventional proof that the new paradigm is really superior to the old'. Though Schmitter used the language of Kuhn, he none the less attempted to assert that his paradigm shift was empirically based.

The main point about the corporatist approach that we would reject is its claim to novelty. There is widespread and long-standing scholarly interest in close group relations with government. A recent survey of the USA concluded that studies are filled with references to sub-governments, policy sub-systems, iron triangles, or 'whirlpools of special social interests and problems' (Gais, Peterson and Walker, 1984). The burden of the argument of the survey is that Heclo's competing, looser concept of 'issue network' better fits the contemporary USA. The important point for us about the argument of Gais and his colleagues, and Heclo, is that in so far as trends can be identified they are away from structuring and regularity in policy-making (as expected by corporatism). The key word in the Heclo article is 'fragmented' rather than 'segmented'.

Heclo argues (1978, p. 105) that

> Social security, which for a generation has been quietly managed by a small circle of insiders becomes controversial and political. The Army Corps of Engineers, once the picture book example of control by subgovernments, is dragged into the brawl on environmental politics. The once quiet 'traffic safety establishment' finds its own safety permanently endangered by the consumer movement.

Similarly, Gais and his colleagues say (p. 162) 'But just as [the] vision of the American system as a frustrating maze of autonomous and impermeable iron triangles has become popular ... several scholars have begun to question its utility as a guide to the policy-making process'.

The argument rests on accepting Ripley and Franklin's idea (1976) that sub-governments thrive best in areas where politics is distributive – there is no direct conflict between groups. The cost payers of the policy (usually the general tax-payer) see no immediate cost link with the benefits distributed. Gais, Peterson and Walker argue that an increase in redistributional and regulatory issues has made the political system less segmented and 'cosy'. Relevantly, Steen (1985, p. 61) has noted – in a comparative study of the politics of agriculture – that 'The basically consensual agricultural policy-making in Norway and the UK is a consequence of the indirect distribution of burdens implied in the support schemes in the two countries. The state budget hides the essential relationship between the payer (the tax payer) and the payee (the farmer).' Certainly, the cosy embrace of government is less problematic when there are no obvious counter groups.

Writing in Britain in 1975, Mackenzie (p. 79) described policy-making in agriculture as less 'a lobby' and 'a pressure group' than a series of 'arenas' by commodity and by area. He likewise identified 'arenas' or 'communities' of the Health Service, of local authority associations, and so on. He noted that, like Indian castes, such communities cut 'through British government (to take the health case) from the House of Commons and its "specialist members" and consultative bodies, down through associations and structures to the Regional Health authorities, the Area Health Authorities, the Districts and the Family Practitioner Committees'. In fact, he uses the metaphor 'vertical mosaic'. Such a metaphor of complexity is necessary for contemporary policy-making. Different cases will deserve more or less rigid analogies; few would seem to merit the corporatist strait-jacket. The drift of the policy style in the USA and in Britain is hardly in the direction of corporatism.

However, the American case does more than give some backing to claims that policy-making is increasingly complex. It shows that sub-government, policy communities, segmentation, incorporation, sectorization – whatever label is preferred – can emerge without the centrally determined incomes policies and central tripartite (government, labour and employer) decision-making which are found in Europe. Our contention is that the factors which lead to segmentation need not be the same, or as demanding, as the attempt to control the economy through central agreement. In this connection Lehmbruch's recent distinction (in Goldthorpe, ed., 1984), between 'sectoral corporatism' and 'corporatist concertation' is important. The former concept seems very similar to the idea of sub-government/policy community. Even those who find no grounds for applying the notions of corporatist concertation, will readily recognize what Lehmbruch now calls 'sectoral corporatism'. If sectoral corporatism is merely segmentation, the specialization needed in modern policy-making will make it omnipresent. The specialized knowledge held by groups will encourage departments to build up relationships – as will a wish for support for the priorities of the department. In his classic *The Politics of the Budgetary Process* (1964, p. 66), Wildavsky wrote that informing 'one's clientele of the full extent of the benefits they receive may increase the intensity with which they support the agency's request'. The relationship between pressure group and department is by no means always one of unwanted pressure.

Another kind of issue in the pressure-group literature concerns the basis of membership. At one time, this was not an issue for debate. Self-evidently, a pressure group would exist when a number of people with shared interests joined together to further their cause. In the work of David Truman (1951), the two main scenarios for group emergence were: (1) there was an increasing specialization in society – which demands new and more specialized groups to cater for this; (2) that developments (for example, the creation of one group) will create disturbances which will (possibly) stimulate new counter-groups to create a new balance.

However, the publication of *The Logic of Collective Action* by Mancur Olson in 1965 uncovered a theoretical puzzle. Olson (p. 2) suggested that

> If the members of a large group rationally seek to maximise their personal welfare they will not act to advance their common or group objectives unless there is coercion to force them to do so, or unless some separate incentive, distinct from the achievement of the common group interest is offered to the members of the group individually on the condition that they will bear the costs or burdens involved in the achievement of the common group interest.

Thus Olson's economically derived model was suggesting that the rational actor would not join with like-minded others in support of a group, but would free-ride. He proposed that political activity is a 'by-product'. Successful groups exist for other purposes and members join for the selective (personal) benefit of these other services.

The significance of the Olson argument was that it attacked the comfortable pluralist assumption that some balance (albeit, rough and ready) existed in the group struggle. The group contest had been held to be a reasonably effective form of democracy since any significant interest would naturally aggregate and make itself felt. Olson's work questioned the 'automatic' mobilization of shared interests in group form.

The reaction to Olson has been voluminous and varied. Richard Kimber (1981), for example, has re-examined the claims of logic at the core of Olson's scheme and concludes that where there is doubt about the existence of the group (and the collective good) it is still rational for the individual to participate. Kimber's rule is: if the supply of the good is uncertain, join; if it is certain do not join. Later, with Keith Dowding (1984), Kimber also questions the selective good/collective good distinction which is so important for Olson's argument.

Whereas Kimber challenges Olson's interpretation of what is, or is not, logical, another approach has been to distinguish between the gains to the member and the gains to the organizer (or group entrepreneur). This line of argument is principally identified with Salisbury (1969) and Frohlich, Oppenheimer and Young (1971). This is yet another approach derived from economics, in that the organizer is presented as an entrepreneur who invests in a set of benefits which he or she offers to members in return for support. In Salisbury's article, the broad conclusion is that members join for benefits other than economic – notably, solidarity feelings or the opportunity for expressive action. Lobbying behaviour by entrepreneurs is presented not as stemming from member demands, but through the personal choice and values of the leaders.

Another dimension to the issue that has been filled out by empirical work is patronage. J. Walker (1983) extends a point made in Salisbury (1969) and shows that groups are often funded (at least in the US context) by patrons – even, of course, by government departments themselves seeking political support or administrative assistance. By acknowledging the patronage possibility, at least for some organizations, painstaking logical analysis about allocation of resources by members in deciding to join is made inappropriate. Salisbury (1984) makes another contribution to reducing the problem by noting that the conventional concept of the pressure group (for example, RSPCA, NUT) omits individual corporations, state and local governments, universities, think tanks and most other institutions of the private sector. Likewise unnoticed, he says, are the multitudes of Washington representatives, free-standing and for hire, including lawyers, public relations firms and diverse others. This important reminder of the non-membership basis of many actors in the pressure politics process, again means that for large numbers of groups Olson's objections are scarcely relevant.

A final point which can be raised in rebuttal of Olson is that the economic decision is often so trivial that the rigorous rules of logic which are set out are inappropriate. Our instinct is to say that long before any economic borderline decisions have to be made the costs of strict analysis exceed the benefits and time will not be spent in reckoning on the margins. In a major study of why companies in Leeds join their local Chamber of Commerce, R. King (1985) concluded that firms paid their subscriptions with very little thought, as these were, in business terms, low. Many respondents (one-quarter) had no idea why their firm was in membership, others felt that what was important was 'being part of business life' or 'wanting to be involved in the business community'.

This might be an explanation for the (in Olson's terms) theoretically unexpected emergence of the public-interest-type group in the 1970s – most conspicuously in the USA with groups such as the Sierra Club, Common Cause, and the Consumers' Union. For the largely middle-class membership, the subscription of $20 or less might be a marginal consideration – and well worthwhile in terms of the emotional rewards of 'doing the right thing'.

The most sophisticated work in the group literature has been critical of the pluralist assumption that group conflict is a reasonable means to establish a practical interpretation of the public interest. However, the corporatist literature – with its picture of a political system that is hierarchical, simple and disciplined – seems at odds with empirical work that far more often discovers tendencies to bureaucratic accommodation and stability under threat from newly mobilized groups. The highly influential Olson work has faced its own problem of logic. Why did lobbying groups mushroom when the theoretical argument was against such 'selfless' behaviour?

PART THREE

Allocation and Implementation

CHAPTER NINE

Budgetary Politics

Introduction

Few public policies can be implemented without public expenditure. In turn, public expenditure cannot take place unless a government raises finance through general taxation, specific charges, or through borrowing. This simple and perfectly obvious fact is the foundation for a huge, complex political process within the government machine for deciding on resource allocation. Equally, it gives rise to a complex process of bargaining between government and outside groups. A glance at any daily newspaper reveals the constant pressure by groups, individuals, public agencies and the media for more public spending on their particular policy areas. In the process leading to the Budget, a 'Schedule of Representations' is compiled by the Treasury, listing all the suggestions received. This will typically have 400–500 items. The demand for spending is infinite, although the willingness to pay for it in the form of taxation is not. Moreover, the process of 'getting and spending' (Pliatzky, 1984) is conducted in the context of an environment in which ideology and economic theory are at times influential.

Thus, the student of the British resource allocation process should not expect to see a process of objective, rational decision-making at work. The fact that the process is highly politicized, that bargains are struck, that U-turns are made, that targets are not met, and that an extended network of actors is involved in the resource allocations process, should not surprise us. The process is one of bargaining and bidding. For example, when Joel Barnett (1982, p. 126) was Chief Secretary at the Treasury he discovered that, on a certain issue, the Department of the Environment would ask for £600 million, it might then settle for £400 million and it might even go down to £230 million. He calls this the Persian bazaar style of negotiation. With regard to the financial limits for British Railways in 1974, he started by offering the Minister for Transport £1,000 million when the minister wanted £2,000 million. All along he knew his final figure would be £1,500 million.

In another example Barnett (p. 103) says:

> It turned out that John Morris, Secretary of State for War, was the luckiest Minister in that we did not reach his programme until late in the proceedings. I asked for £30 million, but because we were already so near our target, Jim [the Prime Minister] asked John for an offer. He raised £5 million and to his astonishment had it promptly accepted. I had no doubt that he was ready to be pushed to £20 million. I had one last try . . . but the Prime Minister pushed it aside – it was nearly lunchtime.

As we have argued in Chapter 6, spending ministers tend to 'fight their own corner'. Heclo and Wildavsky (1981, pp. 135–6) wrote:

> This rule of ministerial advocacy knows no party boundaries . . . The tendency was put to the test in 1970. Few governments can have started out more devoted to government economy . . . But a year later the economising Minister of Education, like other Conservative spending ministers, could be found in the usual political operation of commending herself to a client audience citing increased spending. 'I have,' she said, 'done everything possible to show my confidence in the future of higher education. In my monthly battles with the Treasury, I managed to get another £76 million for student grants and last week announced the biggest ever development programme for further education and the polytechnics.'

The Minister was, of course, Margaret Thatcher in a spending minister role.

Why should we expect resource allocation policies to be any less politically determined than other public policies – such as education, health, or transport? Without wanting to exaggerate the importance of national policy styles, one might expect 'getting and spending' decisions to be made in similar ways to other decisions. Thus if Parliament is relatively weak in the areas of, say, education or defence policies, then we should not expect it to be very effective in influencing the raising and spending of money – even though constitutionally and historically it appears to have a central role. If policies normally change only incrementally, why should we expect governments to make very big changes in the allocation of resources between programmes or in the way in which revenue is raised?

This is *not* to suggest that changes do not take place. For example, as we shall see in later sections of this chapter, Mrs Thatcher's government, elected in 1979, has managed to change significantly the balance of spending *between* programmes, with the reductions in spending on housing and education used to pay for increases in defence and other policy areas, such as unemployment benefit. The Thatcher government has attempted to disprove the British conventional wisdom that the spending process was merely about adjustments at the margin. (This view that economic change was essentially on the fringe of budgets was summed up by one permanent secretary quoted by Heclo and Wildavsky [1981, p. 22] who said, 'Ninety-eight per cent of the expenditures are committed. All we did is mess about at the margins.')

Resource Allocation Mechanisms

The most famous landmark in the present system of resource allocation was the Report of the Plowden Committee in 1961 (Cmnd 1432). Prior to that report, there were two main budgetary weaknesses. First, decisions were taken in isolation, one from the other, with little sense of aggregated consequences. Secondly, decisions were taken on a single-year basis – ignoring their long-term financial consequences. Thus a project could be approved because the relatively low start-up costs could be met – but this meant that in subsequent years the higher costs would be an inherited obligation. The Sixth Report of the former Estimates Committee of the House of Commons in 1958 (HC 254–1), followed by the Plowden Committee Report, brought fundamental changes in the expenditure process – essentially that a more co-ordinated view should be developed with a planning horizon of several years ahead. Thus the Public Expenditure Survey Committee (PESC) process was adopted.

There were two main aspects of PESC to meet the two weaknesses identified above. First, within the annual cycle there was an attempt to secure agreement on the desirable spending total. Then, in theory, the normal spending minister requests would have to take place within this ceiling. Boyd-Carpenter (1980, p. 162) who had been a Conservative Chief Secretary to the Treasury, suggested that the underlying PESC aim was to look at claims for spending together. He neatly claims that the effect was rather similar to that type of hotel menu from which one can choose eggs, or fish, or meat, but only one main dish.

The second PESC aspect was to examine future commitments in the context of future resources. An estimate of future growth in the economy (and tax revenue) is made to ensure that programmes of spending could be contained within these totals. It had been noted that there was a 'scissors problem' in which the public spending graph was still increasing – while the GDP was flatter. Apart from the financial consequences of paying for more and more public services as a greater proportion of income, at various points it was argued that liberal democracy and the mixed economy were threatened – by a change in the nature of the economic regime. The PESC comparison of revenue horizons and spending commitments was intended to prevent an upward drift of spending. Certainly, a government could decide under the PESC system to consciously increase public spending, but at least accidental increases were now supposed to be avoidable.

The Public Expenditure Survey Committee is thus an interdepartmental committee, chaired by a Treasury official and consisting of other civil servants (departmental finance officers). The objective of PESC is to produce a picture of spending patterns in the future (currently, 1985, three years ahead) if existing programmes were to continue. Ideally, ministers will then be able to take key policy decisions, according to the government's policy priorities, in the light of these projections. Understanding the annual nature of the cycle makes sense of the annual pattern of newspaper headlines. It is in the late summer that departments bid for their resources and leaks of Whitehall battles occur. However, both of the supposed strengths of PESC have run into trouble.

The notion of a rational, considered, collective allocation at Cabinet, in line with agreed targets, has been frustrated. As Heclo and Wildavsky describe it (1981, p. 238), what has resulted is 'incrementalism to the n'th power'. They support this view by noting that 'If PESC helps prevent departments from going beyond established bands, it also commits the Treasury in public to keeping their expenditure going at the projected rate. Both sides find it more difficult to depart from the historical base.' Incrementalism is also reinforced, they say, by making each department more conscious of its own fair share of the total. Thus, they argue, 'fair play [in Cabinet] can easily come to mean equal marginal changes . . . PESC has simply enforced an earlier tendency for each dog to get its share . . . Each permanent secretary can test his virility for next year by seeing whether he got the required x plus percentage like everybody else.'

If PESC as a facility for central political choice and priorities has been distorted to provide a broad guarantee of departmental equality, then its claimed virtue of matching future resources to future plans has also been frustrated. Joel Barnett illustrates the problem when he observed that in the 1974 White Paper it was assumed that GDP would grow at 7 per cent per annum in 1973–9. Spending plans were allowed which matched this growth. But, as the growth never materialized at anything like this rate, growth in services could not be financed without tax increases. This overestimation was not a single-year instance. Indeed, it is difficult for a government to be other than optimistic about growth – their policies are self-evidently bound to succeed.

Therefore, far from producing a new realism about what could be afforded, the PESC forecast of growth tended to overestimate future resources, and spending commitments were entered into which were to be financed by growth which never materialized.

Maurice Wright (1980, pp. 89–92), in an excellent review of the development of PESC, has highlighted another aspect in suggesting that 'since its inception, PESC has comprised elements of five processes: planning, allocating, controlling, evaluating, and accounting' and that the relative importance attached to them has changed over time. He sees an important change in the public expenditure process after 1974/5. Prior to that date, it was assumed that borrowing would fill any gap between expenditure and resources. Thus in Wright's view, public expenditure financing played a *subordinate* role (our emphasis) which changed after 1974/5 when the scale of the Public Sector Borrowing Requirement (it increased very rapidly indeed – by 85 per cent between April 1974 and April 1977) became one of *the* key issues in the process.

This shift in attitude to borrowing is a particularly dramatic illustration of a point which we raised earlier, namely, that ideologies and theories influence policies. The point is neatly captured by Wright (1980, p. 92) when he argues:

> In contrast to the 1960s and the early years of the 1970s, the financing of the resources allocated to the public sector, or pre-empted by it, had become a crucial factor in deciding its share *vis-à-vis* other claims, for example, private investment, privately financed consumption, and in deciding how those resources are to be allocated within the public sector, for example, decisions to reduce certain programmes, maintain some at about the same level and increase others.

A radically different dimension has now been introduced into the politics of resource allocation. 'Getting and spending' is not just simply a process of bargaining between departments (supported by their respective client groups) and the Treasury, with the government then agreeing to find the necessary resources by taxing and borrowing, but it is also heavily influenced by the perceived need to control the Public Sector Borrowing Requirement.

Events from 1974/5 onwards have placed the system under very considerable strain – sufficient for Wright (1977, p. 143) to argue in an earlier article that there was a 'crisis of control'. In that article he suggested that, 'Whereas it was possible to claim in 1973 that PESC was the most sophisticated budgeting system in the world, today [1977] it is difficult to resist the contention of a former senior economic adviser to the Treasury that public expenditure is neither planned nor controlled'. Heclo and Wildavsky's second edition of *The Private Government of Public Money* (1981) was less flattering to PESC than their 1974 version. They play down PESC as a planning process and assert, 'If the budget could not keep up with a changing world there was nothing left but to keep changing the budget' (p. xvi). Instead of Britain being presented as *the* example of a sophisticated budgetary approach, they now present Britain's 'repetitive budgeting' in the same breath as their description of the desperate budgetary improvisions of an underdeveloped country – 'the budget is not made once and for all when estimates are submitted and approved; rather as the process of budgeting is repeated it is made and remade over the course of the year' (p. xvii).

The causes of this failure to control expenditure are complex. One factor considered above which has been of tremendous importance, whatever the intention of PESC as an instrument of *selective* choice, is that, as already mentioned, 'ministers fight their corner'. In Wright's terms (1977, p. 153),

It is difficult for the Treasury to resist the individual and collective pressure of ministers to maintain and improve the level of service provision in their programmes. Ministers find it easier to surrender putative cuts in the planned rate of growth of expenditure on their programmes for the distant years four and five in the expectation that such cuts can be re-negotiated and, with a little luck, restored, in two or three years time.

It was this practice of 'unreal' cuts in years four and five that forced the Conservatives to shorten the effective time horizon of the operation to three years.

The other major reform in the PESC process was the introduction of 'cash limits' by the Labour government in 1975/6 (see Wright, 1977, and Cmnd 6440, 1976). The central concept of the cash limit was that departments could not complete programmes agreed (that is, volume) even if costs rose – there was no automatic re-pricing. They were allowed to spend fixed sums (though for some programmes – most importantly unemployment – spending had to be open-ended: the government could not just stop paying unemployment benefit when a growing number of claimants exhausted the kitty). The controversy over cash limits was over the assumptions of levels of inflation and pay increases built into the cash limit. Politically, it would be impossible for the government to say that we expect x inflation and y pay settlements: instead of their best estimate of what *would* happen, they again substituted their optimistic targets of what they would *like* to happen. A more technical problem was that inflation in the areas where departments are operating can be different (usually greater) from the normal run of inflation. Thus the normal x per cent increase for defence might be inadequate if inflation in that sector was running at $x + 10$ per cent.

Thus Heald (1983, p. 194) concludes: 'By setting cash limits incorporating (impossible) factors which were much below actual inflation rates, the volume of expenditure could be squeezed without ever making explicit how large cuts were planned.' Heald goes on to point out that another consequence of the cash limit was that, as managers conservatively kept within budget, they actually underspent. This phenomenon underlies subsequent criticism that the Labour government cut more harshly than it intended: managers in practice failed to spend as much as ministers intended. Heclo and Wildavsky (1981, p. xl) say that the underspending in 1977/8 was nearly £4 billion – double the cuts that caused such anguish to the Cabinet the previous year. (Cash planning has replaced cash limits – the effects are similar.)

The operation of PESC is thus far from being a simple and uncontroversial process. There is political choice in the use to which PESC is put (control or planning) and there is politics within PESC as departments attempt to maximize their resources. Joel Barnett's account of his period as a Treasury minister gives an inside view of how the politics of the process is more important than procedural mechanics. Thus he gives an account (1982, p. 131) of struggles over pensions increases in 1977:

> David Ennals had asked for pensions increases of £2.50 single, £4 married, and I had offered £2 and £3.20. The difference in expenditure in a full year was a hefty £310 million. I felt strongly that we had done well by pensions, while those in work had seen their real earnings fall. Feeling so strongly, I used every conceivable argument, including the normally clinching line that what was a modest amount to pensions would be a substantial claim on the Contingency Reserve, limiting the claims of other Ministers, including some that would be politically popular. It did not wholly work, and it did not surprise me too much that a majority opted for the inevitable compromise, costing £99 million in a full year.

This very political view of economic decisions is endorsed by two of the top civil servants of the past decade. Sir Leo Pliatzky (1985, p. 2) has quoted his former Treasury colleague, Sir Douglas Wass, as saying that when it comes to dividing government spending between the various expenditure programmes, decisions were governed by two well-entrenched principles. The first was 'as things have been, so shall they remain'; and the second was 'he who has the muscle gets the money'.

In this game of resource allocation, well-established tactics have been identified – with a new language to describe them. Howard Glennerster's list of techniques (in Hood and Wright, eds, 1981) can be summarized as:

POLITICAL RATIONALITY: OPENING GAMBITS

'Fairy gold' – cuts in the future (which can perhaps be restored later).

'Sore thumbs' – offering up cuts which it is hoped colleagues will find so drastic they will restrain you.

'Sell your assets'.

'Charge' – often what is presented as a cut in the press when a user charge is established or increased, is a departmental way of *preserving* the service. An extension of this charging is when whole new sources of finance can be found by some organizations. Thus a large part of the increase in engineering students in British universities are overseas students who are a new source of revenue.

'Cut capital, not current spending' – capital cuts are often politically easier to do. The life of an existing building or road due to be replaced can always be stretched – and deferral of capital schemes does not mean sacking and direct controversy.

'Protect the base' – the instinct is to conserve the existing. Hence new programmes or improvements are likely to suffer before the existing is affected.

POLITICAL RATIONALITY: REAL CUTS

'Equal pain for all' – is easier to 'sell' than discriminate against particular targets.

'Rough justice' – arguments with little intellectual credibility are accepted.

'Cut bureaucracy' – politicians might wish to pursue administrative cuts, but such available cuts seldom match the scale of the problem. The bureaucrats who are 'available' to cut (as a corollary of 'protect the base') are planners, researchers, and so on – rather than mainstream administrators.

'Cut someone else's budget, not your own' – for example, central government has tried to cut local government spending.

'Cut by cash limit' – the cuts then appear accidental when inflation exceeds forecast.

'Shift public burdens onto private costs' – for example, returning the mentally-ill to the community has the financial appeal of transferring a burden from the state to the affected families.

PROFESSIONAL AND BUREAUCRATIC RATIONALITY

'Defend professional demarcations' – responding to the threat of cuts, the professional response is a series of defensive reactions that mean that instead of greater efficiency, cuts produce lower efficiency.

'Professional restrictive practices' – the mood of threats of cuts is unlikely to gain professional co-operation in reshaping their service (for example, teaching in 1985).

'Beggar thy neighbour' – departments try to pass their problems elsewhere, just as central government passes cuts on to local government, health authorities and other bodies try to pass on clients elsewhere, for example, to local authority social services departments.

'The presumption of organizational immortality' – in cut-back management, the last option appears to be to terminate an activity, for example, close a department in a university. As Glennerster says, 'if public authorities and their duties never die but merely work on reduced funds, their effectiveness must suffer'.

Barnett (1982, pp. 60–2) also gives an example of the external pressures which may lead to a resource allocations process which is more political than rational. In identifying the 'what' and 'who' which influenced budgets he writes:

As to the 'what', the economic and financial environment was naturally the most important, even if it later became clear that the environment was very different from what we had been led to believe. As to the 'who', the TUC came very close to the top of the list. We always ticked off which of their requests we had been able to meet, if only partially.

The specific example of pensions is cited:

Public expenditure priorities were often determined by the strength of pressure from the TUC. Thus we were pledged, largely due to pressure from Jack Jones, General Secretary of the Transport and General Workers Union, first to increase retirement pensions to £10 for a single person, and £16 for a married couple, then to index them . . .

He goes on to explain that if the government had not accepted this commitment, it might not have retained the support of the unions. This clearly worried Barnett who reflects that

> democracy is also about representing the views of those for whom you are elected to speak. The public expenditure policies we were asked to implement did not have the backing of the ordinary trade unionist, particularly with regard to their total cost and its consequences for personal income tax.

Here we see a Labour government having to compromise its policy objectives in order to retain the support of key interests. And not only the unions have influence. Brian Sedgemore (1980, p. 35) has argued that Labour ministers in 1974–9 readily accepted that the City and the CBI had a 'corporate state' veto over such issues as the upper limits of the Public Sector Borrowing Requirement (PSBR) and related areas. This is not, of course, a literal veto, but a realization among all involved that should the City not like the figures, then a sterling crisis could result, interest rates could be pushed up and generally a set of adverse consequences could result that would be better avoided.

In a similar way, for electoral reasons, Mrs Thatcher's government has found it necessary to compromise with its backers – for example, the climb down on student grants, in response to pressure from middle-class parents in 1984 – in order to retain essential political support notwithstanding the government's strategic objectives of reducing public expenditure. The revolt by Conservative activists, in response to the effects of the 1984 rating revaluation in Scotland, forced the Secretary of State for Scotland to find an extra £90 million in order to mitigate the most severe effects of the increases on small businesses and households. The Secretary of State was also successful in defending a continued subsidy to Prestwick airport (which happened to be located in his own constituency), notwithstanding clear evidence that the airport is considered by many to be a white elephant. He was also successful in defending the continuation of the Ravenscraig steelworks for fear of reducing the Conservative vote in Scotland still further, if Ravenscraig was allowed to close as the British Steel Corporation wished.

This 'bargaining model' of resource allocation suggests that the process is indeed very similar to other policy processes. Colin Thain (1984) has argued that, because the Treasury has to bargain both within and outside Whitehall, it is quite wrong to lay the blame for Britain's economic decline at the Treasury's door. Authors like Pollard (1982) have suggested that the Treasury bears a heavy responsibility for Britain's decline. In contrast, writers such as Blank have seen the Treasury as but one actor in a complex process of bargaining. Blank's view, quoted by Thain, is that the Treasury is as much the *victim* of policy consensus (in that case the maintenance of sterling at the expense of domestic investment) as it was the creator of the consensus (Thain, 1984, pp. 584–5). Thain rightly emphasizes the degree to which the Treasury is influenced by 'outside agencies, such as other departments and interest groups'. In Thain's view (p. 592):

Public expenditure policies provide a good case study of how pressure group activities constrain governments. Politicians and civil servants have been influenced by many interest groups which have grown to defend existing programmes and extend the scope of government activity. This is one of the most important factors which has made it difficult for the Treasury to reduce spending even when committed to do so. (See also Wright, 1977, p. 152)

A picture of resource allocation as essentially bargained, reduces the significance of the technical developments such as PESC, cash limits, and the introduction of new evaluation techniques (see later section of this chapter). However refined the system of resource allocation might be, politics cannot be squeezed out of this system. In a battle between votes and technical procedures, votes usually win.

Power relationships can, of course, change over time, as ideology and the 'consensus' on economic policy change over time. Heclo and Wildavsky (1981, pp. 35–6) note the importance of 'political climate' over spending policies. In the period 1979–84 the Treasury was obviously operating in a more favourable climate for achieving cutbacks. However, by early 1985, with falling electoral support for the Conservative government – and with growing demands by the TUC, the CBI, and Conservative back-benchers for more 'infrastructure' expenditure – the climate appeared to be moving against the Treasury again. As we turn to the experience of the Thatcher government, it is useful to quote Thain's judgement (1984, p. 594) of the overall record of a government more determined than any in the postwar period to reduce public expenditure:

Despite severe cutting exercises between May 1979 and July 1983, the public expenditure targets have been remorselessly raised during the course of the strategy. The original MTFS (i.e. Medium Term Financial Strategy) documents projected a three and a half per cent *fall* in the planning total in cost terms over the period 1979–80 for 1983–84. In practice, the total has *risen* by over five per cent. (See also Chapter 4)

By mid-1985, observers were noting that the 'squeezers' were themselves under pressure and on the defensive in Mrs Thatcher's Cabinet – the 'wets' became the 'consolidators'.

Labour and Conservative Governments and the Politics of Resource Allocation

Mrs Thatcher's government, elected in May 1979, came to office determined to radically change the course of economic policy. There is no doubt that she herself was absolutely determined that the image of the 'Iron Lady', which the Russians had helped to create in response to her defence policy whilst in Opposition, would be carried through to reality on the domestic as well as on the foreign front.

A clear indication of the new government's primary objective emerged at least two and a half years before the election itself. A much-publicized statement of Conservative policy, in October 1976, stated that one of the main aims was *'to enable the country to live within its means, through the reduction and control of public expenditure and rebuilding of a healthy and thriving mixed economy in which taxes can be lower and profits can fulfill their proper function'* (*The Right Approach*, 1976, p. 8; our emphasis). The linchpin of the strategy was the view that public spending cuts were essential if 'we are to bring the economy into balance, and avoid an explosion of the money supply and an acceleration of the rise in prices'. The cuts, it was admitted, would in some cases lead to reductions in the scale of public services.

It is important to note that the deep concern over levels of public expenditure was in fact not significantly out of line with the prevailing climate of opinion in Britain – indeed, as we shall see below, a reduction of public expenditure levels was, by then, a policy of the incumbent *Labour* government itself. The 'crowding-out hypothesis' – which suggested that the public sector was consuming too large a part of the Gross Domestic Product – linked up with a liberal article of faith that the market could (by definition) use resources more effectively. The Conservatives felt that their desire to reduce public expenditure was supported by 'politicians and informed opinion across a very wide political spectrum' (*The Right Approach*, 1976, p. 8). An important aspect of the Conservatives' support for monetarism was their belief that 'natural' initiative was being throttled by the regulatory demands of the modern state and by the financial demands made in support of that state.

The philosophical underpinnings were perhaps best articulated in the argument in support of the Enterprise Zones – which were to be the jewel in the crown of neo-liberal economics (see Jordan, 1984a). Sir Geoffrey Howe, for one, had argued about 'legislative pollution' reducing national wealth and how 'every new law, every new regulation, every new code of practice can involve the community in *some* net cost'. (Howe, 1977). A Conservative Political Centre document of Autumn 1978 claimed that if a socialist government remained in office, unemployment could reach 2·5 million in the 1980s! It quoted Sir Keith Joseph's speech in the Commons in 4 July 1978 when he asked, 'Where are the aspirations to full employment which used to be the basis of the Labour Party appeal to the country . . .? All we have is a whole series of failed panaceas.' Among the reasons identified as leading to high unemployment were high taxes which had been used to fund 'unreal' schemes such as the Temporary Unemployment Subsidy.

In fact, this belief that tinkering with natural forces *cost* jobs was not unique to the Conservative Party. Joel Barnett has claimed (1982, p. 46): 'Many of the decisions taken to save jobs, in the short term . . . will probably be ineffective in saving jobs long term while doing serious damage in economic and industrial terms.'

A clear policy *theory* lay behind the Thatcher government's determination to cut public expenditure (which would allow reduced personal taxation), and to reduce regulation – namely, that these changes would unleash a great surge of enterprise and initiative in Britain which would, in turn, lead to the rapid economic growth (and job creation) which had eluded us for a quarter of a century. As we have seen, leading Conservatives (particularly Mrs Thatcher) were convinced by the theory that once taxation reached a certain level, a strong disincentive to work resulted. This is, of course, a theory about which there is much debate. In 1984 *Public Money*, for example, suggested to the contrary that 'It cannot be taken for granted that higher taxes make people less willing to work, . . . They may even act as a stimulus to future effort, in the case of those striving to attain a particular post-tax income.'

It is important to emphasize the fundamental significance of this tax-cut belief. It initially led the new government, elected in 1979, to pursue quite contradictory policies – namely, the financing of the reduction of direct personal taxation by increasing indirect taxation, thus pushing up the rate of inflation, notwithstanding the fact that, as a government, another of its primary objectives was to reduce the rate of inflation.

The Conservatives' approach was thus firmly rooted in two linked theories: (1) that excessive growth in the money supply (resulting from excessive public expenditure) caused inflation; (2) that there was a direct link between people's efforts and their levels of personal taxation. The two policy theories were prominent in the Conservative general election manifesto and in Mrs Thatcher's campaigning for the May 1979 general election. Their presentation was in classic nineteenth-century Liberal terms, with Mrs Thatcher's own brand of populist overtones. Thus her foreword to the manifesto argued that:

> No one who has lived in this country during the last five years can fail to be aware of how the balance of our society has been increasingly tilted in favour of the state at the expense of individual freedom. This election may be the last chance we have to reverse that process, to restore the balance of power in favour of the people.

In specific policy terms the manifesto repeated the pledge to master inflation by 'proper monetary discipline', with publicly stated targets for the rate of growth of the money supply. A gradual reduction in the size of the government's borrowing requirement was also argued to be vital:

> The state takes too much of the nation's income; its share must be steadily reduced. When it spends and borrows too much, taxes, interest rates, prices and unemployment rise so that in the long run there is less wealth with which to improve our standard of living and our social services . . . We shall cut income tax at all levels and reward hard work, responsibility and success.

The problem with home economics writ large and government by homily is not only that it might be more difficult to do than suggested, but that the complexities of a national economy might not be contained in the advice of Micawber. Thus Heald (1983, p. 54) points out that the ramifications of, say, cutting educational expenditure in order to cut PSBR by £1,000 million are complex:

> Although such a policy would reduce outlays on that programme, there may be repercussions upon other programmes. Within a welfare state, displaced employees have automatic entitlements to a wide range of cash and kind benefits . . . lower expenditure on education will be accompanied by higher expenditure on certain other programmes, notably social security. Furthermore, the Exchequer will lose income tax revenue and, if the spending of these now unemployed falls, indirect tax revenues as well . . .
> The net improvement in the PSBR of a £1,000 million reduction in public expenditure programmes such as education will be far smaller than that figure. It is even possible that in the first year the net effect might be negative [that is, cost more than it saves].

One of the greatest ironies here is that a tough radical image has been presented when, in fact, what the Conservatives were advocating was, in principle, little different from the policies of the Labour government which was defeated in the House of Commons on 28 March 1979. The broad economic strategy of Mrs Thatcher's government is, to a considerable degree, an example of *policy succession* rather than *radical policy change* (Hogwood and Peters, 1983). Thus Denis Healey as Labour Chancellor of the Exchequer had been trying to implement just the type of policies which the Conservatives now advocate – that is, a strict monetary policy, with published monetary targets, cash limits in the public sector and a policy of trying to reduce personal taxation in order to increase incentives.

The later years of the 1974–9 Labour government look strikingly similar to the Conservative government since 1979 (see Table 9.1 below). For example, in July 1976 Denis Healey announced that the growth in the PSBR would be held at £9,000 million. In doing so, cuts in aid to industry, defence, health and social services, food subsidies, and local authority loans would be made, and all new local authority housing contracts were to be frozen. By September 1976 the government was seeking additional credit of £2,300 million from the International Monetary Fund and, in December 1976, Mr Healey announced public spending cuts of £2,500 million over two years.

Interestingly, in the context of the current debate on the Conservative government's privatization policies, the Labour government discovered similar attractions. As Joel Barnett (1982, p. 102) reports:

> On the public expenditure side, however, we were boosted by the success we had achieved on our firm control of public expenditure. Even that most perceptive economic journalist, Sam Brittan, had not spotted some of our intended non-deflationary cuts. These involved our plans to re-finance export credits; replace local authority loans counting as public expenditure with building society loans that were not; and sell BP shares that we had bought when saving Burmah Oil.

By the 1978 Budget, the Labour government was looking even more like a Conservative government with the introduction of a £2,500 million tax cut. The tax cuts were seen as a way of encouraging pay moderation and as increasing incentives to industry. There was continued emphasis on the PSBR. The government was anxious to claim credit for the fact that the PSBR forecast was 5 per cent of GDP – 'a long way below the 1975–76 peak of 9 per cent' (*Treasury Economic Progress Report*, No. 97, April 1978, p. 4). The monetarist philosophy of the Labour government was clearly evident in July 1978 when the Treasury published a review of the British economy since 1945. It pointed out that an accommodating monetary policy in

1972 and 1973 (both years of Conservative government) had permitted a rapid expansion of the money supply which contributed towards the subsequent further acceleration in inflation in the period from 1973 to 1978 (*Treasury Economic Progress Report*, No. 100, July 1978, p. 4). Following this experience, it said,

> the focus of monetary policy is now specifically the control of the money supply for which a formal target – in the form of a preferred range for annual growth – was announced in 1976. Control of the money supply, in helping to rebuilt a climate of confidence and stability in financial markets and to reduce expectations of future increases in prices, is now seen as one of the two main strands of counter inflation policy, the other being policy in pay and prices.
> [Italics added]

This statement, with the exception of the reference to pay and prices, could equally have been issued by Mrs Thatcher's government some three years later (and even on the question of pay policy the Thatcher government has had *de facto* pay 'norms' for the public sector). Mr Healey's money supply target for the year ending April 1979 was in the range of 8–12 per cent. By December 1981 the Conservative government was predicting a growth in money supply for 1982/3 of 11 per cent. In January 1982 it had to admit that sterling M3 (one of the indices) had increased by 12 per cent in the first ten months of the target period – equivalent to an annual rate of 15 per cent (though the figures were still being distorted by the effects of a civil service dispute in 1981). By April 1985 the government was still hopeful of reducing the money supply, but the actual figures showed that the outcome for sterling M3 in 1983/4 had been a growth of 9·9 per cent and for 1984/5 was still estimated to be 9·5 per cent. Yet optimistic projections were still produced in the Budget of that year, suggesting that the annual rate of growth in M3 would fall to between 2 per cent and 6 per cent by 1988/9. By then, the use of M3 as an indicator of the rate of growth in the money supply was being de-emphasized, with a new definition of money supply, 'narrow money' – MO – being thought to be rather more useful. It will come as no surprise to learn that the use of the new indicator suggested that the government's monetary policy had been much more successful!

We should therefore be extremely cautious in accepting the popular view that the Thatcher government did, in fact, represent a *radical* departure from previous economic policy in the UK. Apart from its lack of a prices policy and the fact that its pay policy only applied to the public sector, it is more accurate to see Mrs Thatcher and her chancellors as continuing the broad outlines of economic strategy as attempted by her predecessor Mr Callaghan and his

Chancellor, Mr Healey. In practice, it is difficult to see the discontinuity which the adversary model of British politics might suggest.
One minor, if characteristic, example is defence spending. One of the
'leaks' from the Ministry of Defence in 1980 apparently came from a
civil servant 'infuriated at the Thatcher government publicly pos-
turing as more "patriotic" than Labour, while secretly cutting
Labour's own budgetary projections' (Leigh, *Observer*, 3 March
1985). The 1980 plans were, in fact, £189 million *below* Labour's
projections. (Of course, Labour might also have had to slash its
projections – but the simple notion of Conservative *increases* in
defence spending is indeed too simple.) It is to the practical experience of the Thatcher government that we now turn.

Mrs Thatcher's Government in Practice

Sir Geoffrey Howe announced his first Budget on 12 June 1979. The
Budget statement was entirely consistent with earlier Conservative
statements. The new policy was presented as a complete change in
attitude towards the way in which the economy worked. It was
designed to remove the constraints imposed by the tax systems and by:

> the unduly large role previously played by government – releasing
> initiative and enterprise. The government's policy will be to
> establish sound money through firm monetary discipline, and fiscal
> policies consistent with it, including strict control over public
> expenditure. (*1979 Economic Progress Report*, No. 110, p. 1)

Direct taxes (mainly income tax) were cut by £3·5 billion with
consequent increases of £2·5 billion in indirect tax in 1979/80.

As an immediate measure the Minimum Lending Rate (MLR) was
raised in an attempt 'to deal with the immediate problem of monetary
growth being above the target range'. A start was to be made on
expenditure cuts, 'the first stage of a long-term programme to reduce
both the role of government and its borrowing, to re-affirm the place
of the individual and to help finance income tax cuts'. The Budget
therefore included a squeeze on the cash limits already set by Labour
and cuts in programmes, to be followed by a thorough review of
spending for the years ahead.

An important consequence of the Budget, noted above, was that it
had a serious impact on the rate of inflation. Thus the government
admitted that the Budget itself would add approximately 4 per cent to
the Retail Price Index (RPI), which was the main indicator of the rate
of inflation, leading to a rise in the rate of inflation to approximately
16 per cent in the third quarter of the year. (Once the Budget effect

had taken place it was expected that the rate of inflation would fall back to 13 per cent in the following year.) The justification for this hefty push to the rate of inflation was that the tax reduction would 'improve incentives with the objective of raising the sustainable long-term growth rate of output and productivity . . . everything else being equal this will reduce the extent to which a given rise in wages will add to unit labour costs and hence prices' (*1979 Economic Progress Report*, No. 112, p. 2). Initially, at least, the government was prepared to trade off its objective of reducing the rate of inflation against its objective of reducing personal taxation in an attempt to increase incentives.

The problem of conflicting objectives was also painfully evident in the government's relations with the nationalized industries. As we have seen, the government saw controlling the PSBR as a central feature of its economic strategy. The borrowing by the nationalized industries was deemed by the previous Labour government to be within the PSBR. The Conservatives saw no reason to change this decision and so the borrowing requirements of the nationalized industries became of central importance to the government's economic strategy. This has been a point of bitter dispute throughout the government's terms of office.

The government forced many of the nationalized industries (particularly electricity and gas) to raise prices faster than the average rate of inflation in order to generate a high proportion of investment funds internally. (In effect, present consumers were being charged for future investment.) This increased inflation, the reduction of which was the government's primary objective.

In the case of gas and electricity, the rapid increase in prices was partly justified on the ground of energy conservation. However, the rapid rise in the prices charged by the nationalized industries was such that in 1980 they rose by 30 per cent, although by the end of 1981 the annual rise had been reduced to 11·1 per cent, roughly in line with the rate of inflation. The problem returned to the political agenda in 1985, when the Treasury pressed the Energy Secretary, Peter Walker, to raise prices faster than the rate of inflation, as a means of reducing the PSBR.

Another area where the government's own earlier policies contributed to its difficulties in trying to reduce the rate of inflation, was interest rate policy. Thus in November 1979 the government increased the MLR from 14 per cent to 17 per cent. The Chancellor considered it was necessary to take such action 'to bring the growth of the money supply within the target range. The increase in the minimum lending rate, which demonstrated the Government's determination to act with firmness, went beyond the rise in market interest rates at home' (*Economic Progress Report*, No. 116, p. 1). The policy of high interest rates – which has remained a characteristic of the Conservative government's tenure of office so far – has, of course, increased industrial costs, accelerated the rate of bankruptcies and has raised the cost of house mortgages.

In fact, the government did not *intend* to have a policy of high interest rates, as it initially assumed that the money supply could be reduced by other means (that is, reduced public expenditure). The pressure from industry for the government to lower interest rates has, at times, been intense and the government has therefore found a constant dilemma in its interest rate policy of either following its economic theory or responding to its 'natural' allies in industry. As a result of this pressure (and as a result of international money market factors), there have been considerable fluctuations in the interest rate. Each time the rate went down it was greeted by industry as welcome relief only to be greeted by howls of protest when it went back up again.

The link between interest rates and the exchange rate for sterling was also an issue of dispute between government and industry. Thus the high rate of the pound was often blamed on the policy of high interest rates and was cited as causing difficulties for British exporters (particularly in the US markets). As a result, the government was often under considerable pressure to reduce the exchange rate in order to help exports, yet it feared that, if it did so, it could add a further stimulus to the domestic rate of inflation. While the government had clearly stated, in its first Budget statement of 1979, that the exchange rate was a matter for market forces, it had seemingly abandoned this view by 1982, by which time exchange rate policy had come to play a far more central role.

There have been, however, two central themes to the economic policies throughout the period. The first is that the Government has continued to insist that there is no alternative to the strategy, as outlined in the Medium-Term Financial Strategy (MTFS), first published with the Budget in March 1980. (There were, however, 'adjustments' of the MTFS; for example, it has allowed the PSBR to rise well above target.) The 1985 Budget statement by the Chancellor of the Exchequer, Nigel Lawson, maintained, none the less, that the MTFS had been consistently followed by the government. The government's great success was, of course, inflation which had been reduced to 5 per cent (although unemployment had risen to nearly 3·5 million. Other indicators of the success of MTFS (and of the government's resolve in sticking to MTFS) were not so impressive.

The second central feature of the government's period of office to date has perhaps been the well-publicized battles within Cabinet between the 'wets' and 'dries'. Mrs Thatcher's Cabinet reshuffles have been predictably cast by the media in these terms. Thus Jim Prior, who had emerged as the leading Cabinet spokesman for the 'wets', was unwillingly moved to the post of Northern Ireland Secretary. Another prominent 'wet', Sir Ian Gilmour, who had publicly challenged the government's monetary strategy, was simply sacked. Many observers saw the September 1981 reshuffle as a reassertion of Mrs Thatcher's personal power and as a victory for the hardliners in the Cabinet. In fact, the history of the Cabinet under Mrs Thatcher was little different from the history of previous Cabinets – namely, a struggle between the Treasury team on the one hand, and the spending ministries on the other.

Sir Keith Joseph in his time as Secretary for Industry was one of the most spectacular examples of the spending minister phenomenon. While *talking* fundamental monetarism in the Cabinet and being a strong personal supporter of Mrs Thatcher, he left the Department of Trade and Industry with a reputation as a big spender. Whether at any one time the 'wets' or 'dries' were in the ascendancy in the Cabinet, the results in totality seem to confirm the view that the Cabinet was, like its predecessors, as much a prisoner of the fundamental nature of the policy process (and of international developments) as it was master of its own destiny. As different ministers also had different views of the desired destiny, this virtually guaranteed that a process of trading, incremental bargaining and adjustments, and a 'fudged' compromise would result. The particular issues changed, but the process was following a fairly well-trodden path. Thus when defence was threatened with cutbacks in planned growth (the Conservatives had pledged to increase defence spending in their manifesto) the then Secretary of State for Defence, Francis Pym, successfully mobilized the Defence Chiefs and Conservative back-benchers to defend his budget. In other cases, the Prime Minister herself was ready to make concessions which inevitably increased public expenditure. For example, in February 1981 the Prime Minister was personally involved in the decision to give way on the question of the National Coal Board's plan to close uneconomic coal mines. The threat of a miners' strike at that time caused Mrs Thatcher to change her mind and agree to increase expenditure to cover the cost of not closing a number of pits. (By March 1984, however, she was prepared to back the NCB in its renewed attempt to secure pit closures which provoked the year-long strike by the National Union of Mineworkers.)

Spending and taxing disputes cannot be resolved by purely technical means, in PESC-type committees. In the end, there has to be a political resolution of those disputes. Thus, much publicity has been given to the so-called 'Star Chamber' for resolving disputes between spending ministers and the Treasury. The Star Chamber is an inner Cabinet of senior ministers (ideally with only limited budgets of their own) which adjudicates the annual Treasury versus department contests over expenditure.

The Star Chamber in 1984 was chaired by Lord Whitelaw and included Treasury ministers; Leon Brittan, the Home Secretary; George Younger, Secretary of State for Scotland; and John Biffen, Leader of the House of Commons. Their job was to resolve outstanding disputes following bilateral meetings between the Chief Secretary to the Treasury, then Peter Rees, and individual departments – the so-called 'bilaterals'. The difficulty for the Star Chamber is that almost any cuts are politically damaging and thus the room for manoeuvre is generally very constrained.

As we suggested in our introduction, the Thatcher government has, in fact, demonstrated that it is possible, over a period, to change priorities in terms of resource allocation. For example, in its early years, the government kept its pledge to increase defence expenditure in line with the NATO target annual increases of 3 per cent, it increased expenditure on law and order, and on health (notwithstanding the campaign against health 'cuts'). However, there were big reductions in expenditure on housing.

Having achieved some changes in the balance of public expenditure, the government's plans, announced in the Public Expenditure White Paper of 22 June 1985, *The Government's Expenditure Plans 1985–86 to 1987–88* (Cmnd 9428) indicated that further significant shifts were planned. For example, it planned a 40 per cent reduction in the industry, energy, trade and employment budgets over the period 1983/4 to 1987/8, and a further 19 per cent reduction in the housing budget.

However, caution is needed in interpreting spending figures. Different observers come to different conclusions on what has actually happened to expenditure in particular programme areas. For example, the selection of the base year is important; some figures are quoted in 'constant prices', others in 'survey prices'; some allow for general inflation, and others for both general inflation and relative inflation. Also, any one government may behave differently at different periods in its term of office. Sir Leo Pliatzky (1985, p. 3) notes that 'after enormous increases in its first year, Labour was obliged to make big cuts in its third year, though it took the brakes off again in its final year'.

Pliatzky's view (1985, pp. 2–3) is that 'there is a sharp contrast' between spending on individual programmes during the 1974–79 Labour government and under the Conservatives between 1979–83.

Table 9.1   *Labour's Public Expenditure by Programme: 1974/5 to 1978/9 (£ million at 1979 survey figures)*

	1974/5 out-turn	1977/8 out-turn	1978/9 provisional out-turn
(1) Defence	7,462	7,550	7,509
(2) Overseas aid and other overseas services:			
Overseas aid	628	718	786
EEC contributions	−13	632	774
Other overseas services	699	486	400
(3) Agriculture, fisheries, food, forestry	2,454	1,068	896
(4) Industry, energy, trade and employment[a]	5,213	2,461	3,267
(5) Government lending to nationalized industries	1,187	−238	693
(6) Roads and Transport	3,820	3,023	2,980
(7) Housing	7,141	5,507	5,226
(8) Other environmental services	3,541	3,262	3,330
(9) Law and order, and protective services	2,172	2,284	2,370
(10) Education and science, arts and libraries	9,584	9,362	9,567
(11) Health and personal social services	8,326	8,776	9,055
(12) Social security	14,146	16,595	18,213
(13) Other public services	949	975	973
(14) Common services	965	1,022	1,048
(15) Northern Ireland	1,929	2,054	2,232
Total programmes	70,202	65,536	69,321

Source: Amended from *Economic Progress Report*, no. 115, 1979.
[a] Includes purchase of British Petroleum shares in 1974/5 but excludes sales of British Petroleum shares in 1977/8 and 1979/80.

He notes that total expenditure rose under both governments; however, he argues that Labour cut defence whereas the Conservatives increased it, that Labour increased housing and the Conservatives cut it, that Labour increased overseas aid but the Conservatives cut it.

Our own table (Table 9.1) derived from the *Treasury Economic Progress Report*, shows that the actual year selected as a base is crucial. The Labour government appeared to protect defence spending and health while cutting other programmes, including housing. A simple adversary politics interpretation does not fit the patterns of allocation under the past Conservative and Labour governments.

It should also be noted that the incremental nature of the allocations can be exaggerated. Some of the changes – up and down – (for

Public expenditure
% change in real terms 1979–85 est

	1985 plan £bn

```
  30    20  % 10  – 0 +   10    20    30
   |  |  |  |  |  |  |  |  |  |  |
```

Category	1985 plan £bn
Social security	40
Law and order	5
Defence	18
Health	17
Total	134
Education and science	14
Industry energy trade and employment	5
Housing	2

–68

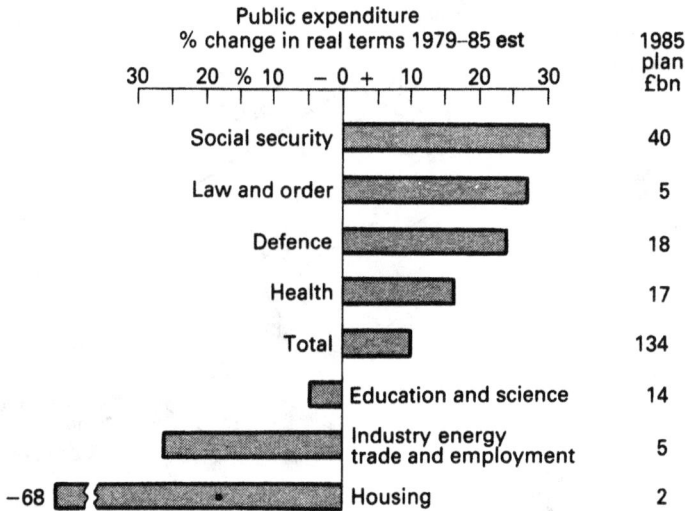

Source: The Economist, 5 October 1985.

Figure 9.1   Changes in public expenditure 1979–85 (estimate).

example, agriculture and housing) have been very dramatic (see Figure 9.1). While incrementalism usefully explains the broad pattern (for example, see Heald, 1983, p. 22), particular circumstances can lead to significant exceptions.

Some policy areas are, of course, much more important than others in terms of their resource implications. The social security programme is easily the biggest single programme of public expenditure, consuming some 30 per cent of planned public spending for 1985/6, compared with 14 per cent for defence and only 10 per cent for education and science. Figures for total public expenditure as a percentaged gross domestic product (GDP) are not as 'hard' as might be imagined. David Heald (1983, pp. 15–16) presents this very vividly in a graph showing how different definitions of public expenditure (all quite recent) give very different pictures. In a famous speech at Llangefni in 1976, Roy Jenkins was so concerned about public expenditure appearing in one Treasury document to be 60 per cent of GDP, that he discussed the imminent crossing of, 'one of the frontiers of social democracy'. Heald shows that other (more reasonable) definitions for 1975/6 were around 50 per cent (using a definition by Brittan); around 45 per cent by the Second Permanent Secretary at the Treasury, Sir Leo Pliatzky; with a similar level when defined by the OECD.

A very high percentage of public expenditure goes on what are

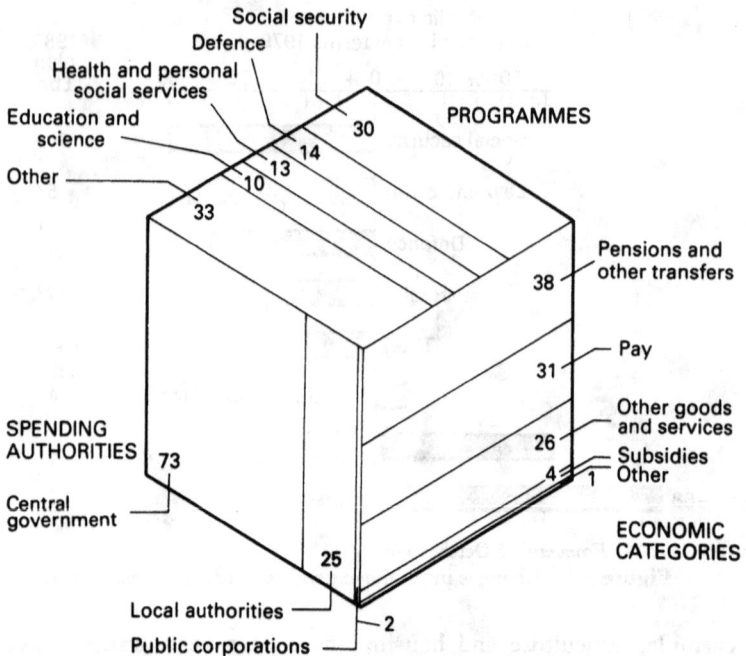

Source: *Treasury Economic Progress Report*, No. 176, 1985.
Figure 9.2   Planned public spending for 1985/6: where, who and what (in %).

called 'transfer payments'. Thus pensions and other 'transfers' account for 38 per cent of planned expenditure for 1985/6 – effectively, money coming into the government's coffers only to be redistributed (often to the same citizens who have paid it in!). If we exclude expenditure on transfer payments and on interest on borrowing, public expenditure on goods and services is approximately 23 per cent of GDP at market prices (Lewis, 1984, p. 58). The balance between spending by programme and by category, and by spending authority is illustrated in Figure 9.2.

An analysis of expenditure by spending authority shows that in 1985/6 central government spending was planned to be 73 per cent of total public spending compared with 25 per cent by the local authorities (and 2 per cent for public corporations), notwithstanding the government's view that the local authorities were the culprits in the failure to control public expenditure properly. In fact, in the period 1980/1 to 1984/5, while central government spending increased as a percentage of public spending, local authority spending fell from 27 per cent to 25·5 per cent (Lewis, 1984, p. 59). Again the embarrassment is for both major parties: the Conservative central government has held its expenditure less well than the much-abused local authorities. And the cuts for local authorities only follow Labour's own cuts in 1974–9.

How then do we assess the total impact of Mrs Thatcher's government in its determined attempts to have a significant impact on resource allocations? Clearly, big changes were made – for example to housing support, defence and local government finance – yet Labour, in its turn, had also had to increase defence spending and to curb local government expenditure. The 'system', and the political bargaining nature of the resource allocation process, has proved extremely resilient. As the *Financial Times* commented on 23 January 1985, since 1979 the Treasury's struggles with the spending departments 'have been marked by setting ambitious targets and missing them'.

In the case of health care, governments are particularly vulnerable to political pressures when the media highlight, say, the closure of a cancer treatment ward, because of so-called 'cuts' in health expenditure. It is extremely difficult for any government to resist pressure to find extra money in such cases. Thus public expenditure seems to have a natural momentum which is extremely difficult to resist in a democracy. By mid-1985 the Conservatives were seeking to claim credit for their spending – whether or not it was deliberate, intended, spending. Chancellor Lawson, in early July, claimed that while the government sought savings, it did spend more where needed: 'On doctors. On nurses. On each pupil at school. On the police. On defence. Our public spending record is a good one.'

Until then the government had managed to devise a remarkable 'no win' position for itself. It trumpeted cuts while delivering increases – managing both to frighten client groups and antagonize those who sought real reductions.

Thain (1985, pp. 228–9) has suggested that the government's economic strategy during the period 1980–4 is best characterized by the phrase 'pragmatism and continuity', and has said that 'the Treasury's most conspicuous failure during the 1980–84 period was the non-implementation of the strategy's public expenditure plans'. It is not surprising, therefore, that governments turn to procedural and technical reforms in the resource allocation process in the hope that a 'solution' might emerge. It is to these technical developments – almost designed to take the politics out of resource allocation, as it were – that we now turn.

Improved Financial Management and Value for Money

Concern with the 'nuts and bolts' of the processes of resource allocation and resource use has increased greatly in the last decade. (For a very useful review, see Peat Marwick, 1984.) The terms value for money (VFM), efficiency audit and effectiveness audit are now very familiar in British government circles. We have also seen the creation of efficiency units, new financial procedures – such as the Financial Management Initiative, MAXIS and MINIS – and changes in the role of the Comptroller and Auditor-General. The auditing process, at both central and local level, has changed markedly; with a shift in emphasis away from concentrating exclusively on financial and regulatory audits towards value for money and effectiveness audits. Thus financial and regulatory audits are concerned with ensuring that systems of accounting and control are efficient and operating properly, and that financial transactions have been correctly authorized and accounted for; and that expenditure has been incurred on approved services in accordance with regulations. Value for money audits are concerned with the avoidance of wasteful, extravagant, or unrewarding expenditure. Effectiveness audits are concerned with whether programmes or policies are actually achieving their goals or objectives. In line with a trend to emphasize VFM and effectiveness studies, the powers and name of the Exchequer and Audit Department (under the Comptroller and Auditor-General) have been changed and the new National Audit Office (still under the Comptroller and Auditor-General) has been created.

Of even more significance, perhaps, is the development of efficiency studies within government departments on their own account. These studies were started in the Efficiency Unit, set up in 1979 under Sir Derek (now Lord) Rayner, who was seconded from Marks & Spencer. The so-called Rayner 'scrutinies' have all been concerned with the *effectiveness* of expenditure (for example, the Rayner scrutiny of the Inspectorate of Schools in 1981). The Efficiency Unit has continued despite Lord Rayner's departure from government and is part of the Cabinet Office, with direct access to the Prime Minister.

Each 'scrutiny' lasts for about ninety days. As the unit is itself very small (approximately six members) the bulk of the work is done by the departments themselves. By April 1983 some 133 departmental scrutinies and six multi-departmental reviews had been conducted with a total of identified savings/income of £400 million. By that date, decisions had been agreed which would produce savings of £180 million a year and £29 million once-and-for-all. These figures need to be set against the total level of public expenditure which is currently (1985) approximately £120 billion a year.

This is not to decry the usefulness of the exercise. Thus if it costs £90 to administer a £100 woodland grant, then clearly something must be wrong with the grant system! Equally, if a government laboratory is spending £30 to breed each rat when it could buy them in for £2 per rat then at face value money is being wasted! But it will take a lot of such savings to buy one Tornado aircraft or one new kidney unit in a hospital. As Michael Lee (1980, p. 442) has suggested, 'it seems doubtful whether Rayner's work can provoke a more general inquiry unless it is linked to wider questions about accountability and audit'. Supporters of the Rayner scrutinies believe that the real benefits will be in the change which is said to be taking place in the 'Whitehall culture', with the result that VFM, efficiency and effectiveness are becoming fully integrated into decision-making processes.

Evidence that the new climate of efficiency and effectiveness is leading to the broader changes advocated by Lee, is said to be in the development of the Financial Management Initiative (FMI). The FMI was officially launched in 1982 with strong prime ministerial backing. The White Paper (Cmnd 8616, September 1982) outlined the central aims of the FMI. These were:

To promote in each department an organisation and system in which managers at all levels have:

a A clear view of this objective, and means to assess and, wherever possible, measure outputs or performance in relation to those objectives;

b Well defined responsibility for making the best use of their resources, including a critical scrutiny of output and value for money;

c The information (particularly about costs), the training and the access to expert advice that they need to exercise their responsibilities effectively.

The thirty-one largest departments were required to produce plans for changes in their financial and management systems. These plans have since been published in a White Paper (Cmnd 9058, September 1983). Great hopes are being expressed for the new system as it is supposed to bring together responsibility for resources and for the work that is actually carried out. 'A prime result of the FMI therefore has been to reinforce and accelerate the creation of a *management* role for senior managers in which they manage both resources and work (in the past the tendency has been for senior management to concentrate on issues and have little involvement in resource questions)' (Peat Marwick, 1984, p. 22). However, as Gray and Jenkins point out (1985, p. 85), departments have tended to concentrate on establishing information systems rather than on elucidating their goals:... they all fail to express the underlying goals or objectives which they are working towards'.

As governments begin to adopt modern management techniques sometimes used in the private sector, such developments sound impressive. But managing government is not like managing the private sector. Even when a commercial organization, such as the National Coal Board or British Steel, decides to discontinue a particular activity because it is not cost effective, then implementation problems are likely. A school, or a hospital, or a railway line cannot be closed without widespread protest – whatever management techniques the particular government department or agency may employ. And certainly a local manager does not have discretion on such matters – at the end of the day the decision will be a *political* decision, not a rational or technical one, on how best to use resources.

Certainly, interest in efficiency did not arrive with the 1979 Conservative government and there has been a succession of attempts – at least from the era of the Fulton Report in 1968 – to introduce greater efficiency in government. (For a review see Gray and Jenkins, 1985.) It is possible to be sceptical of the current 'flavour of the month' reforms, not because of any lack of sympathy with the intentions, but because the record of earlier efforts suggests that any approach to a problem will fail if it underestimates the intractability of the problem. Some of the reasons inhibiting efficiency reforms were ascribed by Gray and Jenkins (1985, p. 131) to the values of the service: '. . . much of bureaucratic politics reflects the values of this system: a stress on political accountability, on short-term and vague goals, on actions rather than evaluation, on inputs rather than on results and outputs'.

One of the most famous of the Rayner reviews, and an example of ultimate failure, was conducted by Clive Ponting. Under the Rayner scheme, the studies were conducted by middle-level civil servants of the department under examination. (This practice was to prevent the department 'freezing out' the examiner – but meant that the investigator might have mixed loyalties.) As described in an article by David Leigh in the *Observer*, 24 February 1985, Ponting was given the task of reporting within sixty days on the purchasing practices of the three armed services. Ponting found plenty of examples of waste – tinned dog food made to military specifications which cost more than Pedigree Chum; a lorry making separate, identical trips carrying food for the officers' mess, for the sergeants' mess and the third time for 'other ranks'. So taken was Mrs Thatcher with Ponting's report and presentation, that he and a colleague (doing a similar project at the Department of Health and Social Security) reported personally to a Cabinet meeting. Apparently, Mrs Thatcher told the meeting: 'We are all agreed that efficiency has to be improved. Sir Derek Rayner's method is clearly going to be the way to tackle the problem.'

However, Ponting found himself with no clear career opportunities after the project. When he met Clive Priestly of the Rayner unit, Priestly acknowledged that he was not surprised and that, 'Sir Derek has always been worried that anyone who criticized his own department would be regarded as unreliable'. Mrs Thatcher again intervened to secure him a promotion, but Leigh concludes: 'Mrs Thatcher's haste to protect Ponting could not mask a deeper failure. Raynerism, like all its predecessors, collapsed as soon as the politicians' self-promoting caravan moved on . . . After a full three years, no major decisions had been taken at all . . .' In 1982 a new junior minister, Gerry Wiggin, wrote a memo confirming there was to be no change: 'There is much to be said for letting people get on with their jobs now, dispelling the uncertainty which has long hung over this whole area of business.'

A second Leigh article also documents how Ponting's efficiency study of military band training concluded that the three separate schools for the three services should be amalgamated – and should be sited at Eastney near Portsmouth. This amalgamation was confirmed in a study by an outside consultant, and by an informal military study. None the less, the Secretary of State, Michael Heseltine, concluded that to avoid a tendency for training to be concentrated in the South-East, a Defence School of Music should be created 'north of Birmingham'. Ponting found suitable (if more expensive) facilities outside Edinburgh, but after Heseltine was lobbied by his Cabinet colleagues and by the Chief Secretary to the Treasury, Peter Rees, it was decided to put the facility in Rees's constituency. Deal was selected, though it was considerably more expensive than Eastney – and not by any argument 'north of Birmingham' (see Leigh, *Observer*, 3 March 1985).

Though current FMI exercise might be more successful than Heath's Programme Analysis and Review (see Gray and Jenkins, 1985, for an account of its collapse) and more successful than some of the early evidence above of the Thatcher approach, we need evidence, as opposed to optimism, to dispel scepticism about the real potential of Rayner, FMI, MINIS or as yet unimagined acronyms which may become the buzz words in the resource allocation process.

As Daniel Tarschys (1981, pp. 54–5) notes:

In the last few decades, methodological innovations with ambitions of this kind have flushed into public administration in wave after wave . . . In the real world, there are several stumbling blocks on the road to synoptic rationality. While approaches of this kind have often been launched as panaceas against public waste, they have seldom led to substantial economies.

While revenue raising and resource allocation systems may become more sophisticated in technical terms, large numbers in the exercise are often not amenable to refined analysis. The disturbances from the outside environment into the Treasury calculations are often crude and crucial. For example, in early summer 1985 the rate of inflation, at 7 per cent was 2 per cent higher than expected. This 2 per cent difference cost the government an additional £700 million on the social security budget. Similarly, the slight rise in the value of the pound against the dollar since the Budget, lopped £2·5 billion off prospective North Sea oil revenues. The real world of resource allocation remains, above all, a political not a technical/rational process, struggling to cope with problems beyond any government's full control.

CHAPTER TEN

The Implementation Process

Introduction

The policy-making process is, as we have seen in earlier chapters, complex but subject to certain rules of the game or cultural norms. Bargaining and consensus are important constraints on policy change. This complex process has been changing in a number of ways – such as Mrs Thatcher's attempt to change the policy style towards a more innovative, less consensual, and more *dirigiste* process. Attention to the way in which issues get onto the political agenda and are then 'processed' into some policy outcomes – either by legislation or ministerial decision – ignores the other side of the policy-making coin, namely the implementation process. Many policies may, of course, be characterized as placebo (Gustafsson and Richardson, 1980) – that is, they are not actually designed to solve problems in society, but are introduced as a means of managing the political agenda. In such cases, we should not expect much by way of implementation effects. But many policies are quite clearly intended to have a positive effect – say, in reducing road accidents, producing better health care, or building more homes. The extent to which these intentions are effected is of political interest.

A decision by the government to 'do something' is often perceived as the end of the matter so far as the public is concerned. For example, a decision to provide state support for low-income families would appear to solve the problem of poverty. But, in practice, the policy decision sets off a long and complicated chain – the implementation process – full of opportunities for things to go wrong. Moreover, there is a tendency for the implementation process to become heavily bureaucratic and rule-laden, as policies are often implemented through large public bureaucracies. For example, the Department of Health and Social Security employed over 95,000 civil servants in 1982. In such huge complex organizations there is ample scope for the original policies to be distorted, for the original objects or goals to be forgotten, for the bureaucrats themselves to substitute their own goals and objectives as they implement the policies. The social security system is possibly the best (or worst) example of the complex systems developed for 'delivering' public policies.

The government's Green Paper, *Reform of Social Security* (Cmnd 9517), reviewing the welfare system, and published in June 1985, revealed that the rules governing the supplementary benefit system ran to 16,000 paragraphs and two volumes, and that 38,000 staff were needed to run it. The Secretary of State for Social Services, Norman Fowler, described the system as 'a leviathan almost with a life of its own'. Thus the implementation process can be rather like the apocryphal story of the First World War when a message – 'send reinforcements, we are going to advance' – was sent from the front line along the trenches back to headquarters. By the time that the message had been passed from one Allied trench to another, it had become so distorted that it arrived at Brigade Headquarters as 'send three and fourpence, we are going to a dance'! The moral of this story, translated in terms of the implementation process, is that policies quite often fail to have their intended effects.

In view of the importance of what actually happens, compared with what was intended, it is surprising that until recently relatively little attention has been paid by governments, and academics, to the implementation process. This picture of relative neglect is, however, changing quite rapidly. There is now a growing body of literature concerned with the nature of the implementation process.

Implementation theory

Hood (1976, p. 6) has described a theoretical model of 'perfect administration' which, if it were adopted in the real world, would produce perfect policy administration. He uses this theoretical model to identify the various constraints which operate in the real world in such a way that implementation is far from perfect. Five main conditions for perfect administration are identified:

(1) A unitary administrative system, rather like a huge army with a single line of authority. Conflict of authority could weaken control, and all information should be centralized in order to avoid compartmentalism.

(2) The norms and rules enforced by the system have to be uniform. Similarly, objectives must be kept uniform if the unitary administrative system is to be really effective.

(3) There must be perfect obedience or perfect control.

(4) There must be perfect information and perfect communication – as well as perfect co-ordination.

(5) There must be sufficient time for administrative resources to be mobilized.

The chances of all five conditions being met are small indeed! Moreover, Dudley (1984, p. 11) has suggested that there are, in any case, some conceptual problems, even in this theoretical model. For example, he suggests that 'perfect implementation' would not be achieved 'if the implementer behaves like an automaton, and carries out the wishes of his controller, even if he sees that the policy objectives are not being achieved'. Thus Dudley argues that this theoretical model, if applied, might actually prevent perfect implementation because, where conditions are changing, the implementer must use his or her discretion if the policy is to be implemented at all. Because policies are implemented in a changing world, a world often beyond the direct control of any government, then the people at the 'coal face' of the policy process must be allowed to modify the policy according to the changed conditions. Dunsire (1978, p. 174) suggests that there can be cognitive gaps in the implementation process and that these gaps can cause discontinuities in the process. Herein lies the tremendous dilemma of the implementation process – namely, that it is difficult to prevent this leeway or flexibility from being exploited by the implementer for his or her own bureaucratic ends.

In a democracy with a volatile electorate, those who are involved in the actual implementation of policies are always likely to bear in mind that the policy could be changed after a change of government – or, indeed, after a ministerial reshuffle. We can take Sir Keith Joseph's 1985 Green Paper on higher education as an example (Cmnd 9524). It advocated a further shift in the balance between science and arts within universities, in favour of science and engineering. Whilst many university academics were keen to implement the new policy (because it suited their own interest), others (those of us in the social sciences, for example) were keen to delay implementation (unless forced to do so) in the hope that a new minister, less radical and more consensual in outlook, might emerge in a future Cabinet reshuffle. The Green Paper was full of inbuilt design problems likely to prevent successful implementation of the Government's objectives. For example, it recommended a shift to science and engineering, whilst also recommending a reduction in resources for universities – yet graduates cost twice as much in science and technology as they do in art and social sciences. Hood's rule no. 5 – the mobilization of the necessary resources – was obviously not considered by Sir Keith!

The policy clearly had gainers and losers within universities and hence there was a struggle over how it was implemented. This behaviour is in accord with a prediction made by Downs, who stresses the competitive nature of the implementation process and the motivational aspects of organizational behaviour (Downs, 1967, pp. 79–91). He is anxious to emphasize the importance of bureaucratic self-interest in helping us to understand the implementation process. Bureaucracies, he argues, wish to expand and, in doing so, often seek to create a 'client group' who will then defend the bureaucracy. Thus bureaucrats and clients can form a powerful alliance to control the implementation process as they see fit, notwithstanding the need for political control. This situation can be extremely difficult for governments to change. For example, any rationalization of the use of resources in the health service – say, the closure of small units and the regionalization of the treatment of certain diseases and disorders, will be met by a determined coalition of doctors and patients who fight to retain existing local facilities. It may be very sensible and natural to have one or two large, highly specialized and well-equipped treatment centres, but exceedingly difficult to implement the policy if doctors and patients go on television to complain that a local children's ward is about to be closed. Because of the emotional importance of the health care system (as well as its political importance), it has proved very easy for the medical bureaucracy to 'wave the shroud' in public, forcing ministers to back down from radical proposals. This is because the medical profession has the power over the implementation of health policy. They can decide how cuts of, say, 2 per cent should be implemented and can cut those areas of the service which are most sensitive politically, for example, children's wards, kidney units, and so on, even though it might be possible to save the 2 per cent in less damaging ways. Hence the saying, 'He who implements, decides'.

A particularly useful theory for our understanding of the implementation process was contained in Pressman and Wildavsky's study (1973) of the implementation of US federal employment creation plans in Oakland, California. They devised the notion of 'decision-points' and 'clearances'. A decision-point is reached when 'an act of agreement has to be registered for the programme to continue' (p. xvi). Each instance in which a participant is required to give his or her consent is termed a 'clearance point'. The theory, derived from their case study, suggests that the greater the number of decision-points and clearances involved in a policy programme, the greater the likelihood that the programme will fail to achieve its objectives. Indeed, they thought that the cards were so heavily stacked against new programmes, because so many decision-points and clearances are involved, that it was, in their view, remarkable that any programmes work at all (ibid., p. 109). If implementation failure results, it may be due to the wilful obstruction of implementers, or it may be due to the fact that the policy-makers failed to appreciate fully the complexity of the implementation process – particularly, the degree of interdependency within that process. Thus we can see a quite different view of the implementation process to the 'top down' perfect implementation view of Hood's model. This alternative view sees the implementation challenge as 'not that of faithfully or efficiently executing enacted policies, but that of increasing our understanding of the depth and complexity of policy issues' (Stone, 1985, p. 489).

This view is best characterized as a 'bottom up' rather than 'top down' view of the implementation process and its problems. The 'top down' view is that implementation failure is often caused by a recalcitrance on the part of bureaucratic implementers (the self-interest model of authors such as Downs). As Barrett and Fudge suggest (1981, p. 4), much of the literature adopts this particular 'managerial' perspective – 'the problems of implementation are defined in terms of co-ordination, control or obtaining "compliance" with policy'.

The contrasting view is that it is perfectly reasonable for imple-menters to change the way a policy is implemented, or even to re-define the objectives of the policy, as they are closer to the problem itself. A balance between the 'top down' and 'bottom up' perspective is that 'policy initiation merely sets the stage for a process of adaptation and potential learning' (Stone, 1985, p. 495). Barrett and Fudge (1981, p. 4) have, similarly, argued that 'rather than treating implementation as the transmission of policy into a series of con-sequential actions, the policy–action relationship needs to be regarded as a process of interaction and negotiation, taking place over time, between those seeking to put policy into effect and those upon whom action depends'. This view of the implementation process is one which places *bargaining* as the key characteristic. Hogwood and Gunn (1984, p. 207) likewise believe that a reconciliation is possible. They sympathize with a 'top down' view, 'if only on the grounds that "those seeking to put policy into effect" are usually elected, while "those upon whom action depends" are not, at least in the case of civil servants and the staff of health services, nationalised industries etc.'. Their own essentially 'top down' view of the implementation process is constructed in the knowledge that the complexity of the policy process, and environmental, political and organizational factors are important. They, rightly, point out that one can find both good and bad examples of 'top down' and 'bottom up' approaches to implementation. They do not deny that it is easy to find examples 'Of national policies so misconceived that they deserved to be stifled at birth'. Indeed, they argue that policies often fail because they are so misconceived in the first place. However, they point out there are just as many problems in being as committed to a 'bottom up' approach. They suggest (1984, p. 208), 'If a Home Secretary is committed to better relations between policemen and black youths, should we view with equanimity the persistence of "street level" police attitudes and actions which are openly racist?'

The need for a process of interaction is readily recognized, with the recommendation that it should take place *before* policy formulation, or during the policy formulation process. Indeed, we suggest (see Chapter 7) that this practice is almost a central philosophy of British government – namely, that you should consult 'interested parties' (that is, those who are directly involved, both 'recipients' of policies and implementer) before deciding on policy. Most British civil servants, and not a few politcans, define feasibility in terms of 'what can I get through?' There are probably more policies which are never introduced because of the *anticipation* of resistance, than policies which have failed *because* of resistance.

How then, can we summarize the practical significance of the growing literature on implementation? In adapting below, Hogwood and Gunn's list of conditions which are necessary for successful implementation, it is useful to remind ourselves just how far we have moved from the notion that ordinary citizens, via voting in elections, can determine policies. The connection between a majority of those voting in a general election, and what actually gets implemented several years later is tenuous.

Hogwood and Gunn (in 1984, pp. 199–206) drawing upon several other major writers on implementation list ten preconditions which would have to be satisfied if perfect implementation were to be achieved. (They, of course, recognize that these preconditions are unlikely to be achieved in practice: perfect implementation is unobtainable.)

(1) *'The circumstances external to the agency do not impose crippling constraints'* (p. 199).
Implementation failure may be due to circumstances quite outside the control of administrators. For example, there may be a failure of political will, there may be national disasters such as droughts, and so on, or powerful interests may veto policies.

(2) *'That adequate time and sufficient resources are made available to the programme'* (p. 199).
They suggest that a common reason for implementation failure is that

positive results are expected to emerge too quickly, whereas many policies take time to work. This is particularly so where policies depend upon a change of attitude. Obviously, a lack of actual resources can cause failure. For example, improved mathematical attainment for schoolchildren will not happen if the supply of trained maths teachers is not increased. Planning controls will be ineffective if there are insufficient enforcement officers, thus allowing builders to break planning conditions and building regulations without fear of being caught. Hogwood and Gunn point out that money sometimes has to be spent too quickly – say, towards the end of a financial year.

(3) *'That the required combination of resources is actually available'* (p. 200).
It is not just a question of providing the right amount of money and resources. They must be made available in the appropriate combinations at the appropriate times. For example, there can be particular bottlenecks. If there had not been sufficient British microcomputer manufacturing capacity to meet the Thatcher government's 'micros in schools' policy, then more foreign micros would have had to be imported, or the policy would have ground to a halt. As it happens, the USSR has such a policy but has been unable to deliver sufficient microcomputers to Soviet schools. As a result many Soviet children have computer lessons without computers!

(4) *'That the policy to be implemented is based upon a valid theory of cause and effect'* (p. 201).
Policies can fail for one very obvious reason – they are bad policies. The failure may be because 'the policy may be based upon an inadequate understanding of a problem to be solved, its causes and cure; or of an opportunity, its nature, and what is needed to exploit it' (p. 201). Every policy has a theory (often hidden or unrecognized) behind it – namely, a theory of cause and effect (such as if you ban international football matches this will reduce football hooliganism). If the policy fails, it might be that the theory is wrong. Thus in Chapter 9 we cited the example of the Thatcher government's belief that reducing income tax for high earners would increase effort and entrepreneurship, and that 'monetary' theory provided the solution to our economic difficulties. The Labour Opposition have argued, of course, that the whole of the government's Medium-Term Financial Strategy is an error based upon false economic premises and that the policy actually worsens the economic situation. (The House of Lords Select Committee on Overseas Trade also suggested that government interest rate policy had actually contributed to Britain's poor trading record! See House of Lords, 238–1, 1985, p. 82.)

(5) *'That the relationship between cause and effect is direct and that there are few, if any, intervening links'* (p. 202).

This condition is similar to the Pressman and Wildavsky observation, cited earlier, that the implementation chain is a long one and that there are many opportunities to break the chain. Any implementation process involves a complex series of events and linkages providing many opportunities for things to go wrong.

(6)   *'That dependency relationships are minimal'* (p. 202).

Successful implementation often depends upon the agreement of a large number of participants, who may block the implementation process. Similarly, A. King (1975, p. 290) has argued that British government is 'overloaded' because there are too many 'dependency relationships'. Boddy's study (1981, p. 102) of the relations between government and the building societies in the 1970s concludes that the building societies' commitment to their own autonomy was such that 'mandatory legislation will be necessary to achieve any real control over their activities'. He concluded that the bargaining between government and the building societies had modified the societies' behaviour slightly, but that those concessions gained from them had been minor. The main effect of the concessions was, in fact, to counter the effective implementation of governmental policy rather than to strengthen it.

(7)   *'That there is understanding of, and agreement on, objectives'* (p. 204).

In real life, the objectives of organizations or programmes are often difficult to identify and are extremely vague. Also, the government's own objectives are often in conflict – as cited in Chapter 9 on resource allocation when the Thatcher government increased VAT in 1979, thus increasing the rate of inflation, despite its other objective of reducing inflation. Very serious implementation problems can arise if those in charge of implementation do not share the objectives of central policy-makers. Thus it is more likely that there will be successful implementation if there is 'good consensus' between policy-maker and implementer (Van Meter and Van Horn, 1975, p. 462).

(8)   *'That tasks are fully specified in correct sequence'* (p. 205).

Hogwood and Gunn suggest that for perfect implementation, it would be necessary to specify, in complete detail and perfect sequence, the tasks to be performed by each participant. Put briefly, everyone needs to know what he or she is to do and when he or she is to do it. It is, of course, necessary to achieve some kind of balance between an excessive number of detailed regulations and a very loose 'steering' mechanism. Montjoy and O'Toole (1979, p. 47) suggest, however, that the benefits from applying rather specific conditions may outweigh the disadvantages. They suggest that 'the surest way of avoiding intra-organisational problems in the implementation process is to establish a specific mandate with sufficient resources'.

(9) *'That there is perfect communication and co-ordination'* (p. 205).

This precondition for perfect implementation is 'that there would have to be perfect communication among and co-ordination of the various elements or agencies involved in the programme'. As with their other preconditions, they recognize that this is impossible to achieve in practice. When discussing Cabinet government we suggest that there are problems of co-ordination because of the fact that ministers 'fight their corner', but we also note that this disintegration of the centre of British government is, in part, counter-balanced by the increasing amount of informal co-ordination between government departments, though the exchange of papers and through more formal machinery such as interdepartmental committees.

(10) *'That those in authority can demand and obtain perfect compliance'* (p. 206).

This precondition is a variant of Hood's term 'perfect obedience'. Thus, policies, especially radical policies, may well meet strong resistance from those who like and benefit from the existing situation or policies. In this sense, implementation is as much about the exercise of political power as is the policy-making process itself. A recent example in Britain is the resistance of Liverpool City Council to the Conservative government's measures to control local authority spending in 1985. This was a classic power struggle between policy-makers (in this case, central government) and policy implementers (in this case, local government).

Implementation in Practice

We now turn to some practical examples – often illustrating problems or policy failures – of the implementation process at work. In highlighting problems we should not assume that all policies fail. Pollution controls have been quite effective (for example, in cleaning up rivers and beaches); the motorway programme started in the early 1950s with the M1, has made it far easier and safer to travel round Britain; consumer protection policies have improved quality and service; and health care is delivered reasonably effectively. The public health system prevents the outbreak of cholera in Britain and even manages to arrange good medical care for those unfortunate enough to catch it on a foreign holiday. As Wildavsky notes (1980, pp. 62–85), few of us would want to live in a society where the public policies which we now have were removed – even though we know that policies do not work perfectly and that they often themselves create quite new problems. An example of the latter, is the urban rehousing programme implemented in the 1950s and 1960s, producing high-rise estates that have, in some locations, been the cause of much distress, violence, and a whole host of new social problems. We emphasize the importance of organized groups in the implementation process. The high degree of integration of groups which is so evident in other aspects of the policy process – such as in the consultations which usually precede policy change – is equally, if not more, evident in the implementation of policies once they have been decided. Again, we should be as aware of the benefits of group participation in these processes as of the costs. We tend to remember only those examples of pressure-group behaviour which disrupt the implementation of governmental policy – such as the resistance of the civil service to the reforms proposed by Lord Fulton in 1968. In that situation, it became clear that it was extremely difficult to force policies through against strong resistance. Civil servants undermined policy change not by confrontational methods but over a long period of time. They were skilled at creating the *appearance* of compliance, without really changing the fundamental nature of the civil service (see Kellner and Crowther-Hunt, 1980).

But there are as many more examples of groups being supportive of public policies, and policy objectives being achieved because of group involvement, than there are of policy failure due to group resistance. For example, the role of voluntary organizations in the provision of various kinds of welfare services, often with government assistance and public money, is very large indeed. Typical of such organizations is the National Association for the Care and Resettlement of Offenders (NACRO) which plays a very practical role in assisting the reintegration of ex-offenders into society and helping to keep them out of gaol. Similarly, much of the Thatcher government's drug addiction programme is 'delivered' via voluntary organizations of various kinds, rather than through the national health service or through other official agencies.

Governments, of course, see great advantages in involving groups in the implementation of public policy. It is one way of securing wider participation in the political system and hence of creating wider support for the system as a whole. It is also a way of securing greater commitment to the success of particular public policies by creating a sense of involvement. And it also enables the government to benefit from the practical expertise which it may lack itself. Further, it is a means of sharing the blame for failure and of 'exporting' difficult problems to private or semi-private organizations when government is finding difficulty in 'solving' a particular problem. The Thatcher government's involvement of firms in the delivery of anti-unemployment schemes and in the creation of local enterprise trusts is a good example of this (Moore, Richardson and Moon, 1985).

It is important to remember that the close involvement of groups in the implementation process takes place even in policy areas which may, at first sight, seem to be of great political controversy and dispute, and which might appear not to be susceptible to a consensual implementation process. The field of unemployment policy is, again, a particularly fruitful example. It is no exaggeration to say that the unemployment issue has developed its own 'industry' (just as race relations and environmental 'industries' have developed). The unemployment problem has itself provoked a proliferating 'issue network' involving literally hundreds of groups in a variety of public policies designed to reduce or to alleviate unemployment (Moon and Richardson, 1984b, p. 397).

For example, the Community Task Force (CTF) has become an important feature of the Manpower Services Commission (MSC) programme provision. Having been established to provide outdoor adventure holidays for children from inner cities it was, by 1984, providing almost 10,000 places on the Community Programme (the adult job-creation scheme introduced in October 1984), and has provided some 2,000 places on the Youth Training Scheme (YTS). Indeed, CTF has completely reorganized its own management structure in order to match the delivery systems of the MSC. Community Service Volunteers (CSV) provides a further example to indicate the scale of the contribution of voluntary groups to the government's job-creation programme. During 1981/2 CSV operated eleven youth training schemes funded mainly by the MSC, for about 2,000, 16–18 year olds. There is a vast number of voluntary organizations being drawn into the implementation of unemployment programmes. For example, in 1981/2 the Glasgow Council for Voluntary Service had a membership of almost 200 organizations. Of these, some sixty-six voluntary organizations and charities provided training opportunities via local community project agencies, set up to provide MSC finance for such initiatives.

If this level of activity is roughly typical, it has been estimated that there are over 3,000 locally based groups providing such opportunities in Britain (Moon and Richardson, 1984b, p. 398). The National Association of Youth Clubs was, in 1984, providing more than 7,000 training places for unemployed youngsters. Such is the level of involvement of the voluntary sector in this key policy area that it has become an essential part of the MSC delivery system.

The level of involvement in the 'delivery' or implementation of unemployment schemes is also reflected in the activity of the big well-known economic groups – such as the Trades Union Congress

(TUC) and the Confederation of British Industries (CBI). The TUC is represented on the MSC itself, and on the fifty-four area manpower boards. This trade union participation in the MSC and its activities has continued despite the extremely bad relations which developed between the TUC and the Thatcher government – even during the temporary withdrawal of the TUC from the National Economic Development Council (NEDC). The TUC has intervened where individual trade unions were resistant to YTS (some unions saw YTS as 'cheap labour'), and has even published its own implementation guide to YTS, emphasizing that trade unionists should co-operate fully in the YTS programme.

Employers' organizations – particularly the CBI – have also been heavily involved in the implementation of unemployment schemes. In addition to being represented on the MSC and its Area Manpower Boards, it set up, in 1980, the CBI Special Programmes Unit (SPU). This was done, at the Secretary of State for Employment's request, because the MSC recognized its own inability to provide sufficient places for the growing number of YOP (Youth Opportunities Programme – the predecessor of YTS) participants. In order to assist the MSC in the successful launch of the new YTS scheme, the SPU became almost the 'marketing arm' of the MSC in persuading large-scale employers throughout the country to provide YTS places. Without the CBI's active co-operation in this policy, it is doubtful if YTS could have achieved the 'success' that it has. The government's decision, in 1985, to extend YTS to a two-year programme, instead of just one year, was again heavily dependent on the assumed close involvement of employers, unions and the voluntary sector in the actual implementation of this policy change. There was no way in which the expansion of the scheme could take place without the willing co-operation of these organizations.

The groups who were involved in the implementation of YTS and the Community Programme (which is also being expanded considerably, along with YTS, as part of the Thatcher government's attempt to 'manage' the unemployment issue) were often involved in the formulation of the policies – via their membership of the MSC itself. The involvement of key groups in the formulation of policy may well increase the likelihood of successful implementation.

Yet close group involvement in the formulation process is not an essential precondition for successful implementation. For example, the rather radical policy change introduced by the Technical and Vocational Education Initiative (TVEI) was not preceded by what we see as the 'usual' consultations. In this case, the policy was *announced*, not consulted about. The normally powerful education 'policy community' was not involved in the emergence of this new policy, and control of the policy was given to the MSC – not to a traditional part of the education industry. The announcement of the policy change marked a considerable departure from past practice and it came as a surprise not only to many of the professional groups who would normally expect to be consulted, but also to most civil servants working in the relevant government organizations and departments. That the style of the policy's introduction is unusual is evident from Kogan's description of the normal working of the education policy community. He writes (1978, pp. 117–18) 'so multiple are the concepts and so potentially conflicting are the claims of different groups that it is surprising that any change at all takes place, change requires alliances to be forged for long enough for action to occur . . . that is why, too, drastic and radical solutions do not work where large scale and long term processes like education are involved'.

The creators of TVEI were obviously conscious of the traditional policy style and were determined to act quickly in order to avoid having their radical ideas smothered in a consultative morass, or at least amended out of recognition (Moon and Richardson, 1984a, p. 25). The MSC chairman commented that, 'supposing we had decided to launch a debate about technical education, or the lack of it. We might have had a Royal Commission and it might have taken five years or ten, to get off the ground. Now we have a pilot project due to start by September next year' (*The Times*, 22 November 1982). Unusually, policy-makers were taking a big risk, as they might have failed to win the support of those bodies essential to the implementation of the scheme – local authorities, teaching bodies, trade unions, Her Majesty's Inspectorate (HMI), the Department of Education and Science and employers who had been excluded from prior consultations. In other words, at first sight there appears to have been unusually little concern, as the policy-makers formulated their ideas, for the implementability of those ideas.

What happened after this bold step is singularly revealing in terms of our attempt to understand the implementation process. Despite initial difficulties, the scheme has apparently settled down well. Why? Two main factors contributed to the successful launch of TVEI. First, the policy – whereby vocationally oriented education for 14–18 year olds was to be provided under several pilot schemes – was actually thought to be a good idea by those who would have to implement it. The objectives of the policy-makers were shared by the implementers. Policy-makers and implementers had developed an agreement about 'the problem' (the poor employment prospects of school-leavers) and about the 'solution' (to make education more 'relevant' and 'vocational'). Secondly, a consultative procedure was, in fact, soon established. Thus a National Steering Group (NSG) was established to provide relevant expertise and advice. The NSG included all of the main interests involved in implementing TVEI. The TVEI case is one where the policy was introduced emphatically in a 'top down' style, but has emerged as one whose implementation, steering and evolution are all highly decentralized, giving scope for local emphasis as desired by the local policy-implementing communities (Moon and Richardson, 1984a, p. 32). In terms of our theoretical discussion of 'top down' or 'bottom up' approaches to implementation, the TVEI example seems one which is a rather subtle combination of the two approaches.

Yet, as we suggested earlier, implementation is often characterized by problems. It is to these that we now turn.

Implementation Problems

Few experienced politicians would subscribe to the view that there is a clear distinction between 'policy' and 'administration', or that 'administration' is somehow depoliticized. The administration of policy is not only a difficult *practical* problem – it is also a difficult *political* problem. A classic example of the high political salience of the detailed implementation was provided by the relatively radical policy, proposed in May 1985, to abandon State Earning Related Supplement (SERPS) in an attempt to control the escalating social security budget beyond the year 2000. This was a rare example of a government trying to be *anticipatory* rather than *reactive* in its approach to problem-solving. Thus, actuarial figures showed that in the early part of the next century the cost of SERPS would be quite enormous. Original estimates of the likely cost of SERPS had been based upon projections to the year 2010. When the Conservatives re-calculated the likely costs up to the year 2033, they discovered that at least 3 million pensioners would be included in the scheme. This is a very good illustration of the importance of the implementation process. Thus the original policy was agreed by all parties, in 1975, that state pensions should be earnings related.

One might think that the rest is quite straightforward, until one realizes that a twenty-year difference in the period used for calculating likely costs makes a huge difference to the whole nature of the scheme. Having discovered the cost implications of implementing the scheme in the next century, the Conservative government set about extracting itself from the commitment. The difficulty in doing that was that their opponents began to argue about the way in which the detailed implementation of the proposed new scheme would affect particular groups in society. When the government published its Green Paper (Cmnd 9517) in May 1985 it decided, as a matter of policy, to deliberately exclude details of how the new scheme would actually affect particular groups. It had calculated the number of people who would lose and the number of people who would gain under the new scheme, but recognized that the losers would soon mobilize in opposition to the policy. News leaked out that the calculations had, in fact, been made, thus causing a political row, which was much to the disadvantage of the government.

The government had readily recognized that implementation would prove to be controversial and was trying, unsuccessfully in this case, to avoid any debate on implementation prior to the policy decision. Such a political tactic risks the introduction of a badly designed policy which could be very difficult to implement, simply because the decision took no account of implementation problems. In the SERPS case, the interest-group pressure – based upon doubts about the practicability of the proposed reforms – led the government to back away, in October 1985, from its radical reform of the system shortly after the president of the CBI publicly suggested that the reform proposals should be 'thrown on the bonfire'.

Thus apparently widely supported policies can rapidly lose friends when the detail of implementation is revealed. For example, it was reported in October 1985 that industry was finding the 1984 Data Protection Act a 'costly bureaucratic nightmare' (*The Sunday Times* 6 October 1985). The Act was designed to protect the individual from misuse of personal details held on computers. The Act was widely welcomed, but its active implementation was fraught with problems – such as firms having to complete a seven-page multiple-choice registration form. One possible consequence was that many firms and other organizations would stop using computers to store such records and would resort to less-efficient manual storage systems rather than face the burden of complying with the new legislation.

Although implementation is often concerned with fine detail, it is surprising just how many implementation problems do achieve considerable political salience. Another example is the way in which the cervical cancer screening test system was being implemented. It became a political issue in early 1985, when a young Oxford woman died after not being told that her test had proved positive. A number of similar cases were reported following this incident, with the result that the Minister of Health then asked health authorities to install computerized call and recall systems and to ensure that women got the results of their tests. He did not, however, propose to supply the necessary funding.

The unintended consequences of policies were illustrated by the effect of changes in VAT rules, introduced in 1984. At this time, VAT was introduced on building repairs. A year later there were protests from conservationists and surveyors that the policy change was having an adverse effect on the nation's historic buildings – the new system encouraged the alteration of historic buildings (zero-rated for VAT purposes) rather than their repair (rated at 15 per cent VAT), notwithstanding the fact that there were other policies in place designed to encourage repair rather than alteration. Even apparently 'successful' policies may turn out to have unfortunate side-effects. For example, the Licensing (Scotland) Act of 1976 was followed by a fall in the number of prosecutions for drunkenness and a generally favourable response from both the public and the police. The good results were noted by the rest of Britain thus increasing the pressure for policy change. While in this example the intended outcome seems to match up reasonably with the actual outcome, there may be undesired and unintended consequences. Medical opinion in Scotland is now concerned with alcohol-related disease. While drink-related nuisance may have been abated, the relatively easy access to alcohol may have long-term medical costs. Therefore the policy-making cycle continues with new policies stimulating the need for change in other areas.

Implementation problems can sometimes lead to legal action. For example, the European Court of Human Rights ruled, in May 1985, that the way in which the British immigration laws were being implemented amounted to sex discrimination. The case arose out of the Home Office policy of preventing women, who were born abroad but were lawfully settled in Britain, from bringing their husbands into the country, whereas men had the right to bring their wives to join them in the UK. In this case the Government's response to the implementation problems was to accept the Court's ruling but to institute a review of the policy of allowing wives to come to the UK in the first place.

This last example is an illustration of the key relationship between implementation and policy-making. Many policy changes are in response to implementation problems. As Pressman and Wildavsky (1973, p. 143) suggest, 'The great problem ... is to make the difficulties of implementation a part of the formulation of policy. Implementation must not be conceived of as a process that takes place after the independent of the design of policy.' Government departments in Britain are very closely involved in the implementation process. Moreover, they spend a tremendous amount of time consulting the affected interests, that is, those who both implement policy and who are 'clients' of the policy. It is rare that a policy is introduced without this prior consultation and hence without prior warning of possible implementation problems. The notion of feasibility is high on the agenda for policy-makers. Of course, there is never perfect information, or governments may press ahead for purely ideological reasons, but the policy process requires a learning capacity and benefits from its mistakes and successes in a process of gradual refinement.

PART FOUR

Conclusion

CHAPTER ELEVEN

Britain as a Post-Industrial Society

Introduction

As Colin Thain (1984, p. 581) has remarked, academics, like journalists, are fascinated by failure, with the result that much energy has been expended analysing Britain's decline. As he points out, one needs to be careful in defining decline. In absolute terms, Britain has not suffered an economic decline, in that living standards have risen faster since the war than in earlier periods. The concern is with Britain's *relative* decline. Thus he quoted Pollard who uses the analogy of the movement of a convoy of ships. On this analogy, Britain's economic improvement has been surpassed by most Western European nations (ranked by output per head), and Pollard predicts that the UK will have been overtaken by Spain by 1995, by Greece in 1998, and by Portugal in 2053 (quoted by Thain, 1984, p. 582). But, of course, such long-term forecasts are subject to considerable error. De-industrialization has, if anything, accelerated in the 1970s and 1980s. Britain is now in that class of society termed post-industrial in that over half of its workforce is now employed in non-industrial jobs.

A spectacular example of industrial decline and de-industrialization is the steel industry. Thus the British Steel Corporation, Britain's main steel producer, employed some 228,000 people in April 1975 but this had fallen to under 75,000 by 1984 – despite the fact that the Corporation had consumed over £3,000 million of taxpayers' money since the early 1970s. Output of steel in 1984 was approximately 13 million tonnes compared with a target figure predicted in the Corporation's ten-year strategy plan (approved in 1972) of over 40 million tonnes. The almost total failure of this particular example of public policy-making has been presided over by two Labour governments and two Conservative governments!

Another graphic illustration of the country's economic decline appeared in a full-page newspaper advertisement by the Engineering Council in November 1984. The Council had been created to strengthen the role, status and quality of engineering in Britain, as it was by then conventional wisdom that the decline in engineering was one of the primary causes of Britain's general decline. The Council quoted some chilling statistics charting Britain's performance as an industrial nation. For example, after the war Britain was the world's third largest steel producer. By 1984 it was thirteenth. In 1900 Britain made 60 per cent of the world's shipping. It now makes 3 per cent. Britain once exported motorcycles to over 100 countries throughout the world. It now imports almost every motorcycle, and over half of the cars, sold in Britain. Having pioneered the machine-tool industry, the country's share of the world market has fallen to 3.1 per cent. Having made the first practical computer, Britain has seen its share of the world information technology market fall to 5 per cent. It once made all of the world's textile machinery and now makes 8 per cent (*The Times*, 21 November 1984, p. 9).

There are few economic indicators which give rise to optimism. Even in the high-technology industries, on which the future is said to depend, the British share of world markets continues to decline and import penetration of information technology products has reached similar proportions to that of the motor-vehicle industry.

The Irrelevance of Politics?

Of central importance from the perspective of this book is to address the question of whether the political system and political factors have contributed to this decline. In raising the question, it should be noted that it is perfectly plausible to argue that political factors have had little or nothing to do with the decline, and that it is caused by long-term structural factors and changes in the balance of the world's economy. Stanislaw Gomulka (1979, p. 169) suggests that 'the innovation rate in the UK industry has been significantly lower than in Japan and Western Europe since at least the beginning of this century'. His conclusions about the relevance of the political process are sobering for those of us who study the political process. Thus he argues that 'The phenomenon of wide and still increasing relative gaps on productivity (especially) and technological levels between the UK and Western Europe and Japan is *essentially unrelated to post-war government policies*' (italics added). He believes that a natural process is at work which will eventually lead to an automatic *rise* in the rate of innovational diffusion from the outside world, and that this will happen irrespective of what British governments do. This automatic rise will take place when the productivity and technological/organization gaps reach a particular point. Gomulka (1979, pp. 170–1) argues that 'the problem of the relative slowness in the expansion of productivity and wages will gradually disappear, but the problem of a lower standard of living will acquire an added emphasis'. Similarly pessimistic conclusions about the relevance of the political system to Britain's long-term industrial decline emerged from an American Brookings Institution study, published in 1980. Based on his study of productivity differences among industries, Richard Caves (1980, pp. 185–6) concluded that:

> because the productivity problem originates deep within the social system, one needs an optimistic disposition to suppose that a democratic political system can eliminate that problem. Perhaps the most useful advice the economist can offer policymakers is for them to recognise the constraints on economic change and progress found in British society . . . and to try to hold Britain's aspirations for consumption in line with what the system is willing to produce.

The Scope of Politics: Alternative Views

The scope for political intervention as a means of influencing underlying economic trends is addressed by Robert Bacon and Walter Eltis (1977). Their theory, that too high a proportion of Britain's resources is being consumed by the 'non-market' sector of the economy, is a good example of what A. King (1985, p. 478) describes as a 'change of mood' so common in the UK. He notes that as soon as their book was serialized in the *Sunday Times*, 'its language and ideas were on the lips of politicians of all parties, including those of the Labour Chancellor Denis Healey'. Bacon and Eltis suggest that those who are involved in economic management are either tinkerers or structuralists. Generally, both politicians and civil servants are tinkerers whereas, Bacon and Eltis argue, fundamental structural change is needed in the UK economy.

Various economists have seen success in dealing with unemployment and inflation as linked with some sort of corporation (using the term imprecisely as a label for interest group/Governmental bargaining). Schott (1984), Cameron (1984) and others have concluded that consensus-seeking Governments have performed better on various indices than their competitors. This literature thus stands as an alternative to the common British view that it was *too much* consensus-seeking behaviour that led to a British decline. Schott (1984, p. 21) concludes that the state should create 'encompassing groups' where they do not exist.

There are, of course, others who see a link between economic growth and governments of the left. For example, Whiteley (1982, p. 20) has suggested that 'economic intervention of one type, demand management, influences the rate of economic growth and operates more effectively in countries with a strong left'. He goes on to conclude that 'Britain's problem is that it doesn't have a strong enough socialist political culture'.

Frank Castles (1982), for another, has been involved in several research projects with the theme 'Does politics matter?', and he has presented conclusions based on comparative research broadly suggesting, 'that partisan control of government is among the factors influencing levels and changes in public expenditure, with strong parties of the Right acting as an impediment to expansion and social democratic and other parties, jointly or severally, serving as a stimulus'. However, he does have to allow exceptions and includes the reservation, 'What it does not imply is that changes in electoral opinion are readily translatable into changed policies.'

The general nature of the Castles argument is such that we prefer the harder evidence of British parties in Office, which show economic allocation surprisingly independent of party control. By 1985 the press was drawing parallels between the boom in credit under Heath's expansionary Chancellor, Antony Barber, and the growth in money supply under Nigel Lawson (April–March 1985, Money supply, M3, grew by 18·5 per cent) (*The Times*, 17 October 1985).

A broader argument than the view that particular ideological dispositions of governments affect the economy, is that the competitive party system itself destabilizes the economy. One of the most prominent debates in the 1970s was the question of governmental overload. The best-known statement of the thesis is Anthony King's article published in 1975, 'Overload: Problems of governing in the 1970s'. 'Not only', he said, 'do parties in office increasingly fail to do the things they said they were going to do; they increasingly do things that they pledged themselves specifically not to do' (1975, p. 285). The overload theorists saw party competition as the engine leading to economic disaster.

King (p. 295) was cautious but gloomy – 'one does not have to be a doom monger to sense that something is wrong with our polity as well as our economy'. Other writers have been more lurid in their descriptions of what might happen. For example, Rose and Peters (1978, p. 63) suggest it could be argued that governments are threatened with 'political bankruptcy' if government spending beyond a certain point continues to grow such that the taxation required to support it will cause a real decline in take-home pay. Yet, as Rose himself recognizes (1979, p. 351), caution is needed in predicting doom. Thus he notes that Clark's (1945) warning about the dire consequences of government spending going beyond 25 per cent of GNP has proved to be ill-founded, and that Milton Friedman's warning about the consequences of public expenditure exceeding 60 per cent of GNP are not supported by any social science evidence (Rose, 1981, p. 11). In practice, governments come and go in Britain, but the system of government seems to survive. Britain is characterized by ineffective problem-solving *and* political stability.

Does Economics Influence Politics?

If there is some doubt about the exact relationship between political choices and economic performance, there is also debate about the impact economics has on politics. The dominant and commonsense view is that economic weakness makes the polity more difficult to handle. Boulding (1973, p. 95) has suggested that in the 'progressive state, the poor can become richer without the rich becoming poorer. In the stationary state, there is no escape from the rigors of scarcity.' Heilbroner (1976, p. 41), also writing on the USA, suggests that the conflict that will emerge will be 'not just between a few rich and many poor, but between a relatively better off upper third of the nation and a relatively less well off slightly larger working class. And fighting against both will be the bottom 20 per cent – the group with most to gain, the least to lose' (both quoted in Lipset, 1979).

However, while such predictions about the 'zero sum society' sound convincing, there is little evidence – and there is every reason to be cautious about such social science 'laws'. Lipset (1979, pp. 11–12) frankly records how his generation of political scientists attempt to explain the phenomenon of McCarthyism in terms of the status tensions of a prosperous society, yet 'The underlying trends that supposedly produced increased status tensions have continued, but McCarthyism disappeared with the end of the Korean War'. Among his many other examples of the fragility of 'futurology' is his discussion of the student revolts of the late 1960s. He concludes: 'The seventies, however, are characterised by a "calm", a period of political quiescence on campus, although the structural conditions that supposedly produced student protest still continue, and if anything have intensified.'

Non-Economic Reforms

Some writers concerned with explaining Britain's decline in political terms have concentrated upon specific institutions – such as the failure of Parliament to contribute effectively to policy-making via proper scrutiny and questioning of government proposals. Over twenty years of parliamentary reform, culminating in the formation of the present select committee system, seem to have had little or no effect either on the distribution of power between the government and the House of Commons, or upon the quality of decisions that have been taken. For the present, the steam seems to have gone out of the parliamentary reform movement, and inadequacies of the legislature have gone out of fashion as explanations of decline. There is, however, a revival of interest in reforming the civil service, reminiscent of the late 1960s and early 1970s. The 1960s saw the setting up of the Fulton Committee on the Civil Service. It reported in 1968, expressing the now-famous view: 'The Home Civil Service today is still fundamentally the product of the nineteenth-century philosophy of the Northcote–Trevelyan Report. The tasks are those of the second half of the twentieth century. That is what we have found, it is what we seek to remedy' (Cmnd 3638). Lord Crowther-Hunt (1980, p. 377), one of the main architects of the Report, said that the recommendations of the Committee were accepted by the then government, 'only to be quickly sabotaged by the civil service as the months and years went by'. He argues that much of the blame for Britain's decline should be laid at the door of the civil service; for example, that 'Britain's abundant ills today owe much to serious defects in our bureaucratic ruling class. Our affairs since 1945 have been so disastrously handled, whether under Conservative or Labour Governments, that were it not for the totally unexpected bonanza from North Sea Oil, our social, economic, industrial and financial problems would be well-nigh insoluble.'

A similarly critical view of the contribution that the civil service has made to Britain's decline is provided by Sir John Hoskyns, former Head of Mrs Thatcher's Policy Unit. He observes (1983, p. 142) that most civil servants are now defeatist about Britain's prospects, suggesting that 'for many of them it must have been like joining Napoleon's army just in time for the retreat from Moscow'. He believes that the permanent civil service lacks the confidence and energy that come from success, and that it is not driven by an urgent need for results. When politicians arrive who want to change existing policies – to 'change the boundaries of political possibility' – the civil servants become uneasy and withhold the last 5 per cent of their commitment. They cultivate 'a passionless detachment, as if the process they were engaged in were happening in a faraway country which they service only on a retainer basis' (Hoskyns 1983, p. 145). The injection of new blood is the main solution advocated by Hoskyns. For example, he advocates the replacement of large numbers of civil servants by politically appointed officials, on contracts at proper rates, so that experienced top-quality people will be available. Hoskyns is clearly of the view that politics *does* matter and believes that better methods, better organization and better people will have an effect.

As we have noted earlier, there is some argument that Mrs Thatcher has quietly taken some of Sir John's advice, to the extent of intervening to secure the promotion of Sir Clive Whitmore to the Ministry of Defence and Sir Peter Middleton to the Treasury. Undoubtedly, Mrs Thatcher did not accept 'seniority' promotions, but whether she made such promotions because of the political philosophy of the individual's rather personal style and effectiveness is not self-evident.

The British Policy Style and Britain's Industrial Decline

We have elsewhere suggested that policy style and policy outcome are related. The way in which policies are decided has some effect on the actual outcomes. Our thesis is that, with some notable exceptions (for example, Mrs Thatcher and the miners' dispute in 1984), there is a natural tendency to bargain, compromise and seek consensus, and that this process is likely to produce incremental rather than radical change. There are, therefore, 'system characteristics' which have important implications for problem-solving in an objective scientific sense. Our system of decision-making is much more likely to produce tinkering than restructuring. The high degree of interest-group accommodation might be seen as particularly relevant in terms of radical versus incremental policy change – as is our notion of policy communities.

The whole rationale of policy communities is that change is by agreement. Unless there is some particular crisis facing the policy community, then radical policy change is unlikely to be agreed. Robert Goodin (1982, p. 55) has analyzed the effects of established relationships between Whitehall departments and outside groups. One of his hypotheses was that 'the older the system of consultation the stronger and more widespread veto powers within the subgovernment should be; and hence the more policy routine should predominate over innovation within policy areas dominated by older, better established systems of consultation'. He found that this did, indeed, explain the level of 'routine' policy-making and the preponderance of routine over innovative policy-making.

Goodin's findings are rather similar to those of the much more ambitious work of Mancur Olson, who has tried to explain the rise and decline of nations. Thus Olson (1982, p. 37) talks of 'institutional sclerosis' caused by a high degree of interest-group involvement. He is especially interested in the question of whether a society can achieve a rational or efficient economy through bargaining among organized groups. His conclusion is that the more powerful the interest-group system (or 'distributional coalitions' in his terms), the less likely a country will be to have an economy which grows quickly. The so-called 'miracle' economies of Japan and West German grew so fast because their 'distributional coalitions' were emasculated or abolished by totalitarian governments after the war (ibid., p. 75).

The logic of his argument is that:

> countries which have had democratic freedom of organisation without upheaval or invasion the longest will suffer the most from growth-repressing organisations and combinations. This helps to explain why Great Britain, the major nation with the longest immunity from dictatorship, invasion, and revolution, has had in this century a lower rate of growth than other larger, developed democracies. *Britain has precisely the powerful network of special interest organisations that the argument developed here would lead us to expect in a country with its record of military security and democratic stability ... In short, with age British society has acquired so many strong organisations and collusions that it suffers from an institutional* sclerosis *that shows its adaptation* to *changing circumstances and technologies.* (ibid., pp. 77–8, italics added).

Olson sees this as a better explanation than others of Britain's *gradual* decline since the end of the last century. Quoting the work of his colleague, Peter Murrell, he notes that 51 per cent of the associations existing in 1971 in Britain were formed before 1939, whereas only 37 per cent of the French, 24 per cent of the West German and 19 per cent of the Japanese associations were. Britain also had a larger number of associations than France, Germany, or Japan. A further characteristic and cause of low growth, according to Olson's theory, is the predominant type of group. He argues that particular and specialist groups will logically look for sectional advantage for their members rather than the general interest in growth. Only those whom Bjurulf and Swahn (1980) call 'generalist' groups will feel compelled to act in the wider interest.

Put at its simplest, the argument is that the existence of strong interest groups (narrowly based, say, compared with the broader-based interest groups in Sweden), which are deeply entrenched in both the public and private decision-making process, will inhibit change, innovation and adaptation. The argument will be familiar to those who have compared the experience of French and British economic planning. For example, Hayward (1974, p. 205) concluded that Britain's attempt to introduce planning was best characterized as 'toothless tripartism', and as a process in which a good policy was defined as one on which there was agreement rather than one which met objective criteria.

One might argue that as an alternative to this consultative style, governments should govern. Such a recommendation is easy to give and more difficult to follow. Moreover, there may be, in addition to broad economic trends which are difficult to resist (for example, the development of steel industries by the newly industrialized nations), some broader cultural factors at work which are beyond the scope of any government – left, right, *dirigiste*, or consensual. It is to this broader cultural explanation of decline that we now, finally, turn.

Culture and Decline

The main proponent of this cultural thesis is Martin J. Wiener in his now classic book, *English Culture and the Decline of the Industrial Spirit* (1981). Like Bacon and Eltis, Wiener's thesis has signalled another of the 'change of moods', as A. King puts it. Wiener's thesis is now the conventional wisdom produced to explain Britain's decline.

In essence the thesis is simple, though difficult to test empirically. It is that the English culture is one which is deeply hostile to industry and commerce and all that it stands for, and that wealth and growth are somewhat distasteful. He argues that industrialists were 'gentrified', and that the élite was open to industrialists if they adapted to its standards. Thus, 'potentially disruptive forces of change were harnessed and channelled into supporting a new social order, a synthesis of old and new. This continuance of the cultural revolution of industrialism lies at the heart of both the achievements and the failures of modern British history' (Wiener, 1981, p. 158).

He detects an inner tension in English culture between wanting to be the workshop of the world and wanting a green and pleasant land. The ideals of 'gentry England' have muffled economic drive, competitiveness and innovation. Ultimately, Wiener argues, 'Margaret Thatcher will find her most fundamental challenge not in holding down the money supply or inhibiting government spending, or even in fighting the shop stewards, but in changing this frame of mind'.

The implications of this dead hand of culture are that it is not a shift in the fundamental nature of the world's economy, or the failure of governmental policies, which is the cause of our decline – but a set of attitudes which values work as a civil servant, lawyer, or doctor, higher than that of an engineer or entrepreneur. The Brookings study mentioned earlier, also drew attention to the importance of the social system, when it argued that Britain's productivity problem – which was argued to be the central cause of our decline – had its origins deep in the social system.

Yet, as Andrew Gamble (1981, p. 236) reminds us, although the effects of the long decline are increasingly serious, there are few signs that Britain is close to a political revolution. Gamble questions whether a viable strategy for reversing decline can acquire the necessary popular legitimacy on the basis of the old electoral system and the old state. Both Labour and Conservatives have failed in their attempts to implement modernization strategies. Major constitutional reform may be needed, especially electoral reform, 'to provide majorities for coalitions of centre parties, so guaranteeing the kind of stability and continuity in policy-making that would enable the working through of a systematic strategy' (Gamble, 1981, p. 220). Whilst not exaggerating the threat to the stability of the system, he suggests that the legitimacy of the state has been tarnished, that the authority and prestige of many national institutions has been undermined, that the parties have weakened, and that opinion has grown more volatile. Analysts of electoral behaviour have also suggested that the traditional party system could collapse because the rock bed of electoral support for the major two parties has been so eroded (Franklin, 1985).

Our view is that the connections between economic performance and the condition of the political system are unclear. On the one hand, the behaviour of governments has been non-adversarial, and the idea that we need to produce a *new* stability is difficult to reconcile with the stability from government to government. And, on the other hand, it seems that, for good or ill, the froth of much political activity simply does not penetrate to the level of economic activity. Enterprise zones and free ports are examples of the current government's belief that *the* switch can be found which will transform economic life. In fact, the policies turn out to be both symbolic and marginal in their effects. They represent only the contemporary version of a series of bright ideas which simply do not begin to cope with the scale and nature of the problems. There is a beating of breasts among ministers over what (with hindsight) appears to be detail; there is lack of sleep, pressure of work, and all this takes place without there being a clear connection between the Whitehall process and the economic world.

Jack Hayward has pointed to this self-delusion of the political class in saying,

> the major source of Britain's difficulties is to be located among the non-state actors and in particular in the failure of both private and public *enterprise* to live up to that proud name ... Politicians in power prate and posture, taking credit and the blame for the diverse fortunes that ensue from the interplay of international and institutional forces, without – in any country – usually being genuinely responsible for either the good or the bad results. (In Gamble and Walkland, 1984, p. vii)

Parties compete with prescriptions which demonstrably differ: policies – such as the rate of tax on high-income earners, or on trade union law – do change. But the prescriptions seem – on the basis of the record, 1970–85 – ineffective on big issues such as unemployment rates. The prescriptions seem ineffective when applied to the particular circumstances – events (and voters) are compelling – and Ravenscraig is saved, student loans are not introduced, soft loans for industry are granted, and so on.

This viewpoint is not to be complacent about the economic problems that exist, but it is to be sceptical that any government can find *the* solution. If it were that easy, we do not believe that our politicians and civil servants of the past quarter of a century would have overlooked it. Our scepticism even extends to any ideas that we might have ourselves, but, at a minimum, the constant adversarial noise of British politics cannot help.

The *potential* for some mass change in our political and social order exists. Yet, so far, the decline has been relatively gradual. Although there have been some exceptions – for example, Northern Ireland, racial disturbances in Liverpool, Birmingham, Bristol, and Tottenham, the miners' dispute of 1984 – the decline itself has been well managed politically. Thus, we should not judge the political system solely by its capacity to deliver economic growth and material well-being, but also by its capacity to run a relatively well-ordered predictable and relatively peaceful society. While the miners' dispute of 1984 was a particularly graphic illustration that all is not well, by mid-1985 we were struck by the resilience of the social and political system: mining had again become part of the 'normal political process'.

We would want to avoid the mental leap that says because there are conflicts – such as that over the closure of pits – the political system is in disarray. For a start, no one should imagine 'beer and sandwiches' solves everything and, secondly, the negotiative political system does require negotiable demands. Now it may be a feature of our current political arrangements that more and more non-negotiable demands are being made, but that problem is not solved by tinkering with political structures.

There is some opinion survey evidence that there is an increase in the number of citizens who can contemplate breaking the law in certain cases of conscience. The 1984 British Social Attitudes Survey showed (see Young, 1984, p. 27) that 48 per cent of male 18–34 year olds and 35 per cent of female 18–34 year olds could conceive of circumstances in which they would break a law of which they disapproved. (Corresponding figures for the over 55 group of respondents were 24 per cent and 15 per cent). Respondents' expectations of political difficulties seem to be on the increase. For example, the percentage seeing political terrorism as likely has risen from 26 per cent in 1979, to 43 per cent in 1980 and 53 per cent in 1983 – although the percentage expecting revolution had declined from 11 per cent to 7 per cent over the same period. Our decline, it seems, may turn out to be a little less smooth and less civilized than in the past, yet the continuity of the political process seems more likely that not to be preserved. Britain may be gradually adjusting to being a post-industrial society in which post-industrialism is seen as a good development rather than a bad one, and in which expectations have begun, as the Brookings study recommended, to be adjusted downwards in line with what is possible. It would be premature to write any early obituaries for the British political system, as its capacity for survival seems considerable.

Bibliography

Allison, G. (1971). *Essence of Decision* (Boston, Mass.: Little, Brown).
Almond, G. (1983), 'Corporatism, pluralism and professional memory', *World Politics*, vol. 35, no. 2 (January), pp. 245–60.
Almond, G., and Coleman, J. S. (1960). *The Politics of Developing Areas* (Princeton, NJ: Princeton University Press).
Almond, G., and Verba, S. (1963), *The Civic Culture: Political Attitudes and Democracy in Five Nations* (Boston, Mass.: Little, Brown).
Almond, G., and Verba, S. (1980), *The Civic Culture Revisited* (Boston, Mass.: Little, Brown).
Amery, L. (1935), *The Forward View* (London: Geoffrey Bles).
Ashford, D. E. (1981). *Policy and Politics in Britain: The Limits of Consensus* (Philadelphia, Pa: Temple University Press).
Attlee, C. R. (1937), *The Labour Party in Perspective* (London: Gollancz).

Bachrach, P., and Baratz, M. (1970), *Power and Poverty* (London: Oxford University Press).
Bacon, Robert, and Eltis, Walter (1977), *Britain's Economic Problem: Too Few Producers* (London: Macmillan).
Bagehot, W. ([1867] 1963), *The English Constitution*, introduction by R. H. S. Crossman, (London: Fontana).
Banfield, E. C. (1963), *Political Influence* (New York: The Free Press).
Banting, K. (1979), *Poverty, Politics and Policy* (Basingstoke: Macmillan).
Barnes, S. H., and Kaase, Max, *et al.* (1979), *Political Action. Mass Participation in Five Western Democracies* (Beverly Hills, Calif.: Sage).
Barnett, J. (1982), *Inside The Treasury* (London: Deutsch).
Barrett, S., and Fudge, C. (eds) (1981), *Policy and Action* (London and New York: Methuen).
Bealey, F., and Pelling, H. (1958), *Labour and Politics, 1900–1906: A History of the Labour Representative Committee* (London: Macmillan).
Beer, S. H. (1955), 'The future of British politics', *Political Quarterly*, vol. 26, no. 1 (January–March), pp. 33–42.
Beer, S. H. (1967), 'The British legislature and the problem of mobilizing consent', in B. Crick (ed.), *Essays in Reform* (London: Oxford University Press).
Benewick, R., Berki, R. N., and Parekh, B. (1973), *Knowledge and Belief in Politics* (London: Allen & Unwin).
Benn, T. (1979), 'The case for a constitutional premiership', reprinted in A. King (ed.), *The British Prime Minister*, 1985, 2nd rev. edn (London: Macmillan), pp. 220–41.
Berrington, H. (1984), 'Decade of dealignment', *Political Studies*, vol. 32, no. 1 (March), pp. 117–20.

Birch, A. H. (1984), 'Overload, ungovernability and delegitimation: the theories and the British case', *British Journal of Political Science*, vol. 14, pt 2 (April), pp. 135–60.

Bjurulf, B., and Swann, U. (1980), 'Health policy proposals and what happened to them', in A. Heidenheimer and N. Elvander (eds), *Health Policy Proposals and What Happened to Them* (New York: St Martin's Press), pp. 75–98.

Boddy, M. (1981), 'The public implementation of private housing policy', in Barrett and Fudge (eds), op. cit., pp. 81–104.

Boyd-Carpenter, J. (1980), *Way of Life* (London: Sidgwick & Jackson).

Boyle, Lord (1980), 'Ministers and the administrative process', *Public Administration*, vol. 58 (Spring), pp. 1–12.

Braybrooke, D., and Lindblom, C. (1963), *The Strategy of Decision* (New York: The Free Press).

Brewer, G. D., and de Leon, P. (1983), *The Foundations of Policy Analysis* (Homewood, Ill.: Dorsey Press).

Bridges, Sir E. (1950), *Portrait of a Profession* (London: Cambridge University Press).

Brittan, S. (1983), *The Role and Limits of Government* (London: Temple Smith).

Bruce-Gardyne, J., and Lawson, N. (1976), *The Power Game* (London: Macmillan).

Buchanan, J., and Tullock, G. (1962), *The Calculus of Consent* (Ann Arbor, Mich.: University of Michigan Press).

Bulpitt, J. (1986), 'The discipline of the new democracy', *Political Studies*, vol. 34, no. 1 (March), pp. 19–39.

Burton, I., and Drewry, G. (1981), *Legislation and Public Policy* (London: Macmillan).

Burton, I., and Drewry, G. (1985), 'Public legislation: 1981/2 and 1982/3', *Parliamentary Affairs*, vol. 38, no. 2 (Spring), pp. 219–52.

Butler, D., and Stokes, D. (1974), *Political Change in Britain* (London: Macmillan).

Caiden, N., and Wildavsky, A. (1974), *Planning and Budgeting in Small Countries* (New York: Wiley).

Cameron, D. R. (1984), 'Social democracy, corporation, etc.' in Goldthorpe (1984).

Castle, B. (1973), 'Mandarin power', *Sunday Times*, 10 June.

Castle, B. (1980), *The Castle Diaries, 1974–76* (London: Weidenfeld & Nicolson).

Castles, F. (ed.) (1982), *The Impact of Parties* (London: Sage).

Caves, Richard E. (1980), 'Productivity differences among industries', in Richard E. Caves and Lawrence B. Krause (eds), *Britain's Economic Performance* (Washington, DC: The Brookings Institution).

Cawson, A. (1982), *Corporatism and Welfare* (London: Heinemann).

Clark, C. (1945), 'Public finance and changes in the value of money', *Economic Journal*, 55, pp. 371–89.

Coates, D. (1984), *The Context of British Politics* (London: Hutchinson).

Cobham, D. (1984), 'Popular political strategies for the U.K. economy', *Three Banks Review*, no. 143 (September), pp. 17–35.

Cockerell, M., Hennessy, P., and Walker, D. (1984), *Sources Close to the Prime Minister* (London: Macmillan).

Cockle, P. (ed.) (1984), *Public Expenditure Policy 1984–5* (London: Macmillan).

Conradt, David P. (1980), 'Changing German political culture', in Almond and Verba (eds), op. cit., pp. 212–72.

Conroy, C. (1981), 'Public demonstrations – a Friends of the Earth view', paper presented at the Royal Institute of Public Administration Conference, 10–11 April 1981.

Cox, A. (1984), *Adversary Politics and Land* (Cambridge: Cambridge University Press).

Crewe, I. (1984), *How to Win a Landslide Without Really Trying: Why the Conservatives Won in 1983*, Essex Papers in Government and Politics, no. 2. April (Colchester: University of Essex).

Crewe, I. (1986), 'On the Death and Resurrection of Class Voting', *Political Studies*, vol. xxxiv, no. 4 (December), pp. 620–38.

Crewe, I., and Denver, D. (1985), *Electoral Change in Western Democracies* (London: Croom Helm).

Crick, M. (1984), *Militant* (London: Faber).

Crick, B. (1968), *The Reform of Parliament*, 2nd edn (London: Weidenfeld & Nicolson).

Crossman, R. (1963), introduction to Bagehot, in Bagehot ([1867] 1963), op. cit.

Crossman, R. (1972), *Inside View* (London: Cape).

Crossman, R. (1975), *The Diaries of a Cabinet Minister*, vol. 1 (London: Hamish Hamilton and J. Cape).

Crossman, R. (1976), *The Diaries of a Cabinet Minister*, vol. 2 (London: Hamish Hamilton and J. Cape).

Crossman, R. (1977), *The Diaries of a Cabinet Minister*, vol. 3 (London: Hamish Hamilton and J. Cape).

Crowther-Hunt, Lord (1980), 'Mandarins and ministers', *Parliamentary Affairs*, vol. 33, no. 4 (Autumn), pp. 373–99.

Dahl, R. (1956), *Preface to Democratic Theory* (Chicago: University of Chicago Press).

Dahl, R. (1961), 'The behavioural approach to political science', *American Political Science Review*, vol. 55, no. 4 (December), pp. 763–72.

Dahl, R. (1967), *Pluralist Democracy in the United States* (Chicago: Rand McNally).

Dahl, R. (1976), *Modern Political Analysis*, 3rd edn (Englewood Cliffs, NJ: Prentice-Hall).

Dahl, R. (1978), 'Pluralism revisited', *Comparative Politics*, vol. 10, no. 2 (January), pp. 191–204.

Dahl, R., and Lindblom, C. [1953] 1976 edn, *Politics, Economics and Welfare* (Chicago: University of Chicago Press).

Davies, A. F. (1972), *Essays in Political Sociology* (Melbourne: Cheshire).

Deacon, A., and Bradshaw, J. (1983), *Reserved for the Poor* (Oxford: Martin Robertson).

Dearlove, J. (1973), *The Politics of Policy in Local Government* (Cambridge: Cambridge University Press).

Dell, E. (1973), *Political Responsibility and Industry* (London: Allen & Unwin).

Dell, E. (1980a), 'Some reflections on Cabinet government', *Public Administration Bulletin*, no. 32 (April), pp. 17–33.

Dell, E. (1980b), 'Collective responsibility: fact, fiction or facade', in *Policy and Practice: the Experience of Government* (London: Royal Institute of Public Administration).

Dempster, M. A. H., and Wildavsky, A. (1979), 'On change: or, there is no magic size for an increment', *Political Studies*, vol. 27, no. 3 (September), pp. 371–89.

Deutsch, K. (1966), *The Nerves of Government*, 2nd edn (New York: The Free Press).

Domhoff, G. W. (1967), *Who Rules America?* (Englewood Cliffs, NJ: Prentice-Hall).

Dowding, K, and Kimber, R. (1984), *The By-Product Theory of Groups*, Keele Research Paper, no. 18.

Downs, A. (1957), *An Economic Theory of Democracy* (New York: Harper).

Downs, A. (1967), *Inside Bureaucracy* (Boston, Mass.: Little, Brown).

Downs, A. (1974), 'The success and failures of federal housing policy', in E. Ginzberg and R. Solow (eds), *The Great Society* (New York: Basic Books).

Drewry, G. (1984), 'The new select committees', in D. Hill (ed.), *Parliamentary Committees in Action*, Strathclyde Papers on Government and Politics, no. 24 (Glasgow: Department of Politics, University of Strathclyde), pp. 30–55.

Drewry, G. (ed.) (1985), *The New Select Committees* (Oxford: Clarendon).

Dror, Y. (1964), 'Muddling through – "Science" or inertia?', *Public Administration Review*, vol. 24, September, pp. 153–7.

Drucker, H., Dunleavy, P., Gamble, A., and Peele, G. (1983), *Developments in British Politics* (London: Macmillan).

Dudley, Geoffrey (1984), *Implementation Dynamics and Discontinuities Within the "Imperfect" Policy Process*, Strathclyde Papers on Government and Politics, no. 11 (Glasgow: Department of Politics, University of Strathclyde).

Dunsire, Andrew (1978), *The Execution Process*, Vol. 1 (Oxford: Martin Robertson).

Duverger, M. (1959), *Political Parties*, 2nd edn (London: Methuen).

Easton, D. (1965), *A Systems Analysis of Political Life* (New York: Wiley).

Eckstein, Harry (1960), *Pressure Group Politics: The Case of the BMA* (Stanford, Calif.: Stanford University Press).

Economist, The (1984), *Political Britain Today* (London: The Economist).

Edelman, M. (1964), *The Symbolic Uses of Politics* (Urbana, Ill.: Illinois University Press).

Finer, S. E. (1956), 'The individual responsibility of ministers', *Public Administration*, vol. 24 (Winter), pp. 377–96.

Finer, S. E. (1966), *Anonymous Empire*, 2nd edn (London: Pall Mall).

Finer, S. E. (1980a), 'Princes, parliaments and the public service', *Parliamentary Affairs*, vol. 33, no. 4 (Autumn), pp. 353–72.

Finer, S. E. (1980b), *The Changing British Party System* (Washington, DC: American Enterprise Institute).

Forman, F. N. (1985), *Mastering British Politics* (London: Macmillan).

Foster, A. (1984), 'Ideology, public expenditure and policy performance', *Public Administration Bulletin*, no. 46 (December), pp. 39–53.

Foster, C. D. (1971), *Politics, Finance and the Role of Economics* (London: Allen & Unwin).

Franklin, M. (1984), 'How the decline of class voting has opened the way to radical change in British politics', *British Journal of Political Science*, vol. 14, pt 4 (October), pp. 483–508.

Franklin, M. (1985), *The Decline of Class Voting* (Oxford: Oxford University Press).

Frohlich, N., Oppenheimer, J., and Young, O. (1971), *Political Leadership and Collective Goods* (Princeton, NJ: Princeton University Press).

Fry, G. K. (1985), 'The career civil service under challenge', paper presented at 15th Annual Conference of the Public Administration Committee, York, 2–4 September.

Gais, T. L., Peterson, M., and Walker, J. (1984), 'Interest groups, iron triangles and representative institutions in American national government', *British Journal of Political Science*, vol. 14, pt 2 (April), pp. 161–86.

Gamble, Andrew (1981), *Britain in Decline* (London: Macmillan).

Gamble, A., and Walkland, S. A. (1984), *The British Party System and Economic Policy (1945–1983)* (Oxford: Clarendon Press).

Gilmour, Sir Ian (1969), *The Body Politic* (London: Hutchinson).

Glennerster, Howard (1981), 'Social service spending in a hostile environment', in Hood and Wright (eds), op. cit., pp. 174–96.

Goldthorpe, J. (ed.) (1984), *Order and Conflict in Contemporary Capitalism* (Oxford: Clarendon).

Golembiewski, R. (1960), 'The group basis of politics', *American Political Science Review*, vol. 54, no. 4 (December), pp. 962–71.

Gomulka, S. (1979), 'Britain's slow industrial growth – increasing inefficiency versus low rate of technical change', in Wilfred Beckerman (ed.), *Slow Growth in Britain. Consensus and Consequences* (Oxford: Clarendon).

Goodin, Robert, E. (1982), 'Banana time in British politics', *Political Studies*, vol. 30, no. 1 (March), pp. 42–58.

Grant, W. (1978), *Insider Groups, Outsider Groups and Interest Group*

Strategies in Britain, Working Paper, no. 19, May (Warwick: Department of Politics, University of Warwick).

Gray, A., and Jenkins, W. (1982), 'Policy analysis in British central government: the experience of PAR', *Public Administration*, vol. 60, no. 4 (Winter), pp. 429–50.

Gray, A., and Jenkins, W. (1985), *Administrative Politics in British Government* (Brighton, Sussex: Wheatsheaf).

Griffith, J. A. G. (1951), 'The place of Parliament in the legislative process', *Modern Law Review*, vol. 14, nos 3 and 4 (July and October), pp. 279–96 and pp. 425–36.

Griffith, J. A. G. (1974), *Parliamentary Scrutiny of Government Bills* (London).

Gunn, L. A. (1978), 'Why is implementation so difficult?', *Management Services in Government*, vol. 33, no. 4 (November), pp. 169–76.

Gustafsson, Gunnel, and Richardson, J. J. (1980), 'Post-industrial changes in policy style', *Scandinavian Political Studies*, vol. 3 (new series), no. 1, pp. 21–37.

Habermas, J. (1976), *Legitimation Crisis* (London: Heinemann).

Hague, Rod (1984), 'Confrontation, incorporation and exclusions: British trade unions on collectivist-post-collectivist politics', in Hugh Berrington (ed.), *Change in British Politics* (London: Frank Cass), pp. 130–62.

Haines, J. (1977), *The Politics of Power* (London: Coronet).

Ham, C., and Hill, M. (1984), *The Policy Process in the Modern Capitalist State* (Brighton, Sussex: Wheatsheaf).

Hanson, H., and Walles, M. (1984), *Governing Britain*, 4th edn (London: Fontana).

Hayward, J. E. S. (1974), 'National aptitudes for planning in Britain, France and Italy', *Government and Opposition*, vol. 9, no. 4 (Autumn), p. 397–410.

Hayward, J., and Berki, R. (1979), *State and Society in Contemporary Europe* (Oxford: Martin Robertson).

Headey, B. (1974), *British Cabinet Ministers* (London: Allen & Unwin).

Heald, D. (1983), *Public Expenditure* (Oxford: Martin Robertson).

Heath, A., Jowell, R., and Curtice, J. (1985), *How Britain Votes* (Oxford: Pergamon Press).

Heclo, Hugh (1978), 'Issue networks and the executive establishment', in A. King (ed.), *The New American Political System* (Washington, DC: American Enterprise Institute), pp. 87–124.

Heclo, H., and Salaman, L. (eds) (1981), *The Illusion of Presidential Government* (Boulder, Colo: Westview Press).

Heclo, Hugh, and Wildavsky, Aaron (1981), *The Private Government of Public Money*, 2nd edn (London: Macmillan).

Heisler, M. (1974), *Politics in Europe* (New York: David McKay).

Heisler, M. (1979), 'Corporate pluralism revisited', *Scandinavian Political Studies*, new series, vol. 2, no. 3, pp. 277–97.

Henderson, P. D. (1977), 'Two British errors: their probable size and some possible lessons', *Oxford Economic Papers*, vol. 29, no. 2, pp. 159–205.

Hennessy, P. (1985), 'The quality of Cabinet Government in Britain,' *Policy Studies*, 6, Pt. 2 (October), pp. 15–45.

Hennessy, P. (1986), *Cabinet* (Oxford: Basil Blackwell).

Hennessy, P., and Arends, A. (1983), *Mr. Attlee's Engine Room*, Strathclyde Papers on Government and Politics, no. 26 (Glasgow: Department of Politics, University of Strathclyde).

Hennessy, P., Morrison, S., and Townsend, R. (1985), *Routine Punctuated by Orgies*, Strathclyde Papers on Government and Politics, no. 31 (Glasgow: Department of Politics, University of Strathclyde).

Herman, V., and Alt, J. (eds) (1975), *Cabinet Studies* (London: Macmillan).

Hewart, Lord (1929), *The New Despotism* (London: Benn).

Higgins, G. M., and Richardson, J. J. (1976), *Political Participation*, Politics Association, Occasional Publication no. 3 (London: Politics Association).

Hill, D. (ed.) (1984), *Parliamentary Committees in Action*, Strathclyde Papers on Government and Politics, no. 24 (Glasgow: Department of Politics, University of Strathclyde).

Hogwood, B. W., and Gunn, L. A. (1984), *Policy Analysis for the Real World* (Oxford: Oxford University Press).

Hogwood, B. W., and Peters, G. (1983), *Policy Dynamics* (New York: St Martin's Press).

Holbeche, B. (1986), 'Policy and influence: MAFF and the National Farmers' Union', Public Policy and Administration, Vol. 1, No. 3, pp. 40–7.

Hood, C. C. (1976), *The Limits of Administration* (London: Wiley).

Hood, C. C. (1983), *The Tools of Government* (London: Macmillan).

Hood, C. C., and Wright, M. (eds) (1981), *Big Government in Hard Times* (Oxford: Martin Robertson).

Hoskyns, Sir John (1983), 'Whitehall and Westminster: an outsider's view', *Parliamentary Affairs*, vol. 36, no. 2 (Spring), pp. 137–47.

House of Commons, Select Committee on Expenditure (1976–77). *Eleventh Report*. (London: HMSO).

House of Lords, Select Committee on Overseas Trade (1985), *Report*, vol. 1. (London: HMSO).

Howe, Sir G. (1977), *Too Much Law* (London: Conservative Political Centre).

Hunter, F. (1953), *Community Power Structure* (Chapel Hill, NC: University of Carolina Press).

Inglehart, Ronald (1977), 'Political dissatisfaction and mass support for social change in advanced industrial society, *Comparative Political Studies*, vol. 10, no. 3 (October), pp. 455–72.

Jay, D. (1980), *Change and Fortune* (London: Hutchinson).

Jenkins, B., and Gray, A. (1983), 'Bureaucratic politics and power', *Political Studies*, vol. 31, no. 2 (June), pp. 177–93.

Jenkins, R. (1948), *Mr. Attlee* (London: Heinemann).

Jenkins, S. (1985), 'The Star Chamber, PESC and the Cabinet', *Political Quarterly*, vol. 52, no. 2 (April–June), pp. 111–21.

Jenkins, W. (1978), *Policy Analysis* (Oxford: Martin Robertson).

Jennings, Sir I. (1961), *Cabinet Government*, 3rd edn (Cambridge: Cambridge University Press).

Johnson, F. (1983), *Election Year* (London: Robson).

Jones, G. W. (1965), 'The Prime Minister's power', *Parliamentary Affairs*, vol. 18, no. 8 (Spring), pp. 167–85.

Jones, G. W. (1976), 'The Prime Minister's secretaries: politicians or administrators?', in J. A. G. Griffith (ed.), *From Policy to Administration* (London: Allen & Unwin).

Jones, G. W. (1985), 'The Prime Minister's aides', in A. King (ed.), *The British Prime Minister* (London: Macmillan), pp. 72–95.

Jordan, A. G. (1978), 'Central Co-ordination, Crossman and the Inner Cabinet', *Political Quarterly*, vol. 49, no. 2 (April–June), pp. 171 and 80.

Jordan, A. G. (1981), 'Iron triangles, woolly corporatism and elastic nets: images of the policy process', *Journal of Public Policy*, vol. 1, pt 1 (February), pp. 95–123.

Jordan, A. G. (1982), 'Individual ministerial responsibility: absolute or obsolete?', *Scottish Government Yearbook*, pp. 121–39.

Jordan, A. G. (1984a), 'Enterprise zones in the UK and USA: ideologically acceptable job creation?', in J. J. Richardson and R. Henning (eds), *Unemployment: Policy Responses in Western Democracies* (London: Sage), pp. 124–47.

Jordan, A. G. (1984b), *The Limits of Planning* (Redhill: School Government Publishing Co. for the Economic and Social Research Council).

Jordan, A. G., and Richardson, J. J. (1982), 'The British policy style or the logic of negotiation', in J. J. Richardson (ed.), *Policy Styles in Western Europe* (London: Allen & Unwin), pp. 80–110.

Jordan, A. G., and Richardson, J. J. (1983), 'Policy communities: the British and European policy style', *Policy Studies Journal*, vol. 11, no. 4 (June), pp. 603–15.

Jordan, A. G., and Richardson, J. J. (1984), 'Engineering a consensus: from the Finniston Report to the Engineering Council', *Public Administration*, vol. 62, no. 4 (Winter), pp. 383–400.

Jordan, A. G., Richardson, J. J. and Dudley, G. (1984), 'Evidence to parliamentary committees access as to the policy process', in D. Hill (ed.) (1984), pp. 107–221.

Judge, D. (1984), *Ministerial Responsibility*, Strathclyde Papers on Government and Politics, no. 37 (Glasgow: Department of Politics, University of Strathclyde).

Kaufman, G. (1980), *How To Be a Minister* (London: Sidgwick & Jackson).

Kavanagh, D. (1980), 'Political culture in Britain: the decline of the civic culture', in Almond and Verba (eds), op. cit., pp. 124–76.

Kavanagh, D. (1981), 'The politics of manifestos', *Parliamentary Affairs*, vol. 34, no. 1 (Autumn), pp. 7–27.

Kavanagh, D. (ed.) (1982), *The Politics of the Labour Party* (London: Allen & Unwin).

Kavanagh, D. (1985), 'Swingometry of the Labour élite', *Times Higher Education Supplement*, 11 October, p. 17.

Kellner, P., and Crowther-Hunt, Lord (1980), *The Civil Servants: An Inquiry into Britain's Ruling Class* (London: Raven).

Kelso, W. A. (1978), *American Democratic Theory* (Westport, Conn. and London: Greenwood Press).

Kimber, R. (1981), 'Collective action and the fallacy of the Liberal fallacy', *World Politics*, vol. 33, no. 2 (January), pp. 178–96.

King, A. (1975), 'Overload: problems of governing in the 1970s', *Political Studies*, vol. 23, nos 2 and 3, pp. 284–96.

King, A. (1976), *Why Is Britain Becoming Harder to Govern?* (London: BBC Publications).

King, A. (1985), 'Governmental responses to budget scarcity', *Policy Studies Journal*, vol. 113, no. 3, pp. 476–93.

King, A., and Sloman, A. (1973), *Westminster and Beyond* (London: Macmillan).

King, R. (1985), *ESRC Newsletter*, no. 55, p. 40.

Kogan, M. (ed.) (1971), *The Politics of Education* (Harmondsworth, Middx: Penguin).

Kogan, M. (1975), *Educational Policy-Making* (London: Allen & Unwin).

Kogan, M. (1978), *The Politics of Educational Change* (Manchester: Manchester University Press).

Kogan, D., and Kogan, M. (1982), *The Battle for the Labour Party* (London: Kogan Page).

Lane, C. (1984), 'Legitimacy and power in the Soviet Union through socialist ritual', *British Journal of Political Science*, vol. 14, pt 2, pp. 207–18.

Lane, R. (1962), *Political Ideology* (New York: The Free Press).

Laski, H. (1931), *An Introduction to Politics* (London: Allen & Unwin).

Lee, M. (1980). 'The machinery of government: the prospects for redefining the issues under Mrs Thatcher's administration', *Parliamentary Affairs*, vol. 33, no. 4 (Autumn), pp. 434–47.

Lehmbruch, G. (1984), 'Concertation and the structure of corporatist networks', in Goldthorpe (1984).

Leys, C. (1983), *Politics in Britain* (London: Heinemann Educational).

Lewis, S. (1984), 'Public expenditure and GDP 1980/81–84/85', *Public Money*, vol. 4, no. 1 (June), pp. 58–9.

Lindblom, C. (1959), 'The science of muddling through', *Public Administration Review*, vol. 19, pp. 79–88.

Lindblom, C. (1964), 'Contexts for change and strategy: a reply', *Public Administration Review*, vol. 24 (September), pp. 157–8.

Lindblom, C. (1965), *The Intelligence of Democracy* (New York: The Free Press).

Lindblom, C. (1977), *Politics and Markets* (New York: Basic Books).

Lindblom, C. (1979), 'Still muddling, not yet through', *Public Administration Review*, vol. 39, pp. 517–26.

Lindblom, C. (1980) (ed.), *The Policy-Making Process* (Englewood Cliffs, NJ: Prentice-Hall).

Lipset, S. M. (1979), 'Predicting the future of post-industrial society', in Lipset (ed.), *The Third Century* (Stanford, Calif.: Hoover Institution Press), pp. 1–36.

Low, S. (1914), *The Governance of England*, 2nd edn (London: T. Fisher Unwin).

Lowe, Philip, and Goyder, Jane (1983), *Environmental Groups in Politics* (London: Allen & Unwin).

Lucas, J. R. (1976), *Democracy and Participation* (Harmondsworth, Middx: Penguin).

Lukes, S. (1974), *Power* (London: Macmillan).

Mack, R. (1971), *Planning and Uncertainty* (New York: Wiley Interscience).

Mackenzie, W. J. M. (1955), 'Pressure groups in British government', *British Journal of Sociology*, vol. 6, no. 2 (June), pp. 133–48.

Mackenzie, W. J. M. (1975), *Power, Violence, Decision* (Harmondsworth, Middx: Penguin).

Mackenzie, W. J. M. (1982), 'The knights of the textbooks', in R. Frankenberg (ed.), *Custom and Conflict in British Society* (Manchester: Manchester University Press), pp. 1–49.

McKenzie, R. T. (1958), 'Parties, pressure groups and the British political process', *Political Quarterly*, vol 29, no. 1, reprinted in R. Kimber and J. J. Richardson (eds), *Pressure Groups in Britain* (London: Dent, 1974), pp. 276–88.

McKenzie, R. T. (1967), *British Political Parties*, 2nd edn (London: Heinemann Educational).

Mackintosh, J. P. (1977), *The British Cabinet*, 3rd edn (London: Stevens & Sons).

Mackintosh, J. P. (ed.) (1978), *People and Parliament* (Farnborough, Hants: Saxon House).

Mackintosh, J. P. (1980), *Specialist Committees in the House of Commons*, Waverley Paper no. 2 (Edinburgh: University of Edinburgh).

Mackintosh, J. P. (1982), *The Government and Politics of Britain*, 5th edn, revised and updated by Peter Richards (London: Hutchinson).

Madgwick, P. J. (1984), *Introduction to British Politics*, 3rd edn (London: Hutchinson).

Marcuse, H. (1965), 'Repressive tolerance', in R. P. Woolf, B. Moore and H. Marcuse, *A Critique of Pure Tolerance* (London: Cape), pp. 93–137.

Margach, J. (1981), *The Anatomy of Power* (London: W. H. Allen).

Marsh, D., and Chambers, J. (1981), *Abortion Politics* (London: Junction Books).

Marsh, D. (1983), *Pressure Politics* (London: Junction Books).

Marsh, R. (1978), *Off the Rails* (London: Weidenfeld & Nicolson).

Marshall, G. (1984), *Constitutional Conventions* (Oxford: Clarendon Press).

Maudling, R. (1978), *Memoirs* (London: Sidgwick & Jackson).

May, T., and Nugent, N. (1982), 'Insiders, outsiders and thresholders', paper presented at Political Studies Association Annual Conference, 14–16 April, University of Kent.

Miers, D., and Page, A. (1982), *Legislation* (London: Sweet & Maxwell).

Miliband, R. (1969), *The State in Capitalist Society* (London: Weidenfeld & Nicolson).

Miller, W. L. (1978), 'Social class and party choice in England. A new analysis', *British Journal of Political Science*, vol. 8, pt 3 (July), pp. 1–19.

Miller, W. L. (1984), 'There was no alternative: the British general election of 1983', *Parliamentary Affairs*, vol. 37, no. 4 (Autumn), pp. 364–84.

Mills, C. W. (1956), *The Power Elite* (Oxford: Oxford University Press).

Minkin, L. (1980), *The Labour Party Conference*, rev. edn (Manchester: Manchester University Press).

Mitchell, A. (1982), *Westminster Man* (London: Methuen).

Montjoy, R. S., and O'Toole, L. J. (1979), 'Toward a theory of policy implementation', *Public Administration Review*, vol. 34, no. 5, pp. 465–76.

Moon, Jeremy (1983), 'Policy change in direct government responses to UK unemployment', *Journal of Public Policy*, vol. 3, pt 3, pp. 301–30.

Moon, Jeremy, and Richardson, J. J. (1984a), 'Policy-making with a difference? The Technical and Vocational Education Initiative', *Public Administration*, vol. 62, no. 1 (Spring), pp. 23–33.

Moon, Jeremy, and Richardson, J. J. (1984b), 'The unemployment industry', *Policy and Politics*, vol. 12, no. 4, pp. 391–411.

Moon, Jeremy, and Richardson, J. J. (1985), *Unemployment in the UK* (Aldershot, Hants: Gower).

Moon, Jeremy, Richardson, J. J., and Smart, Paul (1986), 'The Privatisation of British Telecom: A Case Study of the Extended Process of Legislation, *European Journal of Political Research*, vol. 14, no. 3.

Moore, Chris, Richardson, J. J., and Moon, Jeremy (1985), 'New Partnerships in local economic development', *Local Government Studies* (September–October), pp. 19–33.

Moran, M. (1977), *The Politics of Industrial Relations* (London: Macmillan).

Moran, M. (1984), *The Politics of Banking* (London: Macmillan).

Moran, M. (1985), *Politics and Society in Britain* (London: Macmillan).

Morrison, H. (1954), *Government and Parliament* (London: Oxford University Press).

Muir, R. (1930), *How Britain Is Governed* (London: Constable).

Neustadt, R. (1980), *Presidential Power*, rev. edn (New York: Wiley).

Niskanen, W. A. (1971). *Bureaucracy and Representative Government* (Chicago and New York: Aldine–Atherton).

Norton, P. (1975), *Dissension in the House of Commons 1945–74* (London: Macmillan).

Norton, P. (1980). *Dissension in the House of Commons, 1974–79* (Oxford: Clarendon).

Norton, P. (1984), *The British Polity* (New York and London: Longman).

Oberstar, G. T. (1983), 'Strategies of single-issue groups', *Policy Studies Journal*, vol. 11, no. 4 (June), pp. 616–23.

Olsen, J. P. (1981), 'Integrated organisational participation in government', in P. Nystrom and W. H. Starbuck (eds), *Handbook of Organisational Design*, vol. 2 (Oxford: Oxford University Press), pp. 492–516.

Olsen, J. P. (1983), *Organized Democracy* (Bergen, Oslo and Tromso: Universitetforlaget).

Olsen, Johan, Roness, Paul, and Saetren, Harald (1982), 'Norway: still peaceful coexistence and revolution in slow motion?', in Richardson (ed.), op. cit., pp. 47–9.

Olson, Mancur (1965), *The Logic of Collective Action* (Cambridge, Mass.: Harvard University Press).

Olson, Mancur (1982), *The Rise and Fall of Nations* (New Haven, Conn.: Yale University Press).

Ovenden, K. (1978), *The Politics of Steel* (London: Macmillan).

Parkinson, C. N. (1978), 'Does the civil service expand regardless of the amount of work (if any) to be done?', reprinted in P. G. Lewis, D. C. Potter and F. G. Castles (eds), *The Practice of Comparative Politics* (London: Longman and Open University), pp. 39–45.

Parry, G. (1972), *Participation in Politics* (Manchester: Manchester University Press).

Parsons, T. (1957), 'The distribution of power in American society', *World Politics*, vol. 10, no. 1 (October), pp. 123–43.

Peacock, A. (1984), 'Privatisation in Perspective', *The Three Banks Review*, no. 144 (December), pp. 3–25.

Peat Marwick (1984), *Financial Management in the Public Sector: A Review 1979–1984* (London: Peat Marwick, Mitchell & Co.).

Perrow, C. (1979), *Complex Organisations*, 2nd edn (Chicago: Scott, Foresman).

Pinto-Duschinsky, M. (1985), 'British political funding', *Parliamentary Affairs*, vol. 38, no. 2 (Summer), pp. 828–47.

Pliatzky, Sir L. (1984), *Getting and Spending: Public Expenditure, Employment and Inflation*, 2nd edn (Oxford: Basil Blackwell).

Pliatzky, Sir L. (1985), *Paying and Choosing* (Oxford: Basil Blackwell).

Pollard, S. (1982), *The Wasting of the British Economy* (London: Croom Helm).

Polsby, N. (1963), *Community Power and Political Theory* (New Haven, Conn.: Yale University Press).

Ponting, C. (1986), *Whitehall: Tragedy and Farce* (London: Hamish Hamilton).

Popper, K. (1972), *Conjectures and Reputations: The Growth of Scientific Knowledge*, 4th edn (London: Routledge & Kegan Paul).

Potter, A. (1961), *Organised Groups in British National Politics* (London: Faber).

Pressman, G., and Wildavsky, A. (1973), *Implementation* (Berkeley, Calif.: University of California Press).

Price, C. (1984), 'Ministers, Parliament and the right to know', *Public Money*, vol. 4, no. 3 (December), pp. 25–9.

Pross, P. (1975), 'Canadian pressure groups in the 1970s', *Canadian Public Administration*, 18, pp. 121–35.

Pulzer, P. (1975), *Political Representation and Elections in Britain*, 3rd edn (London: Allen & Unwin).

Putten, Jan Van (1982), 'Policy styles in the Netherlands. Negotiation and conflict', in Richardson (ed.), op. cit., pp. 168–96.

Pyper, R. (1985), 'Sarah Tisdall, Ian Willmore, and the Civil Servant's "Right to Leak"', *Political Quarterly*, vol. 56, no. 1 (January–March), pp. 72–81.

Reagan, M., and Sanzone, J. (1981), *The New Federalism*, 2nd edn (New York and Oxford: Oxford University Press).

Rhodes, R. A. W. (1984), *Continuity and Change in British Central–Local Relations: The Conservative Threat*, Essex Papers in Politics and Government, no. 2, April (Colchester: University of Essex).

Rhodes, R. A. W. (1985), 'Power-Dependence, Policy Communities and Intergovernmental Networks', *Public Administration Bulletin*, no. 49 (December), pp. 4–29.

Ricci, D. M. (1984), *The Tragedy of Political Science* (New Haven, Conn., and London: Yale University Press).

Richardson, J. J. (ed.) (1982), *Policy Styles in Western Europe* (London: Allen & Unwin).

Richardson, J. J., Jordan, A. G., and Kimber, R. (1978), 'Lobbying, administrative reform and policy styles', *Political Studies*, vol. 26, no. 1 (March), pp. 47–64.

Richardson, J. J., and Jordan, A. G. (1979), *Governing Under Pressure: The Policy Process in a Post Parliamentary Democracy* (Oxford: Basil Blackwell).

Richardson, J. J., and Moon, Jeremy (1984), 'The politics of unemployment in Britain', *Political Quarterly*, vol. 55, no. 1 (January–March), pp. 29–37.

Richardson, J. J., Moon, J. W., and Smart, P. (1986), 'Government policy for the acquisition of information technology: the role of the Department of Trade and Industry', in N. Deakin (ed.), *Policy Change in Government: Three Case Studies* (London: RIPA), pp. 63–90.

Richardson, J. J., and Watts, N. J. S. (1985), *National policy styles and environmental policy: Britain and West Germany compared*, Science Centre, West Berlin Discussion Paper no. 16.

Ripley, R., and Franklin, G. (1976), *Congress, the Bureaucracy and Public Policy* (Homewood, Ill.: Dorsey Press).

Rokkan, S. (1966), 'Numerical democracy and corporate pluralism' in R. Dahl (ed.), *Political Opposition in Western Democracies* (New Haven and London: Yale University Press), pp. 70–115.

Rose, Richard (1979), 'Ungovernability: is there fire behind the smoke?', *Political Studies*, vol. 27, no. 3 (September), pp. 351–70.

Rose, Richard (1981), 'What, if anything, is wrong with big government?', *Journal of Public Policy*, vol. 1, no. 1, pp. 5–36.

Rose, Richard (1983), 'Still the era of party government', *Parliamentary Affairs*, vol. 36, no. 3 (Summer), pp. 282–99.

Rose, Richard (1984), *Do Parties Make A Difference?* 2nd edn (London: Macmillan).

Rose, R., and Peters, G. (1978), *Can Government Go Bankrupt*, (New York: Basic Books).

Rose, R., and Suleiman, E. (eds) (1980), *Presidents and Prime Ministers* (Washington, DC: American Enterprise Institute).

Ryan, M. (1978), *The Acceptable Pressure Group* (Farnborough, Hants: Saxon House).

Salisbury, R. (1969), 'An exchange theory of interest groups', *Mid-West Journal of Political Science*, vol. 13, no. 1 (February), pp. 1–32.

Salisbury, R. (1984), 'Interest representation: the dominance of institutions', *American Political Sciences Review*, vol. 78, no. 1 (March), pp. 64–78.

Särlvik, B., and Crewe, I. (1983), *Decade of Dealignment. The Conservative Victory of 1979 and Electoral Trends in the 1970s* (Cambridge: Cambridge University Press).

Schattschneider, E. E. (1960), *The Semi-Sovereign People: A Realist's View of Democracy in America* (New York: Holt, Rinehart & Winston).

Schmitter, P., and Lehmbruch, G. (eds) (1979), *Trends towards Corporatist Intermediation* (Beverly Hills, Calif.: Sage).

Schott, K. (1984), *Policy, Power and Order* (New Haven: Yale UP).

Schumpeter, J. [1943] (1976 5th edn), *Capitalism, Socialism, and Democracy* (London: Allen & Unwin).

Sedgemore, B. (1980), *The Secret Constitution: An Analysis of the Political Establishment* (London: Hodder & Stoughton).

Seidman, H. (1976), *Politics, Position and Power*, 2nd edn (New York, London and Toronto: Oxford University Press).

Self, P., and Storing, H. (1971), *The State and the Farmer* (London: Allen & Unwin).

Sharpe, L. J. (1985), 'Central coordination and the policy network', *Political Studies*, vol. 33, no. 3 (September), pp. 361–81.

Simon, H. (1958), *Administrative Behaviour*, 2nd edn (New York: The Free Press).

Simon, H. (1977), *The New Science of Management Decision*, revised edition, (Englewood Cliffs: Prentice-Hall).

Simon, H. (1982), *Models of Bounded Rationality*, vols 1 and 2 (Cambridge, Mass. and London: MIT).

Steen, A. (1985), 'The farmers, the state and the Social Democrats', *Scandinavian Political Studies*, vol. 8, no. 1 (June), pp. 45–64.

Stewart, J. D. (1958), *British Pressure Groups* (Oxford: Clarendon Press).

Stone, Clarence N. (1985), 'Efficiency versus social learning: a reconsideration of the implementation process', *Policy Studies Review*, vol. 4, no. 3 (February), pp. 484–95.

Tarschys, Daniel (1981), 'Rational decremental budgeting: elements of an expenditure policy for the 1980s', *Policy Sciences*, vol. 4, pp. 49–58.

Taylor, P. (1984), *Smoke Ring: Politics of Tobacco* (London: The Bodley Head).

Thain, C. (1984), 'The Treasury and Britain's decline', *Political Studies*, vol. 32, no. 4 (December), pp. 581–95.

Thain, C. (1985), 'The education of the Treasury: the Medium Term Financial Strategy, 1980–84', *Public Administration*, vol. 63 (Autumn), pp. 260–86.

Truman, David B. (1951), *The Governmental Process* (New York: Knopf).

Van Meter, D. S., and Van Horn, C. E. (1975), 'The implementation process: a conceptual framework', *Administrative Sciences Quarterly*, vol. 6, no. 4, pp. 445–88.

Vogel, D. (1983), 'Cooperative regulation: environmental protection in Great Britain', *Public Interest*, no. 72, pp. 88–106.

Wade, D. (1978), *Behind the Speaker's Chair* (Leeds and London: Austicks Publications).

Walker, J. (1983), 'The origins and maintenance of interest groups in America', *American Political Science Review*, vol. 77, (June), pp. 390–406.

Walker, P. Gordon (1972), *The Cabinet* (London: Fontana).

Walkland, S. (1968), *The Legislative Process in Great Britain* (London: Allen and Unwin).

Walkland, S. A., and Ryle, M. (eds) (1977), *The Commons in the '70s* (London: Fontana).

Waltz, W. (1968), *Foreign Policy and Democratic Politics* (London: Longman).

Ward, H. (1984), 'The anti-nuclear lobby: an unequal struggle?', in Marsh, D. (1984), pp. 182–210.

Wass, Sir D. (1984), *Government and the Governed* (London: Routledge & Kegan Paul).

Welch, S., and Studler, D. (1983), 'The policy opinions of British political activists', *Political Studies*, vol. 31, no. 4 (December), pp. 604–19.

Wheare, K. C. (1975), 'Crichel Down revisited', *Political Studies*, vol. 23, nos 2 and 3, pp. 268–86.

Whiteley, P. (1981), 'Who are the Labour activists', *Political Quarterly*, vol. 52, pp. 160–70.

Whiteley, P. (1982), *The political economy of economic growth*, paper presented at the Political Studies Association group on Political Economy, University of Kent, 14–16 April.

Whiteley, P., and Winyard, S. (1984), 'The origins of the "new poverty lobby"', *Political Studies*, vol. 32, no. 1 (March), pp. 32–54.

Wiener, Martin J. (1981), *English Culture and the Decline of the Industrial Spirit 1850–1980* (Cambridge: Cambridge University Press).

Wildavsky, A. (1964), *The Politics of the Budgetary Process* (Boston, Mass.: Little, Brown).

Wildavsky, A. (1980), *The Art and Craft of Policy Analysis* (London: Macmillan).

Wilkinson, P. (1979), 'Terrorist movements', in A. Yonah, D. Carlton, and P. Wilkinson (eds) (1979), *Terrorism: Theory and Practice* (Boulder, Colo.: Westview Press), pp. 99–120.

Williams, M. (1983), *Downing Street Perspective* (London: Weidenfeld & Nicolson).

Wilson, G. K. (1977), *Special Interests and Policy-Making* (London: Wiley).

Wilson, H. (1976). *The Governance of Britain* (London: Weidenfeld & Nicolson/Michael Joseph).

Wilson, James Q. (1973), *Political Organisations* (New York: Basic Books).

Wright, Maurice (1977), 'Public expenditure in Britain: the crisis of control', *Public Administration*, vol. 55 (Summer), pp. 143–69.

Wright, Maurice (1980), 'From planning to control: PESC in the 1970s', in M. Wright (ed.), *Public Spending Decisions – Growth and Restraint in the 1970s* (London: Allen & Unwin), pp. 88–119.

Yates, D. (1982), *Bureaucratic Democracy* (Cambridge, Mass.: Harvard University Press).

Young, Hugo, and Sloman, Anne (1982), *No Minister: An Inquiry into The Civil Service* (London: BBC Publications).

Young, Hugo, and Sloman, Anne (1984), *But, Chancellor* (London: BBC Publications).

Young, Ken (1984), 'Political attitudes', in R. Jowell and C. Ainey, *British Social Attitudes. The 1984 Report* (Aldershot, Hants: Gower).

Zey, W. (1985), *The impact of interest groups under legislation and implementation*, paper for Extended Legislation Session at the World Congress of the International Political Science Association, Paris.

COMMAND PAPERS

Cmnd 1432 (1961), *Control of Public Expenditure* (Plowden Report).

Cmnd 3638 (1968), *Report on the Civil Service 1966–68.*

Cmnd 4506 (1970), *The Reorganisation of Central Government.*

Cmnd 6440 (1976), *Cash Limits on Public Expenditure.*

Cmnd 6601 (1976), *Committee on Financial Aid to Political Parties.*

Cmnd 7794 (1980), *Engineering our Future.*

Cmnd 7797 (1980), *Report on Non-Departmental Bodies.*

Cmnd 8616 (1982), *Efficiency and Effectiveness in the Civil Service.*

Cmnd 9058 (1983), *Financial Management in Government Departments.*

Cmnd 9428 (1985), *The Government's Expenditure Plans 1985–86/1987–88.*

Cmnd 9521 (1985), *Scientific Procedures on Living Animals.*

Cmnd 9517 (1985), *Reform of Social Security.*

Cmnd 9524 (1985), *The Development of Higher Education in the 1990s.*

All published by HMSO, London.

Index

For Product Safety Concerns and Information please contact our EU
representative GPSR@taylorandfrancis.com
Taylor & Francis Verlag GmbH, Kaufingerstraße 24, 80331 München, Germany

9 781032 949666